A War in Ba

At Home and at Sea, 1807-II

by

John G. Cragg

©2024 John G. Cragg

A War in Baltic Waters: At Home and At Sea, 1807-II

Copyright © 2024 by John G. Cragg

All rights reserved.

Dedicated to

Michael Cragg
Nina Cragg
Kobe Cragg
Jack Cragg

Who all face

Big Changes this Year

Table of Contents

Preface	vii
Principal Characters	ix
Chapter I	11
Chapter II	19
Chapter III	31
Chapter IV	43
Chapter V	59
Chapter VI	69
Chapter VII	81
Chapter VIII	95
Chapter IX	107
Chapter X	121
Chapter XI	137
Chapter XII	153
Chapter XIII	173
Chapter XIV	189
Chapter XV	209
Chapter XVI	225
Chapter XVII	243
Chapter XVIII	261
Chapter XIX	279
Chapter XX	291
Chapter XXI	303
Chapter XXII	317
Chapter XXIII	333
Glossary	343

Preface

This book is a work of fiction, both in terms of events and characters. It follows on from the first seven volumes in this series: *A New War: at Home and at Sea, 1803, A Continuing War: at Home and Sea, 1803-4, A War by Diplomacy: at Home and Sea, 1804, A Stalemated War: at Home and Sea, 1805, A Changing War: at Home and at sea, 1805-II, A Widening: at Home and at sea, 1806,* and *A War in Home Waters: at Home and at Sea, 1808-II*. They are available at Amazon.com and other Amazon sites by searching for my name or the title. The present tale takes place in 1807.

A great many things have changed in the more than two centuries that have elapsed since that date, including items and phrases that may be unfamiliar to many readers. A glossary is provided at the end of the book to help those who are curious. Items in the glossary are flagged on their first appearance in the text by an * as in, for example, tack*. A few notes on terms or institutions that may not be familiar to readers are found in the Author's Notes at the end of the text, organized by the first chapter to which they are relevant.

The period, places, and major activities involved in these novels are well covered by historians, both professional and amateur, to whom I am indebted for the factual and political background of the tales. I try to keep to one rule: The activities described should not alter the significant historical events of the era or significantly change the subsequent history of the period.

As always, I am indebted to my wife, Olga Browzin Cragg, for her encouragement and meticulous help in trying to make a readable manuscript. Many readers have also helped with their comments and criticisms.

Principal Characters

Betsey	Daphne Giles's lady's maid
Blenkinsop, Hector	Captain in the Royal Navy, captain of *Cicero*, junior to Giles
Bolton, Catherine	Giles's half-niece and married to Captain Bolton
Bolton, Captain	Married to Giles's niece Catherine
Beaver, Mr.	Designer of the changes to Camshire House
Brooks, Mr.	Master of *Glaucus*
Bush, Captain Tobias	A Royal Navy Post Captain, formerly Giles's first ieutenant
Bush, Midshipman	Nephew to Captain Bush, on *Glaucus*
Carstairs	Giles's Cockswain, operator of the Dipton Arms Inn
Darling, Mrs.	Cook at Dipton Hall
Downing, Mr.	Chief Magistrate of Westminster
Dunsmuir, Mr.	Midshipman on *Glaucus*
Emery, Sir Titus	A High Court Justice who spends much of his time as an agent of the government
Evans, Garth	Carpenter on *Glaucus*.
Findlay, Michael	Portrait and landscape painter
Foster, Rev. Angus	Curate at Dipton
Giles, Daphne	Countess of Camshire
Giles, Richard	Earl of Camshire Captain in the Royal Navy and husband of Daphne
Griffiths, Henry	Stablemaster at Dipton Hall
Hatcherley, Lord	First Lord of the Admiralty
Jackson, Mr.	Apothecary/physician at Dipton
Jenks, Roger	Junior midshipman on *Glaucus*

Lester, George	First lieutenant on *Glaucus*, on *Cicero*
Macauley, Lieutenant	Lieutenant of Marines on *Glaucus*
Macreau, Etienne	Commander of *Stout*
Marianne, Lady	Giles's half-sister, and Major Stoner's wife
Marsdon, Mrs.	A bawdy housekeeper and procurer
Moorhouse, Daniel	Daphne's father, Owner of Dipton Manor
Moorhouse, George	Daphne's invalid uncle,
Moorhouse, Hugh	Son of Harold and Nancy, eight years old
Moorhouse, Mary	Daughter of Harold and Nancy, five years old
Newsome, Mr.	Second Secretary to the Admiralty
Philman, David	Giles's servant on *Glaucus*
Richardson, Joseph	Midshipman on *Glaucus*
Shearer, Bill	Bosun on *Glaucus*
Snodgravel, Mr.	Lawyer in London, Giles's agent
Steves	Butler at Dipton Hall
Stoner, Major Ralph	Retired Indian Army Officer, married to Lady Marianne
Strangway, Lady	Society lady, social climber
Strangway, Lord	Her husband
Struthers, Lady Gillian	Giles's maternal aunt
Struthers, Lord Walter	Giles's uncle-in-law, a member of the government
Stewart, Daniel	Second lieutenant on *Glaucus*
Ted	New coachman at Dipton Hall
Tisdale	Butler at Dipton Manor
Walters	Dispatch rider at Dipton Hall
Weaver, Nanny	Giles's and Daphne's nanny
Whitley, Ralph	Master's mate on *Glaucus*
Wilson, Mrs.	Housekeeper at Dipton Hall

Chapter I

"Camshire, I thought that I would find you here."

Captain Sir Richard Giles, OB, RN, Earl of Camshire, looked up from the paper he was reading in the library of his club. As he guessed from the voice, Sir Titus Emery was the man greeting him. Sir Titus was a good friend. He was also a high court judge on leave of absence to serve as some sort of government fixer. That was probably his role today: it had been in the past when he had run Giles to earth in Giles's club. The last time Sir Titus met Giles there, it was to persuade him to undertake a tricky task for the Government using his frigate *Glaucus*. Giles's response to the greeting was not very warm.

"What do you want this time, Emery?"

"You are right, Giles. I did run you down here on government business, at least partially.

"First, the Government wants me to extend their very warm thanks for nipping that rebellion in the bud," Sir Titus declared. "They are especially grateful because the task was so much more complicated than they expected as a result of their information turning out to be significantly incorrect. Because officially, no rebellion was even contemplated, they can't publicly reward you for dealing with it, but indirectly, they want to do something."

"Just what do they have in mind, Sir Titus?"

"I am sure you remember your voyage to St. Petersburg."

"Of course. That was not one of the Government's most shining endeavors. Got me kicked out of St. Petersburg because of that ass, Sir Walcott Lainey."

"Yes, true. But apparently, the Tsar was most impressed by your going to the rescue after the disaster in the race you organized."

"I didn't have any choice in that matter. Had to do something when those ships ran afoul of each other."

"Apparently, that is not how the Tsar sees it. Instead, he wants to give you a medal, the Cross of St. Nicholas, of all things. I can't believe it: you will be a member of the Order of Father Christmas, but there it is. The Government feels that, diplomatically, it would not do to have the Russians recognize you without them also providing you with major recognition, even though they cannot explain it for your service in that Jacobite business or in dealing with the lascar slavers. So, in addition to permitting the award for your Russian success, they will add in your rescuing the East India Company captives and your undertaking the mission to Hanover, even though that was not a success. The King insists on the latter recognition since he realizes that he put you in a most embarrassing position."

"Good Lord. In earlier times, I would have lost my head over that fiasco."

"The Government is taking a long view of that matter. They regard you as re-establishing our claim to Hanover, which could be helpful after we kick Napoleon out. Between you and me, I think that that is a ridiculous hope. Unfortunately, Napoleon is, if anything, getting stronger and stronger, but what do I know about grand strategy?

"Anyway, since you already are a Knight of the Bath, and they can't make you a Knight of the Garter anytime soon, they have decided to make you a Marquess. They will announce it in the next Gazette. And no, you cannot refuse it since the King is strongly behind the award. Of course, becoming a marquess doesn't bring anything material with it, and you'll have to buy yourself new robes. A jump in the order of precedence, but if you and Daphne regard it as an excuse to live more lavishly, then that spending will come from your existing resources."

Giles reflected on this information, which came out of the blue, for several minutes before replying: "I don't for a minute think that I can refuse that honor, Sir Titus, though you and I know it is really in gratitude for pulling some government irons from the fire and keeping my mouth shut about it. I will consult Daphne, of course, since she will also be stuck with a new title right after she has come to terms with being a countess after the shock of becoming viscountess. She married a man with no hereditary title and never wanted me to have one. Well, I think I will tell her that she will soon be Marchioness of Dipton, and there is nothing she can do about it."

"This honor doesn't come without a hitch."

"I wonder why I am not surprised about that," Giles replied. "What do they want?"

"You may not like this," Sir Titus answered. "The Tsar wants to award the cross to you in person."

"In person? Can't he just put it in the diplomatic pouch or something?"

"Of course, he can't. You will have to pick it up in person. My masters also want you to accept and go to St. Petersburg as soon as possible. Doing so might improve our relations with the Russians and remind them that we have a powerful Navy and Napoleon does not."

"How am I supposed to get there? After the French victories last fall, the easy route through Prussia is not available."

"We presume that you will go in your frigate, *Glaucus*. After all, the award is in gratitude for what *Glaucus* did. It shouldn't be a dangerous or demanding trip. Though Napoleon now controls Prussia and Brandenburg, he didn't acquire a serious navy in the Baltic that could challenge *Glaucus*. The Swedes are still on our side, and the Danes are not hostile, though they are being careful not to threaten Napoleon. You won't be leaving at once. The Baltic, and especially the approaches to St. Petersburg, is not yet guaranteed to be free of ice, though if you left now, you would almost certainly get through. But we have to communicate with St. Petersburg that you are coming. Maybe the middle of June would be a good time to aim for you to arrive, or even early July."

"Yes, that sounds very sensible. Of course, I still have to talk to Daphne about it. I suppose that since this voyage may help cement relations with Russia, I should undertake it. Still, I have to check the state of the repairs to Glaucus after the damage she suffered while playing the government's misdirection games. I was intending to do that soon, anyway, and was only waiting to hear about the court martial of that fool Blenkinsop. I presume that you can have lunch with me here."

Giles walked to the Admiralty after lunch. The days of sitting in the notorious officers' waiting room to see someone seemed to be over for him. When Giles announced in no uncertain tones that he had come to see Mr. Newsome, he was ushered into the Second Secretary's room immediately.

"Congratulations, my lord, on being made a marquess."

"Thank you, Mr. Newsome. But I still want to adhere to the practice that in naval matters, I prefer to be addressed as 'Captain.' I must say that on this subject, I never expected to be honored for an unpublicized venture and two failures."

"I wouldn't call any of them that, my lord. The King himself pushed for you to be honored, I know. He also insisted that I be rewarded for arranging that expedition, even though some members of the Government thought that I should be hanged, drawn, and quartered for it."

"I am glad that that did not happen! How did they reward you?"

"They made me a knight baronet. So, I will now be 'Sir Joseph.'"

"Congratulations. It is well deserved, Sir Joseph."

"Don't call me that, please, my lord. Not until I have actually been knighted. I am afraid that if I allowed the title to be used now, it would jinx the bestowal of the knighthood."

"Very well, you will remain plain, Mr. Newsome, until the honor is confirmed. Now, what is happening in Portsmouth?"

"I imagine that you know that *Glaucus* has been taken to Butler's Hard to have the bowsprit examined."

"Of course, I authorized it. Have you heard anything about Lieutenant Marceau's being given his step?"

"It is still hung up in the process of being approved. Some blockheads want to review it because of his French background. These things always take too long. However, you remind me that I should speed it along.

"Mr. Marceau's step does raise the question of your officers. And I would like you to take on a couple of promising midshipmen. The war is far from over, and we need to keep up the officer core for the time being.

"You will also need a new first lieutenant, Giles," Mr. Newsome continued. "Certainly, Mr. Stewart is hardly experienced enough to be a lieutenant, let alone your first lieutenant. I'll have to think about it. Do you have any suggestions?"

"I do," Giles replied. "And no, it is not some relative of mine or someone who can do me a good turn. I do think it is in the best interests of the service."

"Now you have me curious, Giles." Mr. Newsome interjected. "Not that I would have ever expected you to have anything else in mind than the best interests of the service. If you were susceptible to the game of interest, you would live in a much more prosperous mode."

"Thank you, Newsome. The man I have in mind is Lieutenant. Lester."

"What? The first lieutenant in *Cicero*? He did well at Pendrag*, but even so, he will be lucky not to be court-martialed over the fiasco of *Cicero* being captured."

"Still, I can understand. I have looked into his situation as part of the preparation for Blenkinsop's court-martial as much as for any concern about himself. It turns out that Lester was appointed to *Cicero* in the hope that he could make up for Blenkinsop's weaknesses. Blenkinsop's claim to advancement was based on his being the only commissioned officer still alive after *Cicero*'s victory over a French ship, whatever her name was. Blenkinsop was, therefore, hailed as a great hero when we were very scarce of them. News of your triumph, Giles, had not yet been received.

Lester's original appointment to the navy resulted from influence, a highly complex path of influence, I believe, starting with a Viscount's third son, the rector of Lester's parish church. Lester is a physician's son who was lucky in his original appointment as a midshipman in a frigate. He made a name for himself and got appointed to a frigate on his own merits at the earliest date possible without bending the rules, even though the chain of his influence was broken when the vicar was made a prebendary of some cathedral. Anyway, all our investigations revealed that the only reason that the crew of *Cicero* was able to participate so usefully at the battle of Pendrag was because of Lester.

"Lieutenant Lester," continued Newsome, "seems to be an ideal first mate for *Glaucus*. Knowing you, Giles, that appointment is not open to being filled by interest, but you will look for merit. I think Lester has shown such merit. If you take him, it may rescue his career; if you don't, with the fiasco of *Cicero* hanging over him, the navy is bound to lose an excellent officer."

"Is he tied down indefinitely waiting for Blenkinsop's court-martial?" asked Giles.

"No. It is happening next week. You should be getting a subpoena to attend as a witness very soon. Of course, if you don't want to testify, the claim of unspecified business is always enough to get a peer of the realm off the hook."

"No, I should go, in case some blockhead has decided to sweep it under the carpet for the 'good of the service.' I'll talk to Lester when we are both there and see if he is interested in the position. I presume that he is not going to be court-martialed."

"No."

"Then I'll wait until after we have both testified. We don't want any hint that Lester's testimony was purchased with the promise of a good position, do we?"

"Quite right, Captain Giles."

"I hope I can get you to drop the 'Captain' part of that, Newsome. Especially as you won't allow me to call you 'Sir Joseph' just yet."

Giles left the Admiralty and decided to walk home. Camshire House was nearby, and his business for the day was finished. Indeed, he had nothing that needed to be done in London right now, while Daphne still had many things to arrange for the ball they were to give later in the Season. He knew she was not as keen on hosting a ball as she had been when she first proposed it, but she still claimed it was an absolute necessity if they were to enjoy their proper place in society. Her enthusiasm seemed to be waning. Would it revive with the news that she was about to become the Marchioness of Dipton?

Chapter II

Giles paused on the portico of his newly renovated mansion in Mayfair. Now, he could revel in the sight his grandfather must have intended when he built the mansion, looking out on Camshire Square on a sunny day that promised that spring would come despite the bare branches of the trees in the square. The wind was steady from the west, and it had chased away the smoke, especially the coal smoke that so darkened the area when an easterly wind blew. The stench of the city was also much less than when the wind was from the east. All in all, Giles was content with his refurbished residence; it didn't hold a candle to Dipton Hall, his home in the country, but since he had to be in London to fulfill his duties in the House of Lords, this was a satisfactory abode. It certainly could be worse. Usually, his frigate stank far worse than what he was experiencing now, and neither it nor Dipton had the plays, opera, concerts, and lectures that London had on offer, especially in the Season.

Giles turned and opened the front door. No sooner had he got it half open than he was tackled by a good-sized boy who almost bowled him over. It was his eight-year-old nephew, Hugh, whose guardian he had become recently after the boy's parents died.

"Uncle Giles! Uncle Giles!" Hugh cried. "Someone has stolen Scruffy. You have to do something about it!"

"Easy does it, Hugh! Easy does it." Giles told the lad who had almost knocked him down. "What is this all about?"

"Scruffy ran out when Mr. Collins opened the door, and some people on the street scooped him up and walked away with him, even though he was barking. Henry and Robert went after them, but the people had disappeared."

"That's it?" queried Giles. "They just looked around the square from the front door?"

"Yes, my lord. There was nothing else worth doing."

"Oh? And how long after Hugh announced that Scruffy had been stolen did these footmen go outside?"

"Not more than ten minutes, my lord. They were very quick about responding from the kitchen when I summoned them."

"And you didn't think to go outside yourself, Collins?"

"Of course not, my lord. You can't have your butler rushing about into the street to rescue that mongrel from some ruffians. Of course not!"

"Come along, Hugh." said Giles, realizing that he would learn no more while talking with his butler in the entry to his mansion." We'll see if we can learn anything about where Scruffy has gone. I'll deal with you later, Collins,"

Giles took Hugh's hand, and they went down the front steps of the mansion. There was no one on the sidewalk around Camshire Square.

"In which direction did the men with Scruffy go, Hugh?" Giles asked.

"That way, Uncle Giles." Hugh pointed to the east.

"Come along, then. Let's ask the crossing sweeper if he saw anything."

At the corner where the street entered the square, Giles found the crossing sweeper who could be engaged to clear away horse dung and other unpleasant things that made crossing the roadway unpleasant. The crossing sweepers were not hired directly by the residents of Camshire Square but swept the way for people crossing the street in the expectation of getting a gratuity for their efforts. The only problem with this service was that the sweepers could not be counted on always to be present when their services were required.

"Did you see some people walk off with a dog?" Giles demanded without any preliminary greeting to the crossing sweeper at the corner nearest to Camsire House.

"Well, my lord, I noticed a group of ruffians who, surprisingly, were carrying a dog rather than having him on a rope or leash. I suppose that might be the one you are interested in."

"Yes. That was likely my dog. Which way did they go?"

"They turned east at the next corner, my lord. They'll be long gone now, my lord. I doubt you can catch them before they get to the rookery. They were a pretty rough, mean lot. I live near them, in Seven Dials, and I wouldn't cross them, my lord."

"I see. So you know these men?"

"Not really. But I recognized them from seeing them near my local. That bunch has a nasty reputation, even in the rookery, where things are pretty rough."

"What is your name?"

"Jarvis, my lord, but I'm usually called 'Jerker.'"

"I see. Thank you, Jerker." Giles reached into his pocket and found a shilling, which he passed to the crossing sweeper. "Come along, Hugh. We have to go home before we can do anything about finding Scruffy."

"My Lord, it wouldn't be safe for you to go looking for those men by yourself. Not in Seven Dials. They don't like people messing with their business. I give their type a wide berth even though I live close to them."

"Thank you, Jerker. I'll keep that in mind. But if I decide to take the matter further, I may want your help. Now come along, Hugh. We are going back home."

Giles turned away and started to walk towards Camshire House with Hugh in tow.

"Uncle Giles, can't we go and get Scruffy?"

"Not right now, Hugh. It wouldn't work without planning and getting some help. The men who took Scruffy are not nice people."

"Why is he called Jerker?"

"I expect that it is because he jerks his head from time to time. I am sure you noticed how he does it."

"Why does he do that?"

"I don't think he has any choice. It's just the way he is."

"Why is that, Uncle Giles?"

"I don't know, Hugh. You can ask Nanny Weaver," Giles replied. 'How could Nanny Weaver cheerfully put up with the endless string of questions children could ask,' he wondered.

Daphne had returned to Camshire House while Hugh and Giles were seeking news on Scruffy. She must have sized up the situation quickly and acted promptly on entering her home, for the butler Collins was nowhere to be seen.

"Giles, Hugh," she said the minute they entered the door. "Any luck?"

"No, except we now know a little about the men who snatched Scruffy," Giles replied.

"I've just dismissed Collins," Daphne announced. "The man is totally useless as a butler—my mistake for not checking him out more carefully. Let me finish with dealing with the immediate problems getting rid of our butler has caused, and then you can tell me what you learned.

"Henry," Daphne addressed one of the footmen hovering nervously, "ask Mrs. Harvey to come here."

"Daphne, why do you want the housekeeper right now?" asked Giles.

"I have to ask her to be in charge of all the servants and the house until I can find a replacement for Collins. He was obviously useless in a crisis and not really good as a butler. Now, what did you and Hugh discover?"

"That Scruffy was seen being carried off by some rough men. The crossing sweeper said he knew they lived in a rookery near Seven Dials."

"Rookery?"

"Yes. It is a squalid and dangerous part of the city. The crossing sweeper lives there, I discovered."

"What? That nice man who is so helpful when Betsey and I have to cross the street. He shouldn't live there. He is one of our servants, after all."

"Not really. He works for the tips people give him."

"What are you going to do about Scruffy?" Daphne changed the subject. "You can't just go rushing out to challenge these people. From what you have told me, it is too dangerous."

"Yes, it is, but I am not going to let them get away with it. I will contact that magistrate who helped me when I had that trouble at Green's Club. I'll also see if Sir Titus Emery has any suggestions."

"Good. I don't want you going into danger without knowing what it is. To that end, the only person we know who knows the rougher parts of London is Carstairs. Elsie told me that he is in London to straighten out some matters after his brother's death. You know that he has kept up some of his contacts with the shadier parts of London even after he became your cox'n and then left the sea to be at the Dipton Arms full time. He might have some good suggestions."

"He might. But how to contact him quickly is the problem."

"Elsie also told me where he is staying. I'll send a note to him right away."

"I'll send a note to Sir Titus, asking him to meet me at my club for lunch and telling him how we could benefit from assistance from the magistrate."

"Can't we do something about finding Scruffy sooner, Giles?" Daphne asked.

"I don't see how, my love. That rookery around Seven Dials is a dangerous place to try to get the dog back by myself. It is a hopeless tangle of streets, alleys, and houses with open doors and exits where dozens of families live, all piled on top of each other. The most likely outcome is that I wouldn't find hide or hair of Scruffy unless the thieves wanted me to, and it could be dangerous if I tried to follow any leads into the crowded houses. We need to make some preparations first to close off the area to prevent the thugs from disappearing or attacking us in overwhelming numbers. That is what talking to Sir Titus is all about — how to confront them to get our dog back safely."

"Yes, I see that."

"Now, what is this about dismissing Collins?"

"Yes, I did terminate his employment without notice. I didn't like his attitude towards cooperating when unusual circumstances arose and his standing on his elevated position and status as our butler to avoid pitching into whatever task was needed."

"I'm glad you did. I intended to do the same thing when I returned from looking around with Hugh. What will we do while we get a replacement, and how will we find someone better than Collins?"

"I'll be asking around and placing an advertisement. In the interim, I'll have Richards, the first footman, handle as many of Collins's tasks as he can while I'll have Mrs. Harvey oversee his work. Richards doesn't have the experience to be a bugler yet."

"Good, though I will look after the wine cellar. I don't know where Collins got that wine, but it won't do. It's enough to make a man give up drinking wine!"

"That would be a pity!"

"Giles, I have been thinking about the danger to the children when we are here," announced Daphne.

"What? Are they not safe? No one could easily break into this residence, even with a poor butler."

"True, but it is easy for them to go outside without Nanny Weaver or the nursemaids knowing. We are just lucky that Hugh didn't chase after Scruffy right away, or those men might have taken him too."

"You are right. I never thought of such dangers. One can't count on the parish constable or even the Bow Street magistrate and his runners to make sure we are safe. We will have to do something to protect our children — and, I suppose, ourselves."

"Maybe you should raise the subject with our neighbors this evening."

"This evening?"

"Yes, don't you remember? Sir Nottly Absenter, or, rather, Lady Absenter, asked us to dinner tonight to meet the other residents in Camshire Square. It should be a pleasant evening. I, of course, have visited all the women, courtesy visits, you know, but this is to include the men too. Lady Absenter had heard that you play the violin and that we play duets, so she wanted you to bring your violin."

"I'd forgotten all about engagement, but now I *am* keen to go. When you ladies withdraw, I can talk with the other men about how to protect ourselves better.

"It's a good idea for you to raise the subject with the man. Especially since trying to arrange things like that with the wives would get nowhere. Now, we had better get changed," Daphne concluded.

However, that wasn't the last they would hear about Scruffy that day. Mary appeared, sucking her thumb vigorously. "Aunt Daphne, will you get Scruffy back? I miss him."

"Uncle Giles is doing everything he can. Unfortunately, it's now dark, and we can't find him in the dark. Tomorrow, your uncle will do everything he can to find him."

"I want him to find Scruffy."

"I know, sweetheart. I'm sure that Uncle Giles will do his best."

Sir Nottly Absenter was a baronet whose title was predated by centuries. The sales of the title had been available since the time of James I, from whom his forefather bought the title. The Absenter family had never been distinguished, though their holding onto the family estate in Derbyshire through many national turmoils was in itself a notable feat. Sir Nottley was the second son of a third son, and only the most fortuitous of unfortunate events had made him the owner of the ancient title when those ahead of him in line for the honor had died. Before that, Sir Notley had been a highly successful solicitor. So successful, in fact, that he had no problem affording the second-largest mansion in Camshire Square.

Daphne had met Sir Knottly's wife when she introduced herself to the other residents of the square. Even though Lady Absenter had been startled by having a countess drop in to introduce herself, she and Daphne had instantly formed a friendship since she came from approximately the same level of society as Daphne and her father. Daphne was much more inclined to downplay her having risen to the highest levels of the aristocracy rather than assert her recently acquired status. Daphne had met some of the other ladies of the square and made friends with them, but this would be her first meeting with the husbands.

Night had fallen before Daphne and Giles were ready to set off across the square. Camshire Square was very well-lit, and the residents kept the streets and sidewalks better than most places in London. There was enough of a nip in the air that they felt glad to enter the warmth of the house across the square. It took a while for the initial awkwardness of people of ordinary status to get over being in the presence of members of the upper level of the aristocracy. To Daphne's relief, that soon passed, mainly because Giles, as usual, did nothing to emphasize his status and showed more interest in finding out about his fellow guests than impressing them with how important he was. By and large, they were nearer to the social status in which Daphne had grown up than were the people she had met at dinner parties at the residence of Giles's uncle, Lord Struthers.

When the ladies had withdrawn after dinner, Giles raised the issue of safety around Camshire Square. Only two other families had children and could see any point in having watchmen during the day to protect them, but even those two did not think the threat very serious and were reluctant to spend money on the project. The others could see no point at all and weren't prepared to contribute any money to have any daytime guardians.

Giles was disappointed, even though he could understand the reasons. In the mornings, each residence had servants in the street to clean the streets and sidewalks in front of their buildings, and, for the rest of the day, there were usually enough tradesmen and delivery people of one sort or another that one should be safe. On some occasions, there were, of course, rather undesirable-looking men cutting through, but surely the crossing sweepers would keep an eye on them. It was just bad luck that Giles had lost his dog, but it was a situation that was very unlikely to arise again.

Giles's proposal was a new suggestion as a way to spend money, and most of the other residents had no reason to fear for their children. On the other hand, Giles was very well known, and reports in the newspapers suggested that he was as rich as Croesus. He was more likely than the others to be the object of plots to extract money from him. He was surprised to learn that some of the other men expected that Giles would soon receive a ransom demand for the return of his dog. If he met the dog snatchers' demand, that would be the end of the story – none of them thought that paying ransom would just encourage others to try to kidnap Giles's children as well as his pets.

Giles was not convinced they were right. Paying the thugs off would surely encourage them to try to extract money by seizing the children, which would be terrifying for them even if they were promptly rescued and dangerous since the criminal enterprise could go wrong in ways that getting rid of the evidence might seem to the kidnappers the best solution to a difficult situation.

"Daphne," Giles pronounced as he joined her in bed. "I am more convinced than ever that we must act firmly so that kidnappers and thieves know that the consequences of raiding Camshire House are dire."

"I agree," Daphne replied, "but do try to stay safe yourself as you go after them. I am afraid, though. I never expected to have to worry about your safety when you are not on your ship. Now, what did you do today before the excitement of Scruffy being kidnapped distracted us?"

"Quite a bit, actually," Giles replied. "Sir Titus Emery tracked me down at my club."

"What did he want this time?"

"Can't he look for me just out of friendship?"

"I suppose, but the way in which you mentioned it indicates he had something on his mind."

"Several things. The Government, with the King's enthusiastic endorsement, wants to make me a marquess."

"Why do they want to do that? Is there any real difference between being an earl and a marquess?"

"Not really. Marquesses are higher in precedence than earls, but since I have the most ancient of earldoms and the newest marquessate, we follow the marquess with the next youngest title, and we are followed by the earl with the next oldest title, so it makes no difference to our precedence. You will, of course, be a marchioness. We can, however, change the place name of our title."

"What do you mean?"

"Well, we could make it the Marquessate of Dipton. I would still be the Earl of Camshire, and it might be less confusing if the two titles had different place names."

"I like that, but I confess that I find it all rather silly. I still feel like plain old Daphne Moorhouse, who got the title of 'Lady' by marrying my true love. Did Sir Titus explain why they want to give you this new title? I presume it doesn't come with any land or money or something of value."

"No, it doesn't. It is partly, probably mainly, because of what I did in stopping the silly Jacobite rebellion. But, since officially that can't be recognized to have occurred, they have invented a couple of other reasons. One is for trying to help the King on that hopeless mission to Hanover. The other is because the Russians have given me a medal for what I did when *Glaucus* was in St. Petersburg. They feel that they have to recognize it, though why, I don't know.

Chapter III

Long before dawn, Betsey, Daphne's maid, crept into her mistress's bedroom, where Daphne was asleep with Giles. Daphne woke at once when her maid opened the door as quietly as possible, bringing a bit of light with her candle. Giles simply rolled over and started to snore lightly.

"What is it, Betsey?" Daphne whispered.

"A note was shoved under the front door sometime in the night, my lady. It must have been before the outside workers started to clean the streets. Richards found it when he went to open the door to check that the cleaning had been done. He thought the message might be urgent."

"Do you have it, Betsey?"

"Here it is, my lady."

"Raise the candle so I can read it."

Betsey complied, and the change in light woke Giles.

"What is it, Daphne?" Giles asked. As always, he woke up alert. Years of being awakened to danger at sea had instilled that in him.

"A note was delivered earlier this morning. Betsey thought it might be important."

"What does it say?"

Daphne read the note scrawled in the almost illegible handwriting of someone who obviously was not accustomed to writing frequently. "It says, 'To get your dog back, bring £100 to the Black Cat in 7 Dials at 6 o'clock today.' Do they really think we would pay one hundred pounds for that dog? We could buy dozens of them for that price."

"They probably guess that Scruffy is a treasured pet," Giles replied. "He certainly isn't worth anything like that amount as a foxhound, but I don't know how to put a price on him as a pet."

"My brother's children certainly latched on to him after their parents died. They will be devastated if we don't get him back."

"Yes, they will be. I have seen Mary telling Scruffy about her loss and how her parents are in heaven waiting to meet him. We can't let that sort of comfort be taken away."

"I hadn't heard about the second part of what you heard, but both Hugh and Mary seem to have become very fond of him for the comfort he gives them just licking their faces. But Giles, you can't go into that crowded area all by yourself to get Scruffy. There is too much danger that the thugs would simply beat you and take the £100. They might even kill you without you even getting to see Scruffy."

"I know. That is why I am contacting Carstairs and Sir Titus. Only if we can overwhelm these men and be confident that Scruffy won't be killed will we go ahead with any action. Even if paying these creatures £100 would get Scruffy back, the news would be out, and we would have many more attempts to hold us up."

"So what will you do?" demanded Daphne.

Before Giles could answer, there was a light knock on the door. Betsey opened it a crack to find Richards looking nervous. "Mr. Richards," she whispered, "What are you doing here? My lady's still in bed."

Soft as the maid's voice had been, Giles heard the words and called, "Richards, come in and tell us what is afoot. I know it is important since, otherwise, you wouldn't dream of bothering us at this hour."

"Yes, my lord." The acting butler was glad not to have to wonder how to wake the Earl with important news without bothering the Countess. "Sir Titus Emery and Mr. Carstairs are downstairs and want to see you as soon as possible. They mentioned that they are here at your request."

"Yes, they are. I did not expect them so early. Is breakfast ready yet?"

"Not quite, my lord. Most of the dishes are still in the kitchen, though we were about to bring the food to the breakfast room."

"Excellent. I'll be down as soon as I can wash and put on some clothes. Show our visitors to the breakfast room and tell them to start as soon as the dishes appear. I suppose that the hot water is not yet up here."

"I am afraid not, my lord. It is still very early in the morning."

"No matter. I am sure that Cook can come up with some tea, and they may prefer small beer for breakfast. I know that Carstairs does. Just ask them rather than waiting until you can provide them with the usual full range of choices. I can wash in cold water; I've done it often enough at sea. I'll be down in a few minutes."

Giles entered the breakfast room ten minutes later to find that Carstairs and Sir Titus were engaged in a lively debate over whether the government was doing enough to protect the ordinary citizens of London. It must have arisen from Giles's messages to them mentioning the theft of his dog.

"There you are, Giles, snuggling in bed when others are hoping to get you out of a jam," Sir Titus welcomed him.

"I suggested we meet for lunch, Titus, not before the crack of dawn. Carstairs, thank you for coming even sooner than I expected."

"You're welcome, captain. I wanted to get here before you do something stupid."

Sir Titus was startled to hear Carstairs, who he certainly did not regard as an equal either to himself or to Giles, speak so bluntly to his former commander. Of course, Carstairs' presence at this ungodly hour did show the respect that Carstairs had for Giles. Then Sir Titus realized that that had also been his reason for rising so early and coming to Camshire House. "I quite agree, Camshire," he said. "Going against the denizens of that rookery can be fatal. I have asked The Chief Magistrate of Westminster to come here as soon as possible to advise us. You will remember him from his help when you were clearing out those imbeciles running Green's Club. He'll be along here as soon as he can."

"Maybe we should wait until he arrives," suggested Giles. The ensuing conversations centered around his two guests sounding out what the other was like. They were from very different walks of life and experiences, united only by their respect for Giles. Their only previous meeting had been very casual when Giles and Sir Titus had stopped in for a drink at Carstairs's Dipton Arms. Sir Titus realized that Carstairs's former shipmates and other acquaintances would be an ideal unofficial force for righting wrongs in the rookeries. Carstairs, who had been puzzled about Sir Titus's role in taking on the denizens of Seven Dials, realized that he was the ideal man to ensure that any actions of dubious legality in retrieving Giles's dog would not come back to haunt them.

They only had to wait twenty minutes before Richards announced the arrival of the Chief Magistrate, Rudolf Downing.

"Lord Camshire," the Chief Magistrate opened the discussion after the welcoming formalities had been dispensed with and he had selected his breakfast, "I am alarmed by the crime you described, though I am not sure that I can do much to retrieve your dog successfully. A raid by my Runners* would be spotted immediately, and the offenders would be warned before we could get near them. We are not a large force, and the rookeries are impossible to police. The thieves would, I am afraid, kill your dog and leave him in the street somewhere, and we would have no evidence on which to convict them or even arrest them."

"I am not surprised by your reaction, Mr. Downing," Giles replied, "but I had something different in mind. I was thinking more of a private brawl to which you would turn a blind eye if there were injuries or even more regrettable outcomes. Between my outside servants and former shipmates of ours that Carstairs has kept in touch with, I believe that we have a group that can rescue Scruffy, the dog, though at the possible cost of some cracked heads."

"I should be clear," Carstairs broke in, "that some of the people would be residents of the seven Dials area who have become fed up with the behavior of these crooks but don't want any steps necessary to put them in their place result in your arresting them if they are not entirely legal."

"I understand," stated the magistrate. "As long as what you do is related to getting Lord Camshire's dog back or protecting yourselves, you have nothing to fear. I give you my word on that. Now, what do you have in mind, Lord Camshire?"

"Well, Mr. Downing, I was thinking that I would take my outside workers to the Seven Dials area to meet up with some of Carstairs's friends. The rest of his friends, the ones who live in the immediate area of Seven Dials, would station themselves to prevent the cretins from slipping away when we show up. Carstairs says that with many of the buildings having several entrances, Seven Dials is a rabbit warren where it is all too easy for people to disappear when they want. These men would intercept the kidnappers as they try to get away from the ones who declare that they are coming for the dog.

"That sounds like a very sensible plan to me," responded the Chief Magistrate. "Now, I have brought a map of the Seven Dials neighborhood with me. It is already a complex area, with all those roads meeting in a small circle, but it is made worse by the way the old buildings have been divided up so that you can enter by one door and get out somewhere else. This map may help you to plan.

"Do you have that ransom demand, Lord Camshire?"

"Yes, of course, it is right here."

Mr. Downing scrutinized the message. "The Black Cat. Even though Seven Dials is quite close to my office, I don't know it very well, including just where this place is. It might be a flash house, but there are a great many in that area, and I don't know where this one might be. It would be nice to know its location before we plan our attack. Do you know, Mr. Carstairs?"

"I am afraid not, sir. There seem to be dozens of pubs in that rookery."

"I know who would know," said Giles. "Jerker, the crossing sweeper, lives in that area. I'll go fetch him."

Giles rose from the table and headed for the front door. The Chief Magistrate stared after him, wondering what had come over his host.

"That's the Earl of Camshire for you," stated Sir Titus."I don't imagine any other earl in England would know the name of their crossing sweeper, let alone where he lived."

"And would go to ask him a question rather than have a servant bring him to his house," added Carstairs.

Giles, quite unaware of anything unusual in what he was doing, ran out the front door and saw Jerker leaning on his broom, waiting for people who would appreciate him clearing the way for them.

"Jerker," said Giles, "Do you know where the Black Cat is in Seven Dials?"

"Yes, my lord. It's in Mercer Street, a few doors down from the Seven Dials circle. It's the local I mentioned to you yesterday."

"Could you show us on a map where it is?"

"I don't know. I've never looked at a map, and I can't read, my lord. Surely, you do not intend to go looking for your dog there."

"I am. Those men have my dog and want money to give it back."

"That's madness, my lord, if you will pardon my bluntness. Those men would just as soon slit your throat as give you back your dog. They'll take your money and demand more."

"We're doing it anyway. Will you help us?"

"My lord, I have to live there. If I help you, I won't be able to sleep easy at night."

"Do you have a family, Jerker?"

"Not anymore, my lord. I lost them to cholera. I lost my home after that — drinking."

"You seem to have that under control. If I hire you as an outside servant, responsible for the street crossings, with, of course, a room in the mews* and meals in the servant's hall, would you be interested in helping us with this problem of getting the dog back?"

"Yes, I would jump at the chance to get out of Seven Dials."

"Good, come along then."

Giles, accompanied by a rather nervous Jerker, returned to the breakfast room to discover that Daphne had joined the other two men."

"Daphne, I am sure you remember Jerker, the crossing sweeper. He has just joined our staff as an outside worker. He has agreed to help us root out these cretins who have stolen Scruffy. Jerker, you recognize Lady Camshire, I am sure. This is Sir Titus Emery, Mr. Downing, and Mr. Carstairs. We intend to teach the denizens of Seven Dials a lesson so that they will not interfere with us again. They have summoned me to pay them ransom for our dog at the Black Cat, and we want to surprise them and get the dog back. If a few heads have to be broken in the process, that is all right with us, including Mr. Downing, the Chief Magistrate of Westminster. But we don't know exactly where this Black Cat pub is. Can you explain that to us and show us on the map, please."

"I'll try, my lord, but I am not used to looking at maps, and I can't read that writing."

"Let's see if I can help," said Mr. Downing. "I have some idea of what the map should be showing. Yes, here is Seven Dials, and here is the church, St. Giles in the Fields."

Jenkins studied the map, nodded his head, and placed his index finger very close to where Mr. Downing had pointed out Seven Dials.

"I think I understand it now," he said. "Yes, here is the way I go when I come back from Camshire Square. Yes, into the circle of Seven Dials and then down this way to get home, which is up this little alley. Let me see —the Black Cat is about here." Jerker put his finger on a point on the map quite close to the Seven Dials circle. And this little lane is how I get home."

"Do you know how many ways there are out of the Black Cat?" asked Mr. Downing.

"Let me think. There is a back door, of course. And once out of it, you could go through any of the passages onto this street or that one, the next one leading out of Seven Dials. Also, you could go along this little alley to either street or even likely through the passages of any of the other houses. They never close their doors, except at night, and you can still always get in then."

"I see," said Giles. "So, if we came in by the front entrance from this street to get the dog back, they could easily disappear into the tangle of passages behind the building."

"Yes, my lord," replied Jerker.

"That's always the major problem of policing the rookeries," added Mr. Downing. "When we try to arrest them, they just melt away into the buildings."

"Well, you will just have to take control of the back door before we approach the front door," said Mr.

Downing. "Somehow, these people always seem to know we are coming."

"That's because you people are easily recognized, and your coming is never good news," muttered Sir Titus.

"Yes, that's true," Carstairs agreed while Jerker nodded his head.

"So what do you want? Not have my men come at all?" enquired Mr. Downing. "If we are not there, you are at hazard of being blamed if anything goes wrong, even criminally blamed if someone is seriously injured. If we are there, or at least near, it can be claimed that you were just helping us to enforce the law."

"Might I suggest, Mr. Downing," broke in Sir Titus, "that you remain a short distance away until the other have succeeded in cutting off the escape routes except down this road, where you can be coming along at a very brisk pace?"

"That makes sense to me."

"Good, then that's what we will do," Giles cut off further debate. "Carstairs, you will come along this road, the next one counterclockwise from the main one, with your group, possibly well spread out so that you don't look as if you are looking for trouble. And then slip into this lane as if that was your intention all along. Maybe you should spread yourselves out a bit, Carstairs, so that you don't look like a large group looking for trouble. Just a few sets of pals not connected to each other who happen to take the same turn. Once into that alley, it shouldn't be too hard to find the back entrance of the Black Cat. Jerker, please go with Carstairs to show him how to get to the back of the Black Cat.

"Jerker, can you hear St. Giles's clock striking from this road?"

"Yes, my lord. Both the hours and the quarter hours."

"Good, I am supposed to come to the Black Cat at five by St. Giles's clock. Carstairs, time your entry into the alley to start at quarter to five by that clock. At five minutes to five, I will come along here on the circle to get to the Inn a couple of minutes before five. I'll have a couple of the men from my stables with me, and the others will be about two minutes behind. Mr. Downing, can you arrange for your men to be about ten minutes away from the Black Cat, preferably seeming to be investigating something else, and set off at five to be at the Black Cat by ten past? If we haven't sorted out the problem by then, we may need your help. If we have, you can take away any that we think deserve to be punished beyond being beaten by us."

"Are you sure, my lord? It is a way, maybe the only way, to get these miscreants before the law, but you are taking a risk."

"I know, but I want it known that no one can threaten the Earl of Camshire without there being very serious consequences.

"Well, that seems to complete our planning. Sir Titus, if you are wise, you will stay well away from the mayhem."

"Then I am not wise, Giles. I will accompany you. After all, I owe you for coming to my rescue in Shropshire — well, it was Daphne, of course, who saved me. However, I wouldn't miss the fun for anything."

The meeting broke up after that. The three men went about their regular activities. They would not meet up until the raid on the Black Cat, and then only if it went as planned.

Daphne had said nothing during the breakfast meeting, eating her bacon and eggs, toast, and kippers in silence while listening to the plans being formulated. She was not happy about the planned attack, but she wasn't about to argue with Giles in front of his friends and acquaintances. Once they had left, she had no hesitation in challenging him.

"Giles," she began, "is it really necessary to go after these thugs in this way? Scruffy isn't a valuable dog; we can always get another one. The children will soon become attached to a different one."

"It's not that, my love," Giles replied. "We cannot let people snatch our property and try to blackmail us without response. We will be living here when we are not at Dipton. And you will be here by yourself when I am at sea. If the rabble in that rookery, or other such places, think we are an easy target, they may cause us any amount of harm and damage. I need it to be known in the rookery that attacking Camshire House is not without great peril for the attackers. We have to nip this thing in the bud."

"But Giles, none of the other people living here have reported that sort of theft."

"There have been a few, though they were never traced to the source or have been a severe problem. I found that out at last night's dinner from the men after the ladies had withdrawn. They had just shrugged it off, saying they could realistically do nothing about it. They figure that it is cheaper just to take the losses and make sure their locks are as secure as they can make them."

"But there you are. We can do that too."

"No. Two things are different in our case. None of the others are spectacularly rich, and no one has thought to try to kidnap their children — yet. Stealing Scruffy and holding us up to ransom is bound to get people tempted to try it again if they get away with it this time. It's not only our dog. What if they want to take one of the children next? No. I have to put an end to this, even though I wish I didn't have to. The fortuitous presence of Carstairs with his connections makes this the ideal time to act."

After hearing this, Daphne knew that trying to stop Giles would be hopeless. She had had to worry about his safety while at sea. She would just have to put up with this foolishness on land. Or would she? Could she at least help in some way? She certainly wasn't going to share these thoughts with Giles. He would forbid her from trying to take part, as was his right. That didn't mean she couldn't think about it.

Chapter IV

The breakfast meeting broke up after everything about their plans was clear to all. Sir Titus went off on whatever mysterious business he had. Mr. Downing left to assemble his runners and to do whatever else his job required until it was time to join the attack on Seven Dials. Carstairs took his leave to go and assemble his friends. Giles took Jerker to the stables to arrange for his new job, which would mainly involve continuing as the crossing sweeper but with responsibilities to keep his eyes open for anyone who might seem to want to steal from or harass the residents of Camshire Square.

Daphne stayed in the breakfast room for several minutes thinking. She wasn't happy about Giles charging off into the notorious rookery looking for Scruffy, though he could understand Giles wanting to get the dog back. She was less convinced that this would ensure that thieves would not target them after Giles had taken on the thugs. Even if that were true, was it worth the danger? However, there was no stopping Giles, she knew, without creating a lasting resentment; he was used to putting his life on the line in the course of duty. He would see no reason not to if it was necessary to protect his family and home. He might agree if she tried to dissuade him, but it could lead to a lasting rancor. In addition, he had already gone too far to pull out with his self-respect unharmed.

If Giles must go to Seven Dials, then Daphne felt she should also be present at the confrontation with the kidnappers. She would not stand idly by. However, she couldn't go with Giles or in a guise in which he would recognize her. Then, he would be distracted by thoughts of keeping her safe, which would put them in more danger.

What sort of a woman would be seen in Seven Dials naturally, and what would she look like?

Daphne could not go to Seven Dials with her maid Betsey as if she were going shopping in Piccadilly without drawing a lot of hostile attention in Seven Dials. She could not look like one of the ladies of the house in Mayfair, nor even like one of their lady's maids. The more modestly dressed wives of professional men, prosperous merchants, and even shopkeepers would also be vastly out of place.

Daphne realized that she didn't know what women in a rookery might look like, though she must have seen them while being driven around on the edges of some of the more unsavory parts of London. But who might live there while working elsewhere? On the basis of no evidence, Daphne guessed that it would be maids of women whose husbands could only just scrape together enough wages to allow hiring a maid of all work, or maybe washerwomen. Such speculation was all well and good, but where would she find a costume that would fit her needs? She had no idea. Would Betsey? Betsey was from the country, but, in her visits to London, she had enjoyed exploring the metropolis on her days off despite her perennial problem with corns. And she was willing to accompany Daphne on what she regarded as stupid errands or activities far below her mistress's proper activities.

Daphne asked Richards to summon Betsey. She showed up almost immediately. Had Betsey been flirting with Richards, Daphne wondered. Probably, she had been. Betsey had enough experience to know that her job would be made much easier if she had the butler on her side.

"You wanted me, my lady?" Betsey asked, giving no hint about what she had been doing.

"Yes. What do you think respectable women walking through the rookery near Sr. Giles would typically wear?"

"I wouldn't know, my lady. I have never been there. It is supposed to be a terrible part of town. Everyone there is impoverished. And I am told it is not a good place for women to be."

"That is true, I have heard that too. But there must be some respectable women who live there or who at least do not want to invite unsolicited lewd approaches. Someone like a washerwoman, perhaps, or a maid of all work who is paid very badly."

"Ah, I see what you mean. Being poor, those women's clothes would be grubby, I expect, and a dingy headscarf would hide their hair. Why do you ask, my lady."

"Giles wants to stage a raid on Seven Dials to rescue Scruffy and put the thugs who want money for him in their places. He is quite determined to do so."

"I heard about it. My lord must really have the bit firmly between his teeth if you couldn't rein him in. But surely you are not intending to go with him."

"No, of course not. He would never let me, and if he did, he would spend so much time worrying about my safety that it would be much more dangerous for both of us. I just want to see what happens and help if things are going wrong without him seeing that I am there."

"I see. So you need a disguise so that the Captain won't notice you. That is a bit of a tall order, my lady. None of the clothes the women in service here wear when they go out would do."

"Why not?"

"They are all very proud to work in Camshire House, my lady."

"I see. What about the work clothes of the laundry maids, the scullery maids, or even the clothes of Janice, who lights the fires each morning? Surely, she needs something different from the normal clothes she wears the rest of the day."

"I can see if there is anything suitable, my lady. I think Janice just wears her apron and a kerchief over her head. But maybe the kitchen maids have something. Unfortunately, one of the men takes out the ashes from the kitchen stoves in the morning before the fires are lit, but maybe the kitchen maids have something for when they gather herbs from the garden. I'll see what I can find for us."

"For us? Betsey, I can't expect you to take part in my foolishness. Certainly, it would ruin any attempt to be unnoticeable if you trail behind as you do here in London."

"Of course, I wasn't thinking of doing that. We servants usually try to go in pairs, especially when going to the poorer parts of town, and I imagine it is the same in the rookeries. Of course, I'll come with you. After all, Lord Camshire would have my guts for garters if I knowingly let you go off on your own. Anyway, I like adventures. With any luck, I will get to kick some men who threaten us, just like I did in Shropshire."

"Well, I suppose that I don't have a choice if you insist. See what you can find in the way of disguises. I haven't yet determined that I will go, and I won't if we can't disguise ourselves convincingly."

"I'll see what I can do, my lady," Betsey replied, with a smile that said she was determined that the unwise adventure should go ahead.

When Betsey left to look for costumes, Daphne reflected that there was no point worrying about what would happen later. She might as well get on with her tasks. Luckily, the new house seemed to be running smoothly. She should, however, look at all the proposals and quotes she had for implementing the ball that she had announced that she would hold. It was expected of her as the new Countess of Camshire to establish her position in the heights of aristocratic fashion and influence. It would be even more necessary for it to be a great success in light of the news that Giles would soon be a marquess. She reflected that in the ceremonial pecking order of the titled aristocracy, to change from being the most senior earl to being the most junior marquess was no change in the overall ranking. Still, more would be expected of her with the new title, and it was up to her that Giles and she deserved the promotion not only by public service but also by the splendor of their entertainments. Well, for that to happen, she had to keep track of the details as well as the general plan for the ball. That required, today, that she go over the plans and the arrangements that had already been made and possibly verify the continued availability of what she had arranged. She also had to consider whether, in view of the change level of position, she should arrange for an even more splendid orchestra. Or would it be a good idea to have two orchestras to get more variation in the musical offerings? Not incidentally, it would help to keep her mind off what she was planning for later in the day.

Giles returned from the mews and started to practice his violin. Daphne had heard from his crew members that they usually heard the sounds of his violin as he waited to engage with an enemy and had nothing to do until his ship closed with her opponent. Apparently, he used the same mechanism to pass the time before action when on land.

Luncheon was an almost silent meal as Giles and Daphne were lost in their thoughts. The only surprise came at the end when Richards, after some hesitation, addressed Giles: "My lord, I hope that you will allow me to participate in the expedition to retrieve Scruffy."

"Are you sure, Richards? It could be dangerous."

'Yes, my lord, I know. I want to participate. The more men you have, the better, I reckon."

"Well, you can't go in your livery."

"I know, my lord. I talked with Mr. Miller, the stable master, and he can lend me a spare set of clothes he has which look sufficiently worn that I will fit in."

"Well, thank you, Richards. And welcome to our adventure."

Giles went to the mews at four o'clock. Daphne wasted no time going to see Betsey in her dressing room. The lady's maid was already dressed as a maid whose salary hardly covered basic living expenses and had a similar costume for Daphne. The only part of the transformation of her mistress into a similarly poverty-stricken woman that bothered her was the large and somewhat tattered headscarf that she had found. It covered Daphne's hair, which, Betsey prided herself, was among the best dressed of all the high-placed ladies who resisted the temptation of having vulgarly flamboyant hairstyles. There was no hiding the healthy, tanned appearance of Daphne's face, Betsey feared. However, Daphne saw the problem when she checked her appearance in the looking glass and ordered Betwey to powder her face with ashes from the fireplace, which produced exactly the look that both agreed would be suitable for someone who labored all day without much chance to avoid getting dirty. Would Giles recognize her if he caught sight of her while dealing with the crook? She hoped not. She did not want to distract him at a tricky time.

Daphne's musings were interrupted by Betsey showing her a rolling pin and a pastry paddle that they could carry in the bags they would be taking with them. "These are the best weapons I could find in the kitchen. We may need something better than our fists. Last time we took on a group of men, I could just kick them, but now it is different, though remember that kicking a man in the crotch does wonders for making him stop trying to fight you."

"Good idea, Betsey. Where did you get them? They look extra big," Daphne responded.

"Cook gave them to me when I asked for one. I was surprised. I expected her to give me a lecture on how important her kitchen and everything that was in it. Too good for me even though I am a lady's maid."

"That's because she is afraid of you."

"She can't be."

"But she is. In her last place, the lady's maid started to lord it over her, and when she objected to her mistress, the mistress dismissed the cook instead of the lady's maid. I hired her the minute I heard that she had been let go. We needed a cook, and she was one of the best that I had.

Daphne and Betsey left Camshire House as soon as they were ready. It was a bit early to go directly to Seven Dials, but Daphne wanted to avoid any chance that Giles would see them. She also wanted to go by St Giles in the Fields to make sure that she had the right time, as specified. Daphne knew that Giles had set his watch to St. Giles's time. Daphne wanted to be sure that she knew what that version of five o'clock by St. Giles's clock was. She wanted to arrive at the Black Cat a short period before

Giles and his crew were to appear, but she didn't want to have to loiter near the pub any longer than necessary.

St. Giles was an easy walk from Camshire Square. As Daphne and Betsey walked towards it, with Daphne insisting that they walk abreast despite Betsey's qualms, the houses and grounds seemed to be getting steadily more poorly maintained, and streets seemed to be grubbier. St Giles in the Fields was an oasis of well-maintained calm in the sleazy neighborhood.

Daphne and Betsey were more than ten minutes early. The best place to wait, Daphne figured, was in the church itself. Just as they went in, Daphne saw Carstairs hurrying along in a group of several men. He looked straight at her and Betsey but showed no sign that he recognized her.

The clock in St. Giles's tower struck the three-quarters hour. Daphne waited one more minute before she and Betsey left the church and headed for Seven Dials. She had no difficulty finding the circle since Mr. Downing's sketch map had been accurate. At ten minutes to five, they passed the door of the Black Cat. There was no sign of Giles yet, and Daphne did not want to seem to be loitering, suggesting that they expected something to happen. Nor did she want to wander away from the pub since, if they did, they might not be available if needed.

"Betsey," Daphne said in a low voice, "we should argue about something. Just with enough strength to account for us stopping, but not so violently as to draw a crowd."

Betsey replied, "You can't say that about Mrs. Higgins. She isn't a skinflint. Not at all. Why look at what she gave me when she bought a new one." Betsey pulled the pastry paddle which she had brought as a weapon.

"That old thing! I wouldn't throw it in the garbage," Daphne retorted. "It's all chipped. If you try to use it, your pies will be as ugly as sin. Mrs. Lampray gave me this rolling pin, which only has a small chip out of the edge and can make as good pastry as you want."

"Says you! As if you had an oven to bake pastry or a table to roll it out on."

The two women kept up this banter to the amusement of passers-by, but it was not intense enough to warrant anyone stopping in the hope that they would come to blows. It was the perfect way to loiter near the pub without appearing to loiter. Daphne could even keep an eye open as she threw insults at Betsey to see when Giles arrived. Unfortunately, just as she caught sight of Giles approaching them from Seven Giles, the situation changed completely.

One-eyed Dick had set up shop at a table in the Black Cat with the group of his cronies who had been with him when he kidnapped Scruffy. He had Scruffy with him, with a rope tied around his neck. His boasts about his cleverness became more extensive and emphatic as he downed one tankard of beer after another. The toff from Camshire Square was bound to pay him £100 for taking such good care of his dog. Maybe, as the beer did more and more of his thinking for him, he should make it one hundred guineas. That had a more elegant ring to it, didn't it? One-eyed Dick could always use an extra five quid, maybe to buy drinks for all his followers.

Scruffy had been sitting at One-eyed Dick's feet in the pub, gnawing away at the rope serving as a leash. About the time Daphne and Betsey had started arguing near the pub's door, he had gnawed through it entirely but made no move at the time. Then, two things happened at once. Daphne and Betsey raised their voices, and a drunken patron opened the door to stagger out of the establishment. Scruffy heard Daphne's voice. He got to his feet and shot out the door, heading straight to Daphne, reading himself to jump up and kiss her. Was he ever happy to hear that familiar voice and see those two women, even if they were dressed in unusual costumes!

Daphne saw him coming. "Down, Scruffy!" she commanded. Would it work, she wondered. Hugh and Mary had been training Scruffy with the basic commands as well as ones about rolling over and shaking hands.

The lessons had been a success. Scruffy dropped to the ground.

"Stay!" Daphne ordered as she stepped forward, raising her skirt enough so that Scruffy had disappeared under it. Without missing a beat, she continued her dispute with Betsey.

Looking up the street, Daphne saw men with white armbands approaching. Giles had arrived!

Giles was still a couple of hundred feet away, making slow progress through the crowd that always filled the streets in the rookery. One-eyed Dick came roaring out of the Black Cat, having discovered that Scruffy had disappeared. He spotted Daphne and Betsey nearby and roared up to them.

"Where did that damned dog go," he shouted at Daphne.

"What dog?" Daphne answered blandly, secretly hoping that Giles would hurry up before anything got worse.

"That dog that ran out of the Black Cat. You must have seen it, you cunt."

Daphne had no idea why the ruffian had called her a hunt, but she wasn't going to ask him now what he meant.

"Did a dog run out of the pub?" she asked innocently.

"You must have seen it, or you," One-eyed Dick pointed at Betsey. "I'll shake the truth out of you."

He took a terrifying step towards Daphne, apparently intending to carry out his threat.

Daphne was not prepared to let One-eyed Jack near her. She still had the rolling pin in her hand and swung it hard at the ruffian. It hit him solidly on the forehead, and he staggered towards Betsey. She whacked him with her pastry paddle, breaking the implement. For good measure, Scruffy left his pace under Daphne's skirt, jumped up, and bit One-eyed's nose.

One-eyed Jack dropped to his knees, bleeding copiously from his nose, but he was not unconscious. Betsey quickly cured that condition by kicking him in the crotch with a good swing of her leg. Down he went, moaning piteously and grabbing his privates.

"Ouch — ow, ow — that damned corn," groaned Betsey before she remembered herself. She had not thought that she needed to get Mr. Jackson, Dipton's apothecary, to trim her corns before coming to London; now, she was paying the price for her forgetfulness. Of course, she never expected that the opportunity to kick a man with impunity would arise ever again.

Giles arrived on the scene just as One-eyed Dick went down. He stared for a moment at the scene where two poorly dressed women had just overwhelmed their attacker. He was admiring their daring when he realized that one of them looked very familiar despite the clothes. It was

Daphne, no doubt about it. What in the world was she doing here?

Even as Giles rushed towards Daphne, he realized that the other woman was Betsey, Daphne's maid. He had heard that she had kicked a gentleman several times in the adventure she had shared with Daphne in Shropshire. Then he was up to the women, and he wrapped Daphne in his arms.

"What are you doing here?" he demanded. "You could have been hurt."

Before Daphne could answer, Giles was distracted by another development. One of the men who had left the Black Cat behind, One-eyed Jack, saw him put down by the women. This would never do, but instead of rushing over to pay them a lesson, he returned to the pub to yell through the door, "One-eyed has been knocked down by a woman and kicked!"

All the denizens were horrified by the announcement. Being bested by a woman was something that could not be tolerated. Nobody knew where it would stop if women were allowed to get away with such behavior. The situation had to be rectified immediately. To a man, they rushed out of the pub and headed for their fallen hero. In their haste to avenge their leader, they failed to notice the group of men from Seven Dials, all wearing white armbands, approaching. Giles's men fall on the pub dwellers, enthusiastically attacking them unexpectedly from the flank. There were more pub-dwellers than Giles's outside workers, but in a minute, Giles's men were joined by a second group with white armbands emerging from the Black Cat. Carstairs and his friends had arrived. This addition to the attacking forces took the fight out of the pub patrons. Many took to their heels and disappeared into doorways in the houses nearby. The remaining men were rapidly tied up, for both groups had brought ropes.

A few of those running away did not disappear into the warrens that would frustrate any attempt to capture them. Instead, they ran down the street away from Seven Dials. But after a few steps, they met a third group with white armbands. Mr. Downing and his runners had arrived at last. They had brought three carts with them. They had loaded the miscreants into the cart in no time.

When the Chief Magistrate's party was about to leave, Mr. Downing came over to Giles. "My lord, you and your people have done a magnificent job. We are all very grateful, and you have made my job of keeping order much easier. The rookery will have learned a valuable lesson — at least for the time being. I will cart this collection to my offices in Bow Street, where we will prepare for their trials. It would help, my lord, if you could come to provide witness to what offenses they have committed, particularly their ringleader, who deserves much more serious punishment than was already meted out by Lady Camshire and her maid."

"Then I'd better come now so you can get on with your work."

"I was thinking about tomorrow, my lord, though today would be better for me. I presume you must see to Lady Giles's safety before you can come."

"That's not necessary, Mr. Downing," Daphne broke in. "We can fend for ourselves on the way home, especially as Reacher and Richards have volunteered to make sure we get home safely."

"Then, I'll be with you in a moment," Giles agreed. He headed towards the door of the Black Cat, signaling Carstairs to join him.

Inside, they found the pub owner ensconced behind the bar, busily polishing glasses. He knew nothing was better for business than a fight outside his door.

"Landlord," Giles said to the man. "Here are four guineas. Make sure that everyone with a white armband has as much of your drinks and food as they want. Mr. Carstairs, here, will see to it that none of them get too rowdy."

Carstairs was about to protest that four guineas were far too much for the man who had harbored One-eyed Jack and his confederates. Giles was just asking to be robbed since, when he left, the pub owner was likely to skimp and provide inferior refreshments to what four guineas should purchase. Then Carstairs realized that his worries were unwarranted. It would be a long time before people in Seven Dials forgot the lessons that it was extremely unwise to try to steal from the Earl of Camshire and that he could be generous if one offered help. Giles did not need to worry that his associates would not be treated well. Carstairs thought he might demand the change from the landlord when, finally, the festivities broke up. Giles would be amused when Carstairs told him about it. His Captain's reply would likely be, "Keep the change, Carstairs."

Giles returned to Daphne to explain what he had done. He was about to say something to her when he realized that Scruffy was nowhere in sight. "Where is Scruffy?" Giles asked in a loud voice. "Has he run off? Has all this been for nothing?"

Daphne laughed. "Of course not. He has more sense than any of us. When he had done his job to scare the ruffian off, he sought the safe place where he had already been hiding: under my skirts."

"Come out, Scruffy!" she commanded the dog. He pushed his head out to check that all was safe and then emerged fully to hold up his paw to Giles. Mary and Hugh had been teaching him to shake hands when meeting people, and the dog knew that his master knew the drill. Giles bent down and solemnly shook the dog's paw. "Now, go with Daphne, Scruffy," he said. She'll show you the way home."

It didn't bother Giles that some people would think it demeaning to shake a dog's paw. He might even be setting a new trend among ton*.

"Come home as soon as you can, Giles," Daphne said. "Come along, Scruffy," Hugh and Mary have been worried about you."

Daphne and a still-limping Betsey set off to retrace their steps to Camshire Square, side by side since Daphne had signaled to her maid that they did not need to keep to society's stricture that ladies walking in London had to be trailed by a lady's maid. Richards and Jerker fell into step behind them. When Daphne was sure that they were out of sight of Giles, she stopped. "Richards, Jerker, you don't need to see us home. We got here quite safely on our own and are perfectly safe going back together. Go back and enjoy the celebration at the Black Cat. You've earned it."

"Oh, my lady, I can't do that. With all the male servants away, there will be chaos preparing for dinner, and I'll have to see how I can help Cook get some sort of dinner provided to you and the children. Of course, Jerker should return if you are sure he is not needed. I imagine he would like to gather all his possessions and bring them to Camshire House, and now is a good time for him to do it."

"Is that what you want, Jerker?"

"Yes, my lady, but I can do it after we get you to Camshire House."

"No. You had better go. The shock of what happened will likely mean that no one will hinder you, and that may not be true once it sinks in just what we have done this afternoon. Go. There is still plenty of daylight to get what you want safely.

"Richards, come and walk between Betsey and me. We are not dressed appropriately to have a man following us."

The three of them continued towards Camshire Square in line abreast, with Daphne throwing questions to Richards. Betsey was not surprised. She knew, just as Daphne knew, that Richards would like to get the vacant butler's position. This was an informal way to get information that would be helpful in that decision.

Chapter V

Giles stretched his legs as his coach swayed along the turnpike to Portsmouth. In the past, he had gone there by public coach, leaving the traveling coach for Daphne's use. Somehow, despite their wealth, having two full-sized coaches had not occurred to them. But with the newly restored house in London, whose mews had plenty of room for two coaches if necessary, and with no lack of space at Dipton, Daphne had insisted that they have a second coach. It was much more convenient and comfortable than using hired coaches. Having one's own would not be a burden on the limited stable facilities that Giles's uncle had at his London House, as having one would have been in the days when they always stayed at Struthers House when visiting London.

Having an extra coach required an extra coachman, guard, and two footmen. Of course, as Daphne explained to Giles with some amusement, she knew Society's rules, and he didn't: extra servants demonstrated how rich and important he was. According to the Reverand Mr. Malthus, Daphne had added, the superfluous servants constituted a valuable addition to the well-being of the poor. Giles partly avoided these marvelous benefits of having servants on public display by also using the footmen as grooms. The guard was a lame former sailor whose opportunities for gainful employment were very limited. Giles supplied all the servants traveling with him great coats, which took away the splendor of having liveried servants freezing in the winter weather.

The few days that Giles had spent in London had been busy. Mr. Downing required much of his time to sign statements and affidavits about the events at Seven Dials, the preceding theft of Scruffy, and One-Eyed Jack's attempt at blackmail. Providing them released Giles from the need to testify at trial. Also, had he been able to evade his duty of testifying because of other business, as most nobles did, it avoided the need for the Chief Magistrate to stitch up* the kidnapper for the crimes without proper evidence. That was always regarded as unfair by those most affected by the criminal laws, even though it was a common occurrence when the well-do were victims of crime.

Giles had also spent an inordinate amount of time with the College of Heralds over his becoming a marquess. Apparently, all sorts of hoops had to be jumped through so that the superior status could be bestowed on him, and he had to listen to lectures about how the robes differed and various other tedious matters about which he couldn't care less. Of particular annoyance were the coat of arms and the motto. Couldn't he use the old coat of arms? Not really. It should be fancier for a marquess than for an earl and noticeably different. His old status as an earl, just like that as a viscount, could be held by him, but it was common practice for it to be used by his heir, so the coats of arms should be distinct.

Giles could retain the old Camshire moto, "C'est le mien," if he wished. He could also have a new one. Giles had lost his temper at that point since the whole subject struck him as silly, and he told the heralds that he was too busy for this nonsense and that they should consult with Daphne, who was more interested in these things. Daphne had not been happy about that instruction when she heard about it. She was concerned about such things only because she knew that indifference would only produce snide comments about how Giles had married an unworthy woman who was unfamiliar with the time-honored traditions around which the ton's life revolved.

This trip to Portsmouth had several purposes. First, the Admiralty had pushed the admiral in Portsmouth to prosecute Captain Blenkinsop as soon as possible. All sorts of rumors were circulating suggesting that the Government was dragging its feet on shining light on the terrible happenings. The sooner that problem was resolved, the sooner the fascination about the mysterious happenings would die down, or so the officials hoped. The last thing they wanted was for the story of the aborted Scottish rising to become common knowledge. Giles did not believe that Blenkinsop's failures should be papered over for the good of the service. Too many seamen on Blenkinsop's ship, *Cicero*, and on *Glaucus* knew what had happened: rumors would be spreading from the ships if they were at anchor in a home port. Giles did not want to find that *Glaucus* was ordered to some faraway place so that his crew would not be able to gossip about what they had seen.

Attending the court-martial, no matter how inconvenient it was for Giles personally, would prevent a slanted choice of witnesses and a toadying group of captains sitting in judgment from succeeding in sweeping the unfortunate event under the carpet. Was that, in fact, the real reason for the Government's wanting him to go to Russia again as soon as possible? Indeed, was making him a marquess supposed to induce him to keep quiet? If that was the Government's intention, they were going to be disappointed.

Giles's second reason for going to Portsmouth was to make sure that *Glaucus* would be ready to go to Russia as soon as possible. He also wanted to check that Mr. Lester would want to be his first lieutenant and would not be delayed in taking up his appointment by waiting around for the court-martial to conclude its business. He also did not want news of Mr. Lester's new appointment to filter down the system because, if it did, other captains or admirals who wished to advance clients in whom they had interest would protest that no recognition should be given to someone involved in the *Cicero* fiasco.

In addition to these reasons for going to Portsmouth, Giles wanted to see for himself that the repairs to *Glaucus* had been adequate. He remained suspicious that there had been pressure to declare that *Glaucus* was ready before she was truly ready in order to get him out of the country. He would take a detour on his return trip to London to visit Butler's Hard and check with Mr. Stewart, the boat builder, that *Glaucus* really was sea-worthy. She was a relatively new ship, but she had seen more battles and suffered more wounds than most frigates experienced in their lifetimes. The damage to the supports for her bowsprit had been severe, possibly fatal. Giles wasn't about to take *Glaucus* to distant waters with no drydock help available if it should be needed unless Mr. Stewart was certain that she was now completely seaworthy.

Giles had been hesitant about undertaking these tasks for the Navy because the date of Daphne's first London ball had been moved forward. The elaborate entertainment was supposed to have occurred in the dying days of the season when most of the excitement about balls had waned since it was the Countess of Camshare's first ball, and other ladies had priority in hosting balls. Now, Daphne's ball would happen in only two weeks. Lady Camerstom, a veteran member of the ton, had been taken ill with typhoid fever. It was doubtful if she would survive. What was certain was that she could not hold her ball. To have a sudden gap in the schedule was regarded as totally unacceptable, but all the other ladies had stuck firmly to claiming that their planning was too advanced to consider changing their dates. The ladies, led by the Queen as an active participant, concluded that the only solution was to tell the Countess of Camshire that it was her duty to move her ball to the vacant date; of course, they were not hoping that she would refuse: much better for this upstart, only one generation removed from the factory floor, to come a cropper in trying to put on a ball or to ignominiously have to declare that she was not ready.

Daphne wasn't happy about the change in date, but she could hold the ball with some scrambling to obtain the necessary supplies and help. The ball would not be quite as perfect as she had intended for the one she had planned for June. But the new date was a much better one for displaying to the world of the ton the improvements to Camshire House, of which Daphne was very proud, and her ability to host a first-class ball. After all, she had taken the Ameschester Hunt Ball into her hands after it had suffered years of obscurity and made it a local success that drew members of the ton from London. The self-appointed leaders of London Society would get their comeuppance from Daphne's staging a memorable and perfect ball. It was to be held on a date uncomfortably close to that of the Ameschester Hunt Ball, but that event was fully and meticulously planned and could go ahead with no further advanced planning by the hostess.

Giles had offered to help with the sudden rush needed to get ready for the ball, but Daphne had claimed that he was not really needed and the fate of the country, or at least that of Captain Blenkinsop, was more important. She did not have time to instruct him in the event's details nor how to avoid the reefs that other ladies of the highest rank might create. Giles, in fact, was happy to be away for a few days, for he knew that he would be underfoot during the hectic days of preparation for the ball. He did mention that Daphne's insistence that their status required far more servants than were truly necessary for their usual life in London would come in useful after all. In preparing for the ball, they could all be put to work and demonstrate to the world how necessary they were to the functioning of a great London house.

The rocking of the coach soon lulled Giles to sleep, and he only awakened when they pulled up at the pier in Portsmouth. Night had fallen, but that was no reason for Giles not to go to *Glaucus* at once. The footman jumped down. He was supposed to open the door for Giles, but his master forestalled him. All he could do was fetch Giles's bag.

"All right, Jenkins'" Giles instructed the coachman. "Take the horses and carriage to the Spotted Dogge and get yourselves warmed up. I'll send a note there to tell you when I will need the coach again."

Giles turned and walked down the pier. He didn't have far to go before he saw that one of *Glaucus*'s boats was tied up there, with its crew sitting idly in it.

"Dench," Giles called to the coxswain, "what are you doing here?"

"Waiting for Mr. Stewart, who is in the Mermaid Pub, Captain."

"How long has he been there?"

"Maybe a quarter of an hour. He was meeting some friends, he said, Captain. He'll probably be engaged for a couple of hours."

"Then you should have time to row me out to *Glaucus* and go back to pick him up. If he finishes sooner, just tell him that it is on my orders that you were away."

"Aye, aye, Captain. It is good to have you back."

The only officer on *Glaucus*'s deck when Giles arrived was Midshipman Jenks. The master, however, was also on board, so Giles wasn't annoyed to discover that all the other officers and petty officers had gone ashore.

Despite sleeping during most of the journey from London, Giles slept like a log until daybreak when he was woken by the noise of crew members holystoning* the deck above his head.

Giles went on deck with a mug of coffee once he was dressed and was startled to see a captain's barge approaching. Surely, no captain was coming to *Glaucus* when her captain was away. Then he thought for a minute. Probably, his officers had been drinking with lieutenants from other naval ships in port. The way in which gossip spread about the fleet while at anchor when one might expect them to be isolated was quite astounding. A captain might be coming to see him with the delicate business of Blenkinsop's court martial in the offing. There was undoubtedly a captain sitting in the stern sheets* of the approaching barge.

"*Bellona*," called the coxswain of the approaching boat.

"Prepare to welcome the captain with full honors," Giles ordered before the officer of the watch had recovered from his surprise at a ship's captain visiting at this early hour. Only a couple of orders were needed to get Glaucus's crew ready to welcome the post captain. He must be important since his ship was a ship of the line. Despite being at least twenty years older than Giles, the visitor turned out to be a vigorous man. He saluted the quarterdeck punctiliously before taking Giles's outstretched hand.

"Jeremy Singleton of Bellona," the visitor announced.

"Welcome aboard, Captain Singleton," Giles responded. "I'm Richard Giles, captain of this frigate."

"I'd heard that you don't use your title when at sea, Captain Giles. I see that it is true. I come on a matter of some sensitivity. Could we repair to your cabin?"

"Of course. Let me lead the way."

"Thank you. It's a long time since I was on a frigate."

It was a clear day with a light wind from the west. The captain's cabin on *Glaucus* was flooded with bright sunlight, making it look its best.

"Can I offer you some refreshment, Captain Singleton?" Giles asked.

"It's too early in the day for me."

"Then some tea or coffee?"

"Coffee, please."

When the coffee had been brought, Captain Singleton opened the conversation.

"As you may have heard, Captain Giles, I am in charge of the court martial for Captain Blenkinsop. There are some aspects of the case that I am not clear about, but you might be able to help."

"I'm not sure that this is appropriate, Captain Singleton. As you know, I have been summoned to testify at the court-martial."

"Yes, I know, of course, but I expect the questions to you will only have to do with your interaction with *Cicero* in the Mersey and maybe what you learned about *Cicero* off the coast of Scotland, but I can't prevent other members of the court from asking or you from answering."

"Yes, but even there, I am afraid, I arrived after most of the events relevant to the court martial had already occurred. You'll get a more useful understanding of that event from Lieutenant Stewart or Commander Macreau."

"So, Lieutenant Macreau has been given his step."

"Yes, indeed. He unquestionably deserved it, I believe. I am told that he has also been appointed to a brig* of war."

"I won't anticipate his testimony or that of Lieutenant Stewert. What I wanted to ask you about was something that might be connected with your recapture of *Cicero*. I am supposed to keep that off the public record as much as I can."

"Yes?"

"The logs for *Cicero* for the period before her capture have disappeared. I wonder if you know what happened to them."

"Not really, but I have my suspicions."

"Oh?"

"As you will undoubtedly hear, if you don't already know it, Captain Blenkinsop gave his parole as soon as the enemy boarded* *Cicero* after he surrendered her, but his officers refused to do so. They were placed under lock and key immediately. Captain Blenkinsop was given the run of the ship even before the French had finished taking control of the frigate. He could easily have gathered up the logs and taken them to his cabin. I would not be surprised if he did not want them found, especially the ship's log, which might have recorded the warnings to Blenkinsop about trusting the unidentified frigate approaching them. You can ask Blenkinsop about it at trial, but I am afraid I would not take his oath to tell the truth very seriously. If I were you, I'd ask *Cicero*'s master about the logs. You can certainly ask me, though I can only say that they had disappeared."

"I have heard almost nothing about how you came to recapture *Cicero* and the fight you got into using some of her crew. Can you enlighten me?"

"I am afraid that I cannot. The Government treats those events as ones that never happened. I don't think they are wise in this since too many people were involved, but they probably hope that it will be old news of no interest to anyone as it seeps out. I think they are mistaken, but I cannot disobey orders."

"I am not surprised. The members of the court-martial have been instructed to steer clear of that subject, to the extent that the official record should be vague about whatever comes out at the trial."

"Of course, if I am asked specific questions concerning the role of *Cicero* or her crew in the action, I will have to answer without going into detail—two things I should make clear without going into unnecessary detail about them. *Cicero*'s officers and crew participated very eagerly in the event that is supposed to remain secret. They did so without my having to ask them; indeed, they came across to the ship I was on to offer their help. I was sufficiently impressed by Lieutenant Lester's performance that I have asked for him to be appointed as the next first lieutenant on *Glaucus*."

"That gives me useful perspective, Captain, but I am not sure how much I can let such information shape my judgment."

"Quite right, Captain. Good luck with the case."

"Thank you. I wish I didn't have to be involved. Whatever we decide, it is a duty I would not have minded being excluded from, as are you. I appreciate that you did not duck the unfortunate duty of testifying against another officer. I'll see you at the court-martial."

They parted cordially. Each felt that they had gained an ally in dealing properly with the problems that Captain Blenkinsop had created.

Chapter VI

The crew of *Glaucus* was not surprised to hear their captain starting to play his violin as soon as Captain Singleton had left their ship. They knew that it was Giles's practice whenever things about which he could do nothing were stressing him out.

At noon, Giles, accompanied by Lieutenants Macreau and Stewert, went across to *Bellona*. Giles was warmly met by her first lieutenant and shown to the wardroom where the witnesses summoned to testify at the court-martial were assembling. Not surprisingly, Cicero's officers were present. The others waiting to testify were less expected. One was the captain of the French frigate that Giles had captured off Pendrag Island. He could not be required to testify, so he must have volunteered. Another was a merchant captain who widely proclaimed, despite attempts to stop him from divulging his testimony in the presence of other witnesses, that he had been robbed by Captain Blenkinsop of the money that he had obtained to use on his voyage to the slave coast*, so he had had to return to Liverpool. Losing the money meant that he had been ruined since much of it was gold that he had borrowed for trading on his own behalf. Now, he was even delayed by the requirement to testify here in taking up a routine post as a merchant captain, which would do little to restore his fortunes.

Giles felt no sympathy for the slave trader, telling him that his trade was obnoxious and despicable and that Giles, for one, was delighted that his voyage had been terminated. If Giles ever had the misfortune to find him transporting slaves, he would hang him from the yardarm*

.Giles's testimony was peripheral to the main charge that the court-martial was dealing with, Captain Blenkinsop's surrender of *Cicero* without a fight. He was there to supply relevant background material on Blenkinsop's ability to command. He was also summoned so that an officer senior to Blenkinsop would be present to evaluate what he had seen of Blenkinsop's performance. The officer who should have done that, his admiral, had ducked a request to testify, no doubt because the testimony and examination by the court might cast a most unfavorable light on his performance as an admiral. Giles's testimony was requested for his information about the standoff at Birkenhead and his retaking of *Cicero* at Pendrag Island. He had no first-hand knowledge of how *Cicero* came to be captured by the French frigate. However, a frigate captain, and a very successful one at that, would carry weight in the opinion he expressed or conveyed by other means of Blenkinsop's performance as a frigate captain. Since Giles's testimony was peripheral and to support what other witnesses might say, most of those other witnesses were heard before him, their testimony being more relevant to the central issue. When he did get to be heard, Giles left no doubt that he despised the other captain. Surprisingly, since he had been absent for most of the Birkenhead incident, that was where he got the most hostile questioning.

"Captain Giles, why were you not on *Glaucus* when the brush with *Cicero* began?" Captain McDuff, a large, burly man with a prominent red nose, asked.

"I was ashore returning from dealing with some personal matters. I might add that the Admiralty was fully aware of my absence. Indeed, it was discussed and recommended as part of the orders given for the assignment."

"Which remain secret, even from this court-martial," sneered Captain MacDuff. "So, you are saying that the Admiralty approved a cockamamy scheme to have a frigate sailing under very inexperienced officers while her captain gads about on some personal business."

"If you mean, 'Did the Admiralty issue the orders that had Lieutenant Macreau with Lieutenant Stewart take *Glaucus* from Portsmouth to Birkenhead,' the answer is yes. Captain Singleton,. If I may, I would digress to point out that Lieutenant Macreau is a very experienced officer, having served during several successful sea battles. Lieutenant Stewart has shown superlative skills for such a junior officer. Both have been in far more successful sea battles than you, Captain MacDuff, sir."

The last remark was based on the remarks of Mr. Brooks, *Glaucus*'s master, who made a hobby of knowing the battle records of the officers of the Royal Navy. When he heard that Captain MacDuff was part of the court-martial, he had sniffed and said, "That product of interest whose ship is never loose of his adlmiral's leading strings*. He has never seen action, let alone had a victorious encounter with anyone. The one time he was faced with danger, this while he was just a commander, his ship turned tail and ran from an equally powerful French ship, and only interest saved him from being court-martialed himself."

Captain MacDuff took umbrage at Giles's last remark, probably because it was all too true.

"Are you saying that I am shy*, Captain Giles?"

"No, sir. Just totally inexperienced in commanding a ship of war in battle."

"Why, sir, that is an insult! I outrank you, Captain Giles. This is insubordination! I demand satisfaction," roared Captain MacDuff, the effect of his cry being less than might be expected since it came out in a very high-pitched voice.

"Sit down, MacDuff," ordered Captain Singleton, who outranked Captain MacDuff in addition to being the presiding officer of the court-martial. "You should be aware that it is against the Articles of War to challenge a senior officer. It is none of this court's business why Captain Giles was not on his ship when *Cicero* approached her threateningly. The incident is only relevant for assessing Captain Blenkinsop's behavior when he surrendered his vessel very soon after his encounter with *Glaucus*.

"Captain Giles, let's get on to what happened off Pendrag Island, keeping in mind how confidentiality matters constrain us about an undertaking whose nature cannot be divulged. Could you summarize how you recaptured *Cicero*?"

"Yes, sir. *Glaucus* and the captured Berber vessel that we had named *Freedom* were at anchor near Pendrag Island when a French frigate, accompanied by *Cicero*, anchored off the coast of Pendrag Island. Our location was such that the arrivals could not see my ships. It was evident that *Cicero* was a prize of the French frigate, whose name I learned later was *Dordogne*. The wind had dropped just as the French ship anchored, and the current was against *Glaucus* being towed into action against *Dordogne*. *Freedom* is a Berber ship, a xebec, which is somewhat of a cross between a galley and a ship. I might mention that she was captured by *Glaucus* when Lieutenant Macreau was in command, and Lieutenant Stewart sailed her from the Irish Coast to Birkenhead. The former galley slaves volunteered to row *Freedom* to attack *Dordogne*, whose officers and men were largely ashore. We were able to capture *Dordogne* and then recapture *Cicero*."

"And what did you find on *Cicero*?"

"I discovered that her crew and officers had been locked up in the fo'c'sle. The officers had not given their parole and served very willingly in the following action."

"Which, of course, you cannot describe," said Captain Singleton, fearing that Giles might get carried away and mention what the action involved. "Where did you find Captain Blenkinsop?"

"He was sitting in a chair facing the stern windows of his cabin."

"Can you summarize your conversation with him?"

"Captain Blenkinsop remarked, 'You certainly took your time coming to our aid. Now that you are here, I will resume command.'"

"Did you agree to his doing so?"

"No, sir. He had given his parole so he could not engage in hostile acts against his captors, while I intended to use *Cicero* and her crew in my mission."

"Did you take further action against him?"

"Yes, sir. I placed him under arrest. I knew he would face a court-martial for losing his ship, and he had already told me that he took giving his parole very lightly."

"Now, Captain Giles, there are a couple of other matters we have to ask you about."

"Yes?"

"Did you find any sacks of gold coins in Captain Blenkinsop's cabin?"

"Yes, sir. We discovered some sacks of golden guineas, with a label saying they were from a Liverpool Bank for some captain. I have forgotten the name of the captain. We didn't unseal the bags when we saw what they were, so I don't know how many there were. The find was recorded in *Glaucus*'s log for the voyage and my one."

"What did Captain Blenkinsop say about your find."

"He first said they were his, but when I pointed out that they were labeled for some other captain, he came up with some story that he had retained them as surety for some slave trader. I didn't press for the details, just made sure that they were secured."

"Speaking of logs, did you find any of the logs for *Cicero*?"

"No, sir. We looked for them but could not find them, neither the ship's log nor the master's log nor, most surprisingly, Captain Blenkinsop's log. I asked him about it, but he said he had no idea, even though it would normally be kept in his cabin. It certainly wasn't there. We also searched any documents in the French captain's possession but found none of *Cicero*'s logs or other records."

"Thank you, Captain Giles," stated Captain Singleton. "We appreciate that you could easily have ducked an unpleasant duty."

"One moment, please, Captain Giles," interrupted Captain MacDuff. "Do you think Captain Blenkinsop, a captain who had to make very difficult decisions in a great hurry, is guilty of anything?"

Before Captain Singelton could intervene to rule this a most inappropriate question, Giles replied rather heatedly, "I can't say, Captain, without hearing all the evidence. I believe that we captains must be responsible for our actions, and a court-martial should not hesitate to convict if they feel that the evidence points that way clearly and impose as severe a sentence as the Articles of War permit."

With that, Giles rose, saluted the court, turned smartly, and left the cabin. He was rowed back to *Glaucus* with Mr. Macreau and Mr. Stewart, who had already testified about the event at Birkenhead.

Back on *Glaucus*, Giles found it hard to concentrate as he kept an eye on *Bellona,* awaiting the lowering of the court-martial flag, which would indicate the end of the trial. There were numerous charges against Captain Blenkinsop, not just concerning his passive surrender to the French frigate but also having to do with his brush with *Glaucus* and the source of his golden guineas. Giles expected that the merchant captain had been brought to the court to shed light on that matter. It might take some time for the court to decide, with so many different matters to consider.

Finally, after two hours of waiting, the court-martial flag came down. Of course, that indicated that the court had decided; it did not tell what they had decided. *Glaucus* was anchored some distance from *Bellona,* and no boats came close enough to her to spread the news of the results. The members of the court finally appeared on *Mellona*'s deck and left the third-rate with the usual ceremony to return to their own ships. Though their faces were observed with great interest using telescopes throughout the fleet, no one on *Glaucus* could deduce what the court had decided. Then, a boat was observed taking Mr. Lester to Cicero, unaccompanied by any marines, which indicated that the court had not found reason to charge him in connection with the surrender of *Cicero*. Finally, after another long pause, Captain Singleton was observed descending into his barge, and it headed towards *Glaucus*.

"Captain Giles," Captain Singleton announced after saluting the quarterdeck. "You were a great help today. Thank you."

"Did you reach a verdict?"

"Yes, we did."

"And the result?"

"We found Captain Blenkinsop guilty of all charges and sentenced him to be hanged. That sentence will have to be reviewed by the Admiralty, of course, and they may decide on a lesser punishment. We recommended that no further charges be laid against the officers and crew of *Cicero*. Parenthetically, we praised *Cicero*'s other officers and crew for responding so well when *Cicero* was recaptured, even though we were not made privy about what exactly they did."

"I am afraid that I still cannot tell you, Captain Singleton, but I can confirm that I certainly agree with your commendation."

"Now, I have a letter from the Admiralty, which is to be delivered to your Mr. Macreau if we find Captain Blenkinsop guilty," Captain Singleton continued. "I see him over there, carefully pretending that he is not interested in our conversation,

"Mr. Macreau, I am commanded to give you this letter from the Admiralty. I understand that it contains what many would regard as difficult news. I suggest that you read it at once since I may be able to have the doubtful part rescinded."

Etienne took the letter, broke the seal, and started to read. A broad smile broke out after he had gotten through the first two or three sentences, which changed to a look of consternation as he got farther. He then refolded it, seeming to be deep in thought.

"Come on, man," said Giles. "You can tell us what it says."

"Yes, sir. It is quite amazing. First, as I expected, it appoints me as a commander. I must thank you for that, Captain Giles."

"Well deserved, Captain Macreau," Giles said. "Congratulations. I did not tell you because I was afraid that they might not agree to my recommendation to make you commander because of your being French or not experienced enough."

"That is not all that is in the letter. The letter also appoints me to command a brig-of-war and lets me choose my first lieutenant. I am amazed. I hoped to get the step, but I would not have been surprised to have been left on the beach for a while."

"It's entirely deserved, Captain Macreau," said Giles. "Your performance as acting commander of *Glaucus* proved that you are ready for command.

"Now, gentlemen, this calls for a celebration. Lady Camshire has laid in some excellent claret for my next voyage. I hope you can join us, Captain Singleton. You have certainly earned it with your work on that unpleasant court-martial."

It was a raucous little get-together in Giles's cabin. The wine flowed freely, not surprisingly, since it was some of the best that Daphne's canal company had imported legally. Giles and Captain Singleton had both served in the Caribbean in earlier days and could swap stories about various, usually amusing, things that had happened to them there. Mr. Lester regaled them with tales of Blenkinsop's silliest blunders while the newly promoted Captain Macreau told tales of being taken as a French spy in the days when he still had a more pronounced French accent and mannerisms.

"Listening to you now, Captain Macreau, I would never have guessed that you were French," remarked Captain Singleton.

"Ah vell," Etienne responded, "I don' zinc zat I vould get much rezpec if I try to command speaking li' zis."

That sally produced raucous laughter that spoke more of the wine's quality than of the joke's wit.

At the end of the evening, Captain Singleton signaled that he would like a few words in private with Captain Giles, and the other officers left the captain's cabin promptly, if not soberly.

"Captain Giles, "the more senior captain began, "I have noticed that you are remarkably short of lieutenants."

"I am. I have had a series of outstanding first lieutenants who got themselves promoted. My midshipmen have also learned quickly, thanks to having a good Master to teach them. It has worked well for me, but the result is that I now do not have any midshipmen who can be promoted. Indeed, my second lieutenant is so junior that his commission was only confirmed a few weeks ago. I don't really want someone unknown who would be senior to him. In the past, I have found that lieutenants recommended to me by those with interest are as green as grass or have some highly undesirable habits, so, by and large, I have relied on promotion from within. That's not possible now, so I will just have to accept whoever the Admiralty appoints."

"I may be able to help in that situation. I loathe the interest system, having largely been a victim of it rather than a beneficiary, but even so, I will appeal to you."

"Tell me about your candidate, Captain Singleton. I must say, I am always eager to hear an honest recommendation from a colleague, though I discourage the implied tit-for-tat based on no knowledge that too many of my colleagues in the House of Lords indulge in. Now, who do you have in mind?

"He's a young man now serving on *Bellona* who was recommended to me by a close friend of my uncle, so yes, that was the interest system at work. It was also the only interest he could call on, and he wanted to go to sea. I took him on as a midshipman. He turned out to be a first-rate boy, quick to learn and eager to do more than his share. He passed his lieutenant's exam without trouble and has the required (and, unlike many others, real) sea time for promotion. I have more lieutenants than I need, and he won't get what he needs to progress farther by continuing to serve on a seventy-two that spends all its time either in port or else sailing back and forth outside Brest, waiting interminably for the French to come out. He would benefit from being on a frigate, and since his commission was approved only last week, he is junior to your Mr. Stewart, as he should be, if he were to join *Glaucus*."

"He sounds very promising. Send him across tomorrow, and I'll talk to him. In fact, with Mr. Lester sailing on *Glaucus* for the first time, I intend to take her to sea for a couple of days just to check that she is ready to go on a long voyage and that Mr. Lester is, in fact, capable of serving as my second-in-command. If your youngster is as good as you say, I will happily appoint him when we return. Of course, I can't guarantee that he will see action serving on *Glaucus*, but he is likely to have much more varied sea time and a better chance to hone his skills than he would on a ship of the line in which he served his years as a midshipman. Have him come over first thing in the morning, for I intend to sail soon after sunrise. What is his name?"

"Gordon Baxter"

"Then I will look forward to seeing him tomorrow morning."

"Now, Captain Singleton, there is something I wanted to ask you, though, quite properly, you may feel that you can't answer."

"Yes?"

"Was Captain MacDuff as obnoxious a member of the court-martial as he seemed to be when questioning me?"

"More so. I think that MacDuff was put on the court at the insistence of Admiral Bentley, who is the admiral under whom Blenkinsop was serving. His job seemed to be to try to prevent any reverberation of Blenkinsop's shortcomings back on his admiral. He was not successful in that since the court's private recommendation to the Admiralty was that Admiral Bentley should be removed from his command. That's partly because of how the admiral connived with Blenkinsop but more so because most of us who serve under him do not think he is much of an admiral. MacDuff tried to get us not to condemn Captain Blenkinsop because, he argued, it would reflect badly on the Navy. I suspect he is no better a captain than Blenkinsop; I am told he rose to be a captain and was given his ship only through interest and toadying up to his superiors. If he were put in Blenkinsop's position off Ireland, the result would likely have been the same."

Captain Singleton left at that point. Giles guided him gently through the ceremony of leaving *Glaucus*, for he was none too steady on his legs. Then Giles could retire to his cabin. He wrote a long letter to Daphne that night. He thought that he had to explain his sudden decision to take *Glaucus* to sea even though he suspected she would be glad not to have him underfoot in the rush to put on the ball. Writing to her nightly was a habit that Giles had gotten into that cleared his mind of the day's problems. He wouldn't skip it just because this had been a difficult day, or she might not be delighted by the news it carried.

Chapter VII

Giles was up at four bells of the morning watch, just in time to welcome Mr. Lester and Mr. Baxter on board. Gordon Baxter, the lieutenant sponsored by Captain Singleton, was a tall, blond-haired boy. Giles knew that he had to treat his new lieutenant as a man, but he also had to remember how young he was, just the minimum age to be a lieutenant. Mr. Lester had met most of *Glaucus*'s petty officers at Pendrag Island and had some familiarity with the ship. Nevertheless, Giles sent both new officers on a quick tour of the frigate with Mr. Brooks, the master, with formal introductions to the petty officers and important members of the crew as part of the tour.

By the time that task was completed, there was enough daylight to set sail.

"Prepare to leave harbor, Mr. Brooks," ordered Giles. "You may observe our practices, Mr. Lester, and then take us out of here, going east initially."

Mr. Lester looked alarmed at this order for good reason. Taking an unfamiliar vessel to sea from a crowded anchorage was a daunting prospect. All the officers of the other ships at anchor, who had nothing better to do, would be following *Glaucus*'s departure to see how he could mess up leaving harbor. However, Mr. Lester had taken *Cicero* from similarly crowded anchorages any number of times without any help from Captain Blenkinsop, and the orders he should give would be the same. A broad wink from Mr. Brooks restored his confidence. It said that the master knew exactly what to do, and he would surreptitiously transmit any hints the newly appointed officer might require. What Mr. Lester did not realize was that Giles had anticipated how daunting it might be to find the order and had indicated to the master that a little assistance to their new first lieutenant would be a good idea.

All went well. *Glaucus* got underway much more smoothly than *Cicero* ever had, with none of the captain's unhelpful, distracting comments and counter orders that Mr. Lester had grown used to enduring while taking his former ship to sea. In no time at all, *Glaucus* was clear of the anchorage. Giles ordered that *Glaucus* turn south, keeping well clear of the Isle of Wight. He then left the deck, leaving Mr. Lester in full charge of the ship since he was officer of the watch.

Mr. Brooks told the helmsman to steer by the wind unless it changed and became steady by more than three points. He then went below to do whatever ships' masters had to do when not on deck. In *Cicero*, that consisted of drinking, which did not improve the accuracy of his noon sights. Mr. Lester was pretty sure that that did not apply to *Glaucus*: Mr. Brooks appeared to be a very different kettle of fish from the master of *Cicero*.

Glaucus's crew went about the myriad of tasks that had to be dealt with on a ship on active duty. Lester noted that none of the bosun's mates carried rope ends to 'start' the men, unlike those on *Cicero* and other ships that he had served on, where it was standard to drive the men to work by whipping them painfully with short pieces of rope as a way of "encouraging" the crew. Nevertheless, everything seemed to be done promptly and accurately. All the ends of lines were neatly coiled, and, looking about the deck and the masts, one would never have guessed just how much effort had been required to get *Glaucus* sailing so effortlessly, apparently. Serving on *Glaucus*, Mr. Lester realized, promised to be much more pleasant than it had been on *Cicero*.

Mr. Lester had noted in his short time on *Glaucus* that every officer knew every seaman's name. It would do him no harm to start learning all the names now that everything was going smoothly. He started with the helmsmen on the quarterdeck with him. He asked their names and received a friendly answer, not grudgingly at all. Daringly, since Captain Blenkinsop had frowned on his officers having much informal contact with the crew as bad for discipline, he asked where the helmsman was from. He turned out to be from a fishing town in Cumberland and had joined the navy to see the world. He had been lucky enough to secure a berth with Captain Giles after his previous ship had gone aground and was lost.

Further introduction to crew members would have to wait since eight bells were about to be struck. Mr. Brooks and some midshipmen had already assembled to take the noon sightings. Mr. Lester was again surprised. In such familiar waters where there was no question about where they were, Captain Blenkinsop would have considered the ritual an inconvenient nuisance; on *Glaucus,* the question wasn't where they were; it was whether the midshipmen could determine it by examining the sun at noon and checking the chronometer, and then make the necessary calculations. Mr. Lester realized that the truly slack ship had been *Cicero*, not *Glaucus*. He still had a lot to learn — and unlearn — about how to sail a ship successfully.

After the watches below had been fed their dinner, Mr. Lester got his next surprise. The wind was light from the southeast. Giles came on deck and immediately spoke in formal terms to the officer of the watch: "Mr. Stewart. We haven't seen the royals for some time. Let's raise the masts and spars and bend on the sails."

Though it was worded as a suggestion, there was no doubt in Mr. Lester's mind that it was an order. Or was it? What would happen if Mr. Stewert thought there was some reason to question the order? After all, there was no urgency about this voyage, and no prize was in sight that they might try to overhaul. Mr. Lester was somewhat confused about how the loose expression of orders worked on *Glaucus*: if he didn't know better, he would presume that she was an unsuccessful ship.

Mr. Lester did not get an answer to his hypothetical question. Mr. Stewart's reply to Captain Giles was a simple, "Aye, aye, sir," followed by a loud call: "All hands on deck to rig and loose the royals on all masts." Since neither the appropriate royal masts and spars nor the intricate web of ropes that would sustain them and allow them to bear the thrust of the sails were aloft, they all had to be sent up and securely attached to the existing rigging and spars before the additional sails could be attached to the yards. Then the ends of their controlling lines, the sheets* and braces, having been taken up the masts and attached to the appropriate places, had to be sent down again so that, when the time came, they could be hauled in and cleated down so that the additional sails could function. It was a long, tedious process to make the additional sails functional, and it was subject to delays and much annoyance as errors were made and had to be undone before the process could continue.

During his time on *Cicero*, Mr. Lester had attempted to persuade Captain Blenkinsop to practice the drill so that it would go smoothly when the sails were needed. After a fiasco of an attempt the first time it was tried, Captain Blenkinsop never again allowed Mr. Lester to have a full drill, though, on one occasion, he had ordered him to rig the royal masts. After that, the royal sails were furled up when not needed. They were never taken down while *Cicero* was at sea, creating needless windage when not in use and a serious hazard should the ship encounter a storm. The idea that the skysails would ever be used was beyond Captain Blenkinsop's imagination. Perhaps that was because he had served all his time before joining *Cicero* on vessels that did not have the supplementary masts and sails above the topsails.

All went smoothly in the drill on board *Glaucus*. When Mr. Stewart reported that the skysails were drawing properly, as if Captain Giles was not aware of what had been happening, the captain consulted his watch, with which he had been measuring how long the exercise took, before saying, "Very good, Mr. Stewart. Give the crew half an hour's rest before striking it all below again."

"Are we not going to do the skysails as well, captain?" the officer of the watch asked.

"No, Mr. Stewart. We started late. We'll do both soon, but not on this occasion.

"Mr. Lester," continued, "we were a bit slow in getting that drill done. We will have to shave fifteen minutes off the time, at least. *Glaucus* has been engaged in too many other things recently for the standard drills to be kept up properly. We should have plenty of time on our coming cruise for you to get the crew up to snuff again."

"Yes, sir," Mr. Lester replied, wondering how in the world he could get much improvement over the demonstration he had just observed. "I notice, sir, that no one used rope ends to encourage the crew."

"Of course not. The men are not horses who need to be whipped into doing their duty. We can rely on the petty officers to point out any deficiencies and on the crew members to correct anyone slacking off. Incidentally, I avoid flogging to the greatest extent possible, except for theft from fellow crew members."

Giles turned away. "All right, Mr. Stewart, strike the royals and masts below."

Once again, the ship came alive as the crew raced to their places to start the exercise. Again, in Mr. Lester's opinion, the drill was performed flawlessly, though at the end, when everything was stowed away, Giles mentioned a few flaws to Mr. Brooks, Mr. Stewart, and Mr. Lester. The other two officers nodded their heads in agreement. Mr.

Lester was impressed by the attention to detail. This ship was not *Cicero*!

Winter dusk was closing in as the crew finished their exercise with the first dog watch about to begin.

"Mr. Baxter, it's your watch next." Giles addressed the new lieutenant, "Just through the first dog watch, of course. I doubt that you were ever officer of the watch on *Bellona*."

"No, sir. I haven't had that honor."

"I'm not surprised. I'll be on deck most of the time, as will Mr. Brooks. Don't hesitate to ask either of us if you are unsure about anything. There is no shame in asking, only in acting from ignorance."

The new lieutenant had an uneventful watch to initiate his time on *Glaucus*. However, the middle watch, which he also stood as officer of the watch, was informative. Fog, occasionally interrupted by light rain, prevailed, but since the light wind was from the east and *Glaucus* was in no danger of running aground, it was easy to hold the course under only topsails as Giles did not want to go far.

To Mr. Baxter's surprise, Giles came on deck as four bells. A quick look around informed him of what was happening, confirming Mr. Baxter's report.

"Mr. Jenks," Giles ordered the midshipman of the watch. "Rouse Mr. Lester and Mr. Brooks and ask them to come on deck. Better rouse Mr. Stewert and the bosun as well."

When the requested officers had come on deck, Giles addressed them. "We are close to the Isle of Wight, which is a favorite place for smugglers to come ashore and for legitimate cargo vessels to pass on their way up the channel, though they usually stay farther offshore. As a result, French privateers and even ships of the French navy on the lookout for prizes often assemble here. I want to clear for action with a minimum of noise now when it is well before dawn. Of course, we will not run out the guns, but everything else, including the power and balls, will be ready to go when there is a bit of light."

For the next many minutes, Mr. Lester and Mr. Brooks watched as the crew, guided by the petty officers, went about the myriad of tasks necessary to get the frigate ready for combat. When the controlled rushing to and fro ended, Mr. Stewert told Giles, "Cleared for action, sir. Guns not run out, but loaded and ready for action. "

"Very good, Mr. Stewart. Stand down the watches below, though those on the next watch won't get much sleep, I am afraid."

The morning watch was almost over before there was any more excitement. As time wore on, the fog seemed to be thinning, though whether that was real or only due to the slowly increasing light as dawn approached was unclear. Giles had stationed Midship Jenks at the masthead along with the lookout to relay messages without the need to shout, for noise might give their position away to any ships that happened to be nearby.

Suddenly, Mr. Jenks appeared on the quarterdeck with an urgent message for Giles: "Sir, in one of the gaps in the fog, the lookout has spotted a vessel off our starboard bow, only three cables away. He couldn't tell much about her, but she is certainly much smaller than *Glaucus*."

"I'd better go aloft to see what is going on. Thank you, Mr. Jenks. Come with me, for I may still need you to relay messages."

As Giles mounted the ratlines, the fog thinned a bit more. When he reached the top, the lookout pointed towards the shore to starboard of *Glaucus* and somewhat ahead. The fog must also be thinning towards the land; for now, the lookout pointed to where he could see the ghostly outlines of three — no four — small ships. The two ships closest to the shore looked like the luggers widely used for cross-channel trading — and smuggling. The third one looked like a small sloop of war, mounting six guns. It was the sort of ship that many privateers, both French and English, used in the English Channel. Giles suspected he was looking at a privateer hoping to capture some smugglers in the waters where they frequently brought contraband. The fourth ship, nearer to *Glaucus* and closer to shore than the others, was still largely hidden by clearing fog. From what little Giles could see, she did not look like the standard revenue cutter used to try to cut down on smuggling. She might be a brig of war of the French Navy or a strong French privateer. Giles noted with surprise that she had no one at her masthead.

Giles returned to the deck. He first ordered the watches below to come on deck as quietly as possible. Then he ordered all the boats to be made ready. Finally, he assembled his officers and petty officers and picked up the slate, which he had sent a nipper to fetch from his cabin when he learned that there might be ships nearby. He succinctly summarized what he had learned about the other ships. His officers, Giles continued, were to act on the supposition that the strange ships were enemies and be ready to board them in stealth, if possible, but they were not to harm anyone until they were sure they were enemies.

"Mr. Bush," Giles addressed one of his midshipmen, "you can use the jolly boat. Follow the bearing for the farthest ship. We'll give you ten minutes head start. Silently, of course.

"Midshipman Barrow, you can take the next ship, the second farthest away. Use my barge. Be careful. The only British luggers in these waters are likely to be smugglers of wine and spirits or, sometimes, other contraband. The smugglers sometimes try to hide what is really their cargo with a layer of legitimate cargo at the top of their holds. I'll send a master's mate with you to help shift the cargo if necessary.

"Mr. Stewert, use the pinnace* to find out about the third ship. Be prepared for trouble. Presume that she is French until and unless she proves otherwise. Mr. Macauley chose a squad of marines to assist Mr. Stewert.

"Finally, Mr. Lester, you can use the long boat to investigate the ship that is nearest to us. Make sure your people make as little noise as possible, but presume that you will be boarding a hostile vessel unless they tell you differently in a convincing way. Mr. Macauley, take the rest of the marines to ensure the success of Mr. Lester's task."

Off the four boats went in order, with suitable time gaps between them so that they would all arrive at their targets at the same time. Giles had to disguise his nervousness about the operation. Two of his officers were inexperienced in this kind of activity, and many things could go wrong. However, if he didn't give them a chance to experience such ventures, they would never learn, and he did not believe in coddling his officers; they had to learn as quickly as possible to be independent when needed.

On *Glaucus,* the wait seemed to be intolerable. The light was getting brighter, and, at the same time, the fog seemed to be thinning. And moving aside, blown by the slight wind. How long could it take before something happened?

Even though it was expected, a shout followed by a pistol shot broke the silence. It sounded quite close. It must be from Mr. Lester's target, but which side had fired? More pistol and musket shots were heard, and then the clash of cutlasses rang out. The fog about the nearest vessel was still thick. Giles and the others on *Glaucus* could still see nothing, but Mr. Lester must be engaged!

Lieutenant Lester had been very nervous as the long boat rowed into the fog. He had never been on an expedition to cut out an enemy warship or, indeed, to take any kind of ship. He had dreamed about it any number of times during his service on *Cicero*. Now, he was faced with capturing a French brig of war. He didn't dare fail, not after Captain Giles had given him this chance to redeem his naval career.

The pinnace crept through the water as the crew rowed slowly with muffled oars, trying not to make any sounds that would reveal their presence. Then, through the fog, the target started to emerge. 'She's huge,' Mr. Lester thought. 'How could we possibly capture her?'

The cockswain directed the boat to the boarding battens on the side of the ship. It took hardly a moment, Mr. Lester thought, before they were alongside. Mr. Macauley signaled that Mr. Lester should lead the way. Up the side of the ship, he climbed using only one hand since the other one was clasping his pistol, which he had cocked ready to fire.

Suddenly, just before his head could clear the gunnel, an enemy seaman looked over the side, staring right into Mr. Lester's eyes. Without thinking, Mr. Lester cocked his pistol and fired at the man, whose head promptly disappeared. Mr. Lester continued climbing and stepped onto the enemy deck, only to fall flat on his face as he tripped over the body of the man he had just killed. Mr. Lester at least had the presence of mind to roll to one side as a swarm of marines followed him up the side of the enemy brig. More shots were fired, though Mr. Lester could not tell whether they were from the marines or defenders. It seemed to be the marines who dropped their pistols as soon as they had fired, drew their cutlasses, and charged to take control of the watch on deck and of the ways that anyone below deck would have to use to come to the aid of the defenders. A few French sailors got their hands on the ready supply of cutlasses, but they were no match for the marines. Before the slaughter of the unprepared crew became extensive, an officer appeared at the quarterdeck rail and bellowed, "Ve surrender! Nous nous rendons!"

The French sailors threw down any weapons they had succeeded in getting and raised their hands in the universal signal that they were surrendering. It was over almost as soon as Mr. Lester had picked himself up from his fall and drawn his sword. He resheathed his weapon and stepped forward to accept the Frenchman's sword. He had taken his very first prize after years of inaction, and it was not an insignificant one. How he wished that the fog had cleared so that Captain Giles could have witnessed his triumph!

In the mysterious way that fog sometimes behaves, it opened up, leaving only trails of mist about. Giles could see what was happening on the nearest ship. Mr. Lester was accepting a sword from someone who must be the captain while a crew member was hauling down the flag. With little wind and soaking wet from the fog, the flag looked like a soaked blanket, and it was largely guesswork that identified it as the French tricolor. Mr. Lester had indeed taken his first prize, a brig of war!

Farther afield, Mr. Barrow's boat had pulled up to the side of the first of the two luggers. That ship was flying a dripping French flag above a British one. His men had succeeded in getting aboard the prize before the French crew knew of his presence or the pistol shot disturbed their tranquility. The prize crew offered no resistance. It seemed that, somewhere, they had discovered a supply of hard drink and had decided to celebrate their success in capturing the lugger.

"No prize money there," Mr. Brooks remarked as his telescope swept the other ships after he witnessed Mr. Lester's success. "but there might be a little head money,"

"Maybe, but not much," Giles responded.

The fog continued to break apart. Now Giles could see the second warship. Through his telescope, he could see

Mr. Stewert on the deck, clearly in charge of another prize since the Union Jack was just rising to her masthead. How he had secured her with no audible resistance would remain a mystery until Mr. Stewert returned to *Glaucus*.

That left only Mr. Bush. The more distant lugger was now in clear sight from *Glaucus*, and Giles had no difficulty in seeing through his telescope that Mr. Bush's boat was alongside the ship.

"The final merchant ship looks very familiar to me," Giles remarked to Mr. Brooks. "Clearly, she is certainly a lugger, don't you think, and one we have met several times before."

"You are quite right, sir." The master replied. "It is *The Ruddy Fox*. I expect that Fred Creasey is still her captain. I wonder what he is smuggling this time."

"We will soon find out. Mr. Jenks, I see you are the signal midshipman. Signal to Mr. Bush to bring the captain of the ship he is talking with to *Glaucus*. Indeed, signal all the ships to come to *Glaucus* and bring the captured captains here. When they arrive, we can find out what we have acquired."

The signal arrived at *The Ruddy Fox* while Mr. Bush was still in the jolly boat. He had been several cables from her when the first pistol shot announced the commencement of the British attack. Shouts erupted from his target, followed by the clang of cutlasses. The racket died down before he had a chance to board the vessel. Indeed, the noise stopped before he was about to grapple with her. A weathered face looked over the side of the ship at Mr. Bush.

"What have we here, youngster?" The apparition asked. "Have you been sent to free me from the terrible Frenchies?"

"Yes, sir. Captain Giles sent me thinking you had been taken by French privateers."

"So I had been, lad," came the reply, "but in the fog, when the frogs heard that musket shot, they didn't know what to do, so I relieved them of their anxiety and retook the ship. You can take the prisoners back to your ship and tell Captain Giles that the head money is all his."

"Sir, those are not my orders. I have to check your cargo and report back to Captain Giles before I can let you go."

The strange man laughed heartily at this statement.

"Ah, lord, you don't know who I am, do you? Or this vessel?"

"No sir, should I?"

"I suppose not, youngster, since you weren't on that frigate the last time I helped Captain Giles out of a jam. You'll have heard of me and my ship, I imagine. I am Captain Fred Creasey, and my lugger is *The Ruddy Fox*. Say 'hello' for me to your captain. I'll be on my way now."

"I am afraid that I can't allow that, sir. My orders are to verify that your cargo is not contraband."

"Are they? Well, you had better come on board to have a look. I have a load of fancy cloth and dresses from Paris that I am taking into Southampton so they can get to London quickly for some fancy ball. I also have some wine that I will take to the customs house in Harksmouth after getting rid of the cloth. All above board, lad. I have helped Captain Giles in the past, and the Countess of Camshire has been good enough to provide a service where I can sell my wines without the hassle of smuggling them in.

"You had better come aboard and see the items so that you can report to Captain Giles. He can be a bit of a stickler when it comes to smuggling, you know."

"Mr. Bush," interrupted the master's mate whom Giles had sent with his midshipman. "*Glaucus* is signaling to you, sir. 'Bring captain to us.' is what the signal says."

"So that's what he wants," said Captain Creasey. "Well, Mr. Bush, you had better come aboard and see my cargo before we go across. Giles is very strict about such things."

Midshipman Bush didn't know what to make of *The Ruddy Fox*'s cargo. Captain Creasey explained as he took the wrappings off a couple of samples that there was some special ball scheduled for London, unexpectedly, and the highly placed women were all in a tizzy to get new clothes for the occasion. He showed Mr. Bush a selection of the bright bolts of cloth, some plain, but most patterned, of very fine quality if Mr. Bush was any judge, elaborate ball gowns, and some other female clothing. Midshipman Bush had older sisters, and he recognized the last items as underwear. The sort a gentleman never saw, but younger brothers did before they were sent away to school or, in his case, the navy.

Mr. Bush found that part of Captain Creasey's demonstration distinctly embarrassing since it produced naughty thoughts of the sort that were best kept secret, or so his sisters had told him when he had inadvertently discovered them trying some of them on. At least, he would have Captain Creasey with him when he returned to *Glaucus*. Hopefully, the merchant captain would explain to Captain Giles exactly what that part of *The Ruddy Fox*'s cargo consisted of.

Looking towards the frigate, Mr. Bush realized that he was likely to be the last of the officers sent to take ships' captains to return to *Glaucus*. Well, there was no reason to dawdle before reporting to Captain Giles. He had fulfilled his mission, even though it had not involved anything heroic.

Giles was also pleased. The ship had done well after its period in harbor, and the new officers seemed to be working out. The action, limited as it was, would lessen the problems that always crept up when a crew spent an inordinate time at anchor. The modest amount of prize money that they had obtained would please everyone.

The only thing limiting Giles's satisfaction was that the trip had lasted a day longer than he had intended. Daphne's ball was coming up, and he knew she would be nervous about it, and he would like to be on hand. Of course, there was nothing he could do to help with the preparations. His being at a loose end in London might do more harm than good. He would tell her about his thoughts and activities in his letter that evening and not mention his feelings of guilt. He'd be back in Portsmouth the next day and could go to London with plenty of time before the ball.

Chapter VIII

It was well past noon when *Glaucus* led her little captured fleet through the Solent on the way to Portsmouth. Such a victory parade was old hat to most of the officers and crew of the frigate, but it was the first time for Mr. Lester and Mr. Bunting. In the past, they had both been aboard ships enviously watching *Glaucus* bring in prizes, sometimes with clear signs of a hard-fought battle, other times, like now, with no indication other than the prizes that she had engaged the enemy. If they hadn't been sure about their new positions beforehand, this parade demonstrated to them that their careers had definitely taken a turn for the better,

Glaucus turned into the anchorage while the other ships with her backed* their sails to wait. As she did, a mail boat from the office in Portsmouth pulled up to her side, and a small sack of mail was tossed aboard. Soon the frigate was anchored, and *Glaucus*'s barge was seen taking Captain Giles to one of the merchant luggers. The four ships then proceeded to Portsmouth. When they reached the port, the brig and the schooner went to the Admiralty Prize Dock, where the ships would be processed and the fate of their crews decided. There would be prize money for everyone on board *Glaucus* after the authorities had taken their own sweet time evaluating the French ships and counting the number of seamen taken prisoner. The only non-routine matter was whether the letter of marque issued by French authorities was genuine or whether she was actually a pirate ship, as so many alleged private warships turned out to be. All too many enterprising privateer captains saw no reason why they shouldn't be able to take any merchant ship they could catch and then decide for which side they worked or after they had captured a prize and determined under which flag she was sailing.

The two merchant luggers proceeded to the Customs Dock. What could be afoot? Usually, when merchant ships were rescued, they were allowed to proceed, and their liberators received no compensation for freeing them. Captain Giles was known, however, to have a tendency to enforce the customs laws even when there would be no reward for doing so. Most other captains just let them go on their way, often accepting a tub* or two of wine as a goodwill gesture,

Giles was indeed going to the Customs Dock to deal with the laws against smuggling in wine and spirits, but he also was worrying about the situation facing Daphne in London. The letter from her that had just been delivered indicated that things were not going with the smoothness that usually accompanied his wife's ventures. Daphne's plans for the ball, which had recently been assigned to her with her having little time to prepare, were all going disastrously astray. First, her butler, who was, in fact, just an inexperienced footman, was discovered not to be able to plan and direct the elaborate rituals with which the myriad of footmen kept all the guests happy at a ball. Furthermore, he had no idea who were the important members of Society, even though part of his job was to broadcast the arrival of visitors with just the right tone of importance to reflect their position among the gentry.

To make matters worse, Daphne wrote, the cook had come down with a serious illness, and none of the other members of the kitchen staff were in a position to step in. Experienced cooks were not easy to find. Daphne had no idea of how to get one in time. It looked like the ball would be a disaster, much to the delight of Daphne's detractors.

As if all this wasn't bad enough, Daphne wrote that her dressmaker had told her that Baroness Strangway had purchased in advance the entire cargo of the next shipment of fashionable fabrics and patterns from France, for which it had been arranged for the officials to turn a blind eye. As everyone knew, France was the only true center of fashion despite Napoleon being in charge. Getting such goods from France or any other place that had joined Napoleon in going to war with Great Britain was now illegal, but everyone knew that such laws did not apply to what the cream of Society required. They also should pay the customs levy on the goods, which would be avoided by smuggling in the goods. Furthermore, paying the duty would crimp the style of some of the most important ladies. Smuggling also avoided getting a permit to import the material, which could take a lot of time and would be a nuisance in other ways.

The contraband goods could be expected to make a great splash at Daphne's Ball, and she had arranged for her modiste to obtain a pattern and the cloth to make an outstanding ball dress so that she would shine on her most important occasion. Now Daphne could not make much of a splash.

Lady Strangway was to host the next ball after Daphne's. She did not want Daphne's ball to introduce the latest fashions when hers would be a much better venue for displaying all that was *le plus au courant*. Lady Strangway believed it would be best to prevent Daphne's Ball from being where the latest trends were revealed. Their great splendor, gracing the figures of ladies who were Lady Strangway's cronies in the dog-eat-dog world that was the ton in London, should be reserved for the later ball. Lady Srangway not only had expressed such beliefs to her cronies, but she had also taken steps to guarantee that Daphne's ball would be a drab affair, or so Daphne declared.

Lord Strangway was rumored to be fabulously wealthy, so his wife could pay the exorbitant cost of scuttling Daphne's success by cornering the supply of French patterns and fabrics. Indeed, his richness allowed his wife to buy up the best material for gowns already in London so that only those in her coterie could have new dresses for Daphne's Ball. Of course, Daphne knew these actions would do little to raise Lady Strangway in Society's opinion, though it might hurt Daphne. That belief struck Daphne as being the last straw when her ball was already in danger of being a flop.

Giles knew that Lord Strangway's fortune and title were badly tarnished, in Society's opinion, by his wealth having been obtained solely by manufacturing. Worse still, Lord Strangway had been only a very distant cousin of the previous Baron of Strangway. Even the Heralds had been dubious about some of the links that had made him the closest living male relative of the previous Baron. So he might not really be the scion of a noble family, just plain Mr. Strangway, a bumped-up tradesman, not even a professional man. Giles had never seen him take his place in the House of Lords, even though the man had moved to London from somewhere in the midlands when he became the Baron Strangway. Giles would not mind putting him in his place if the opportunity presented itself.

Daphne was sure that the hateful Lady Strangway was deliberately trying to ruin Daphne's ball so that her own would appear more splendid. Unfortunately, with the staffing problems that had arisen, Daphne was sure that her rival would succeed. Her letter to Giles suggested that she was at her wit's end over how to pull it off successfully and not be embarrassed by the whole affair.

Daphne had never written Giles such a distressed letter. While she claimed not to care tuppence about what the ladies of the ton thought of her or the silly games they played to gain status, he knew that she hated to fail at anything. For Daphne, adequate was never enough! How he wished that he was at Camshire House to support her! Well, he wasn't, but he would do what he could, starting with the problem of ballgowns and related supplies. Captain Creasey's cargo must be the one Daphne referred to. Giles would make sure that it was delivered into the right hands. Daphne might even be able to use his intervention to put Lady Strangway in a bad light. He would take the lead in discussions to get Captain Creasey out of the clutches of the revenue service.

"What have you got for us this time, Captain Giles?" the official on duty asked when Giles entered the Customs Office with the master of the second captured lugger and Captain Creasey.

"I rescued *Daisychain*, the first of those two luggers I have just brought to your dock after she had been taken by a French ship. Her manifest claimed that she was taking tin from Cornwall to London, but investigation by the officer who conducted her release from the French discovered that tin goods in crates were only to be found as the top layer of her cargo at the hatches. The rest of her cargo consisted of wine, for which there were no papers, in tubs* so, obviously, the ship's captain was smuggling the wine and had the false papers and the small number of crates of tin as a ruse."

"All right, we'll deal with him and his crew. Do you want to pay the duty and take possession of the goods?"

"No, thank you."

"Right. Now, what about this other cargo?"

"It is the fabric and patterns that Captain Creasey was carrying that may be an issue. I should mention that part of his cargo consists of barrels of wine that are to go to the Customs Dock at Harksmouth, where, as often happens, the canal company I own will pay the duty and then ship the barrels inland. However, some of the cargo is separate from that transaction. Captain Creasey tells me that it is for a London customer, who, I understand, has made arrangements to pay the duty and to obtain permission to import the material from France."

Giles realized that it was rather fun to try to hoodwink the customs. He was doing it for the good cause of making sure that Daphne's ball was perfect, but he was getting an unholy thrill over trying to pull the wool over the customs agent's eyes. His statements to customs were made of whole cloth, but he was making them in a very good cause.

"Captain Creasey is only serving as a carrier, not the principal," Giles continued, ad-libbing as he went. "His understanding presumed that he would be paid when he unloads the material here and that there would be no trouble getting it cleared. That is, he was told that this part of the cargo conforms to what the buyer has obtained a special permit for. Hasn't he contacted you about this and arranged for the shipment to be landed without trouble? I am told that its transshipment to London is rather urgent. Your role, I suppose, is to check that the shipment is what permission was given in the client's import document and reevaluate the duty to check that what has been paid is correct."

"I am afraid, my Lord, that no such documents have been received. What are the goods, again?"

"Ladies' clothes and patterns for making such things, as, I think, I already told you. Ballgowns, and so on. Something to do with the latest fashions from Paris, I understand."

"I see. Yes, such goods are dutiable, even if the buyer has an exception for the ban on importations from France. I can't recall any such permission being sent here, and no one has come in with such a document. Certainly, there is nothing about the owner coming in to pay the duty in advance or accept the goods. I know that no agent for such a cargo has appeared or informed us that the goods and payment are coming. It has been quite some time since we have seen an exemption for such items. Maybe they all ship to London, or maybe the ladies are following the law about not importing such items, but we haven't seen such goods for a long time. You have to have an explicit exemption to bring in such goods, as well as pay the duty on them before they can be landed."

"Oh, no! What is Captain Creasey supposed to do? He was sure that everything would be in the clear when he arrived here. He needs to get on to Harksmouth with his wine. He also needs to be paid for transporting his cargo. Isn't there something you can do?"

"Well, no. There is nothing in my power that I can do to help, and I am the senior person in this office. We have no record of who owns this shipment, so we have to suppose that it should be treated as contraband that has fallen into our hands. Just between us, I can pretend that you didn't know what the problem was, Captain Creasey and I might be able to bend the rules to release the cargo if the duty is paid. The wine, Captain Creasey — you won't sell it again, will you, without going into Harksmouth?"

"Of course not. Anyway, the wine is in barrels, not much use to most smugglers who have trouble handling such large containers clandestinely. I always get a good price in Harksmouth for my wine."

"Well, that's settled then. Captain Giles will pay the duty on the condemned clothing goods and take possession of them. Captain Creasy will unload the clothing and then proceed to Harksmouth, where he can unload his wine at the Customs Dock."

Giles wrote a bank draft on his account at Coutts, which the customs officer accepted without question. "It's all yours now, my lord," he announced.

Giles and Captain Creasey left the revenue office.

"I have never seen anyone deal with the revenuers so easily, Captain Giles," Captain Creasey remarked.

"I'm afraid I rather undercut you and your buyer, Captain Creasey,"

"He knew the risks. And he hadn't hired a reliable crew to bring the goods ashore here. Probably trying to save a bit of money. His people never showed up, so I couldn't unload, and I got taken in the fog by that damn pirate. If I'm asked by the man who commissioned it — a nasty piece of work, I'd say, though he is some sort of lord — I'll just tell them that he knew of the danger that it would fall into the hands of the revenue department and that the transfer boats were not present when I arrived at the appointed shore. That's true enough. I'm not out of pocket, and it serves Lord Strangway for not properly preparing for the smuggling or not hiring experienced agents. He paid me half in advance and half on completion."

"So that's who was behind that shipment. Still, Captain Creasey, you are out the second half of the payment. Let me give you something in thanks for helping me acquire the goods."

"No, Captain Giles. You have got me out of some difficult predicaments in the past, and I'm in your debt."

"Well, it works both ways. Now I insist that I pay you for the transport. I got the goods at a fraction of their worth, thanks to you. I'll mail an order to my company in Harksmouth that should cover it.

"Please, Captain Creasey, in future, try to stay out of trouble with the revenuers. You have rendered Britain invaluable assistance, and I would hate to see you punished for some of your more questionable doings."

I'll try, but no promises, though I confess that this time was a close enough shave to make me think of taking up a less risky trade."

"Then I hope you do. I must say the authorities gave us more trouble than I expected over those ballgowns. Now, where can you unload the items."

"Right here, if you want, but you will have to have something to take the stuff away, a cart or something similar."

"How about a carriage?"

"I think that would do. This cargo is not very bulky or heavy. It might be hard for someone to ride in the carriage at the same time, however. The fabric and the patterns will pretty well fill up the carriage itself."

"Winslow," Giles addressed the ship's boy who had accompanied him, ready for any tasks that Giles might require while on shore. "Go to the Spotted Dogge Inn and tell my coachman, Jenkins, that I need the coach here, ready to go to London, as soon as possible. Oh, and tell the stable master that I will need a good horse to take the first leg of a rushed ride to Dipton. Have him get it watered, harnessed, and ready to go in an hour, by which time the carriage should be on its way.

"Now, Captain Creasey, let's unload this cargo I have just acquired from you."

It was the work of only minutes to board *The Ruddy Fox*, remove the hatch cover, and start unloading the well-wrapped packages. Captain Creasey used an old sail to protect the precious bundles from the muck of the dock. His crew members handled the packages carefully, knowing that their chances of getting any more commissions like this one rested largely on the condition of the delicate goods when they arrived at their destination. Before they were finished, the carriage arrived, so they started loading the conveyance rather than adding to the pile on the ground. When they had cleared the hold, they piled the earlier and more delicate items on top of the ones already in the carriage. They finished by tying the packages down so they would not shift during their journey to London.

"Captain Creasey," Giles said. "It has been good to see you again. Thanks for your help."

"No thanks required, Captain Giles. I know you got me out of a hot spot. I hope your wife realizes how lucky she is to have you."

"I'm the lucky one," Giles replied.

Giles climbed onto the driver's bench of the coach. "Drive on," he ordered the coachman.

The carriage stopped briefly at the Spotted Dog to let Giles off. He checked the waiting horse over, mounted, and rode to the Admiralty Prize Dock.

Mr. Lester had handled the transfer of the French brig of war to the Admiralty officials well. All Giles had to do was sign the documents that would start the lengthy process before the ship's fate and the prize money awarded to *Glaucus*'s crew were determined.

The French privateer, which might be an English pirate ship, had presented a problem for Mr. Lester, which only Giles could resolve. The issue was whether she was a French privateer or an English pirate ship.

In Giles's opinion, it was a matter of little concern to *Glaucus*. Either way, the ship would be considered captured by the navy, and the officers and crew of his ship would receive the same prize money. What happened to her crew and officers was a different matter. They would be treated as prisoners of war if the ship was considered a French privateer and would be exchanged for British prisoners. Unfortunately for them, the Royal Navy had captured far more French prisoners than the French and their allies had British seamen. Their captives would rot in prison hulks where their prospects of exchange were minimal, especially as they didn't speak French. They would likely die from the wretched conditions in the prison ships where they would be held prisoner. If they were found to be pirates, they would be sentenced to hang, but, except for their captain, they were more likely to be sent to Australia, which seemed to have an unlimited demand for prisoners to provide cheap labor.

Giles favored hanging the captain and thought there was not much to choose between the alternatives for the other captives. He decided to present the ship as a pirate vessel unless a more formal tribunal decided elsewhere. Accordingly, Giles ordered the clerk to prepare the transfer documents to conform to that decision. He wondered if the rich investors who funded the pirates, probably getting them the letters of mark to act as a privateer for whichever side was convenient, would pay lawyers to stop the interpretation going through.

Giles then left the Admiralty office and mounted his horse to go to Daphne's assistance. However, he did not head for London; he was going to Dipton. Giles had thought of a way to get the highly trained servants that she so badly wanted in time for her ball, but there was little time to waste. He would ride all night to implement his plan at the very beginning of the following day.

Chapter IX

It was past noon before Giles left Portsmouth. He still needed to hurry, even though he would not arrive in Dipton until well after dark. He wanted to rouse the household well before dawn so that they could depart early the next day to go to London.

The idea of going to Dipton had come to him as he read Daphne's distressed letter on the way to the customs dock in Portsmouth. The servants at Camshire House were unable to put on a ball successfully. The staff at Dipton Hall had considerable experience, and both the cook and the butler had come to Dipton when they were hired from Giles's father's London house and had long experience in the leadership roles that were now lacking. The solution seemed obvious: bring the people from Dipton Hall to serve at the upcoming ball. After this ball was out of the way, there would be plenty of time to hire and train the right servants so that the next extravaganza would be flawless. It never occurred to Giles that his Dipton servants would hesitate to come to London to help out.

Everything went well on Giles's trip home until after the second stop to get some refreshments and to change horses. Then, he mounted his new steed and rode off again. It had been fully dark before he made the stop, but a gibbous moon provided plenty of light, though clouds sometimes obscured it. The horse was not a good specimen, but as long as Giles did not push him too hard, he should be able to reach the next posting inn without trouble.

Giles rode on. The horse was not strong. He could only keep him to an ordinary walk. It was also getting darker as clouds started to obscure the moon for longer periods, and it was getting colder. He had left *Glaucus* that morning wearing only a light coat over his uniform jacket. Maybe at the next stop, they would have a greatcoat for sale and a horse with which he could make better time.

The horse plodded around another bend in the road. The moon peered out for a minute. Ahead there was a coach off the road, not turned over, but with one wheel in the ditch, so it looked very precarious: it might roll over at any moment. Sitting on the step of the carriage was an elderly man with his head in his hands. Over him was hovering a woman, who Giles guessed was not much younger. There was no sign of the coachman, and there was no sign of the horses.

Giles paused for a moment to evaluate the situation. He had heard many stories of coaches in distress used as lures to get travelers into the clutches of highwaymen. It was also the case that coaches often had accidents, especially when driving at night. He took out his pistol, cocked it, and made sure that it was properly primed. He also loosened his sword in its scabbard. It wasn't indeed a sword, a weapon he only used on ceremonial occasions. It was his old midshipman's dirk*, which he had found much more convenient than a usual sword when he was engaged in possibly hazardous activities at sea.

Giles dismounted and approached the coach gingerly. He ignored the man and the woman while he went to see if anyone was on the other side of the coach. The coachman was lying on the ground there, presumably having been thrown from his bench. Giles felt for a pulse; there was none. The man wasn't breathing either, as far as Giles could tell. He must be dead.

Giles blew the priming out of his pistol and uncocked it. Only then did he go to the side of the carriage, where the elderly people waited. They were shivering, especially the old lady, probably from the cold but also, likely, from the accident. The old man seemed to be almost comatose.

"What happened?" Giles asked.

The old woman was rather inarticulate, but the story emerged. They had been waylaid by a highwayman, who must have charged at the carriage, yelling loudly. The carriage horses swerved off the road, and the carriage got stuck in the ditch. As far as Giles could tell, the passengers had been thrown onto the side of the carriage but were not injured. The highwayman had pulled them out of the carriage and searched their persons and baggage. He had cut loose the horses and departed, leaving the old people stranded on the side of the turnpike.

It was freezing cold. Giles was not sure that the victims would survive if he left them to go and seek help. The next inn was a few miles away, he knew. He didn't like to leave the victims where they were huddled next to the stranded carriage. They certainly could not walk to the inn. All that Giles could think of doing was to put the old people on his horse and proceed on foot, hoping for the best. He dressed the man in his coat and the woman in his uniform jacket, which he had been wearing when he went ashore with Captain Creasey. That left him shivering, but he hoped a brisk walk would keep him warm.

Giles helped the old man into the saddle. The prospect of being rescued seemed to have revived the old chap, and he could mount the horse and help Giles position his wife in front of him on the horse.

"Hold on tightly," Giles ordered as he took the horse's reins and set off at a brisk walk with the horse following him. He maintained his rapid pace rather than plodding along shivering. He might not be as young as he had once been, and he had already had a busy day, but he knew that he needed to get to Dipton as soon as he could and that going more slowly would allow the cold to seep into his joints and made the ordeal worse. Even so, it was over an hour later before he spotted the posting inn ahead of him. He then had no trouble traversing the short distance to where his companions could be adequately treated, and he could rest before proceeding on his way.

When Giles reached the inn, only a stable boy, whose job was to welcome visitors traveling at such an outrageous hour, was awake. The servant roused the innkeeper and his wife while Giles helped the old people descend from the horse. Their hosts came out of the inn, bleary-eyed from sleep, wearing warm-looking wool dressing gowns over their night clothes. The innkeeper's wife somehow realized the nature of the situation at a glance: "You poor dears. Let's get you in and get you warm. George, get the fire in the lounge going again. Then, rouse Shirley and tell her to get the blue room ready and light a fire in it.

"Now, you, sir," she addressed Giles. "You do not look much better than these others. Come into the lounge, too, and get warm. Mr. Cobbler," she directed her following words to the innkeeper. "Get this gentleman a coat of some sort to warm him. And he looks like he could do with one of your rum toddies."

Before he knew it, Giles had a warm blanket wrapped around him and a large tankard of ale in his hand as he sat in front of the reviving fire in the lounge, having already downed a powerful rum drink. He was assured that food was coming soon, and the highwayman's victims were also being treated, though they were already lying under warm covers in the inn's best bedroom before being given any warm food or drink.

The innkeeper approached Giles when the immediate needs had been satisfied. "I'm George Cobbler, the innkeeper here, Captain …?"

"Richard Giles," Giles replied. That is how he still thought of himself, not as the Earl of Camshire. "How did you know I am a captain?"

The innkeeper looked taken aback. "The jacket you lent the lady, sir. Not *the* famous Sir Captain Giles, The Earl of Camshire, surely?" he asked incredulously.

Giles was always surprised to discover that ordinary people read the newspapers and remembered what they had read about naval matters, but all he said was, "Yes, the same. Thank you for dealing with us so efficiently."

"I'll be blimeyed!. The Earl of Camshire turning up at my inn in the middle of the night with some worn-out old people! Well, I never….

"May I ask, my lord, how did you come to be traveling at this hour with these poor souls?"

Giles explained how he had come upon the overturned carriage and discovered the elderly couple. He also explained why he had decided to bring them to the inn on the only available horse as quickly as possible.

"You probably saved their lives, poor souls, my lord. We have had trouble on that bit of road with highwaymen," the innkeeper commented. "It's surprising since it is not a much-traveled piece of road, at least not at night. I wonder what Mr. and Mrs. Smithers — that is what they are called, Mrs. Westerly tells me — what they were doing on the road at that hour."

"I didn't ask, I am afraid. I was more interested in getting them to a warm place as quickly as I could. One thing that I should mention is that their coachman was killed when the carriage was wrecked. I am afraid that his body is still out there. I thought it was more important to deal with the living than the dead as soon as possible."

"Quite right, my lord, quite right. But I had better send some of my people to guard the body from wild animals until we can send someone with a cart in the morning. Just let me attend to that, and I'll be back."

The innkeeper returned quickly after loudly ordering two stable hands to harness horses and ride to the overturned carriage. "What a nasty business this all is, my lord. What the highwayman did was murder, plain and simple. I'll have to inform the magistrate and get him to take a hand in this business. He'll want to talk with you, my lord, I am sure."

"I have to get on. I must get to my residence at Dipton as quickly as possible. Lady Camshire urgently needs the assistance that our servants, who are at our home right now, can provide. If I may, I will just have a bite to eat, and then I'll take one of your horses for the next stage of my journey."

"You will do nothing of the sort, my lord," the landlord's formidable wife interrupted the conversation. "You are worn out and still shivering, and it would be madness to continue your journey in the dark. I am sure the Countess of Camshire would not be pleased, either with you or with me, if you kill yourself. No, my Lord. Have something to eat and a few hours of sleep. You will be better off going in the daylight, and Lady Camshire wouldn't want you to fall asleep in the saddle and get injured. I'm sure she would not have been happy if she knew that you were riding to this Dipton place during the night, though it is lucky for Mr. and Mrs. Smithers that you did, for they probably would be dead by morning if you hadn't come along. Now, I'll just see what is keeping your food from coming and make sure that your bed is warmed by the time you have finished."

With that, Mrs. Cobbler turned away to see about fulfilling what she had promised Giles. Mr. Cobbler silently shrugged as she departed. "You can see who rules the roost here, my lord, but she is right. I will send for the magistrate right away. He really needs to talk to you, though I realize that people like you can ignore his wishes if you want to."

"I know what you mean, Mr. Cobbler, about 'people like me.' I am afraid you are correct, but even so, it isn't right. I will wait to see the magistrate, or if he is delayed, make sure to send him a sworn statement about what I observed."

"I can't ask more, my lord."

At that point, Mrs. Cobbler hurried up. "Your food's ready, my lord. It's only some left-over stew, yesterday's cheese, and a heel of bread, I'm afraid. But that and another mug of our ale should sct you up for a rest very well."

Before he knew it, Giles had eaten and been whisked off to a bedroom where a fire was burning in the grate, his bed had been turned down with a warming pan used to take the chill off the sheets, and a nightshirt laid out for him. He hardly had the energy to remove his clothes, climb into bed, and douse the candle before he was asleep. For once, he did not lie awake thinking about the day that had passed and the tasks that would await him on the following one. Nor did he write his usual letter to Daphne to tell her how his day had gone.

Giles slept late, much later than he had intended. The first light of day was creeping around the curtains before he awoke. During the night, someone had taken his trousers, brushed them, and cleaned his boots. His two coats, which he had lent to the old people, were also in the room, newly brushed. When he got out of bed, he found that there was even warm water on the washstand. Mrs. Cobbler might be a bit bossy, but she ran a good inn.

Giles was ready in minutes, but when he stepped into the inn's taproom looking to settle up with Mrs. Cobbler, he found the innkeeper instead.

"Good morning, my lord. I've requested that the magistrate visit as soon as possible. I added that the Earl of Camshire needs to see him urgently and can't tarry at my inn for long. He should arrive at any minute. He would hate to find that I had been talking to you, and he had not."

Moments later, there was a kerfuffle at the inn door as a large, rotund man with a distinctly red nose came in yelling, "I am here to see the Earl of Camshire. Where is he, Cobbler?"

"Right here, Mr. Carruthers," responded the innkeeper. "My lord, may I present Mr. Goerge Carruthers. Mr. Carruthers is the magistrate who lives closest to us."

"My lord," the magistrate started the conversation, "I appreciate your waiting for me to come. I gather you had a problem with a highwayman."

"Not me, personally. I came upon a scene of the aftermath of a carriage wreck that was the work of highway robbers and assisted some victims of the crime."

Giles proceeded to tell the tale concisely and completely.

"Thank you, my lord," said the magistrate when Giles concluded. "A highwayman has been robbing people using that stretch of road, but he's never done anything like this before. Just stopping coaches, usually earlier in the night, and taking money. Hanging offense, of course, but with nothing of substance to follow up on, we have been able to do nothing except spread the word that there might be a reward for information. This is much more serious. There is no doubt that the coachman was murdered, even if unintentionally. That is, nevertheless, a hanging offense. The coroner will want to hold a hearing. If you can, my lord, I am sure that he would appreciate your sending a notarized account of your finding the crime scene. I don't think there will be any further need for your appearance, even if we catch the robber. The courts are always willing to accept sworn statements from military men who may be unable to attend an assize."

Giles was more than happy to agree. He was desperate to resume his trip to Dipton. Even so, settling his bill with the Cobblers, who were reluctant to charge him for anything at all, making sure that the elderly victims would be appropriately taken care of — again, Mrs. Cobbler objected to what she took as Giles's not trusting them to be good Samaritans without needing payment — required more time than Giles liked.

Finally, Giles was on his way. He hoped to reach Dipton by the early afternoon. That would leave enough time for the servants to gather what they needed and be ready to leave first thing the following morning. Even with the short winter days, they should be able to arrive in London on the same day. The sooner he got to Dipton Hall, the more likely this plan could be executed.

The first stage went uneventfully. Giles arrived without problem at the next inn, and it took a minimum of time to arrange a horse for the next section of his trip. Off he went again. It was a fine winter day, with a hint of warmth from the sun signaling that soon spring would be upon them. He hummed to himself the theme of the Beethoven sonata he and Daphne had been practicing. He noticed an unusual number of post riders coming the other way, but he thought nothing of it, giving and receiving a friendly wave or nod as the riders passed without stopping.

When Giles reached the next posting inn, he commented to the hostler on the number of riders he had met. That was greeted by a laugh.

"That's due to Sir William Walters, sir. Randy Willy, we name him around here. He has seven daughters, would you believe it, but no sons. At least there are no legitimate sons, though enough lads around here look like him that there is no doubt that he can have sons, just not with his wife. His lands are all entailed, and his heir is a distant cousin who is supposed to be a nasty piece of work, so there may be no money for Sir William's family when he dies. He's on his third wife now, and two of the daughters are hers, which has just made the situation worse, especially with Randy Willy not getting any younger. Then, just last night, she finally delivered a baby boy. Sir William is cock-a-hoop over it. Nothing would do than that everyone must know about the good news as soon as possible. So he sent messengers to everyone he could think of to tell them of the change in his fortunes. Every one of our horses was used. We have nothing you can use, sir, and you seem to have ridden this horse very hard. You will have to wait a while for it to rest before you can go on your way.

"But I have to get to Dipton as soon as possible. Ameschester isn't that far away. Surely, the horse I have been riding can get me there."

"Well, maybe. But you should let it rest for a bit. Have a feed of oats to help it to continue."

Giles had no choice. He spent some time in the lounge, having one beer and then another. He had nothing to do except worry about how Daphne would hold her ball if he didn't arrange for help soon. After forty-five minutes, he gave up and went out to the stable yard.

"I'll set off now, hostler," he told the servant. "What do I owe you?"

"Oh, thrupence will do, sir. But, sir, I haven't had a chance to check the horse over yet. Give me a few minutes, and I'll do it."

"No, I'm in too great a hurry. I'll take him now."

Giles left immediately, going at a good canter. He had traveled this road many times in the past and knew he was getting close to Ameschester. With only a few more miles to go, the horse stumbled and almost threw him. When Giles regained his saddle, he realized that the horse was limping badly.

Giles had no choice but to stop the horse and dismount. The problem was obvious the minute he examined the horse's hoofs. The creature had cast the shoe off his right front hoof. It already looked tender. Giles could not ride him farther. He would have to lead the horse as it hobbled along to Ameschester since he knew of no blacksmith nearby, and reshoeing would not allow the horse to be ridden immediately. His hoof would still have to recover before he was functional.

Giles set off on foot with the horse limping along behind him. It was only about two miles to the inn at Ameschester, but it took Giles an hour to reach it. Then, finally, his luck changed. As he entered the inn yard, there was Mr. Griffiths, the stablemaster of his hunting-horse breeding enterprise.

"Lord Camshire," Mr. Griffiths exclaimed. "What are you doing here?"

"Trying to get to Dipton Hall as quickly as possible. This miserable horse lost a shoe. It's been one delay after another, and Daphne needs me to get some people from Dipton Hall as quickly as possible."

"Then I suggest you take my horse, and I will deal with the one you have."

Giles wasted no time mounting Mr. Griffiths's horse. It was one of the ones they had bred, and both men were very proud of it. Dipton Racer, they had named her, for she was very fast. Giles had no hesitation in setting off at a gallop. Finally, he was moving rapidly. Even so, the winter sun was setting as he rode up to the entrance to Dipton Hall. He jumped off the horse and tossed the reins aside as he charged up to the door. Dipton Racer had been trained not to wander off when her master left her unhitched.

Giles raced through the front door, not waiting to see if any servant was on duty to open the door for visitors. "Steves," he bellowed, "Mrs. Wilson, Mrs. Darling,"

The butler, the housekeeper, and the cook all came running. Whatever could be the matter? Lord Camshire had never summoned them in that way. Something serious must be at hand. They listened patiently as Giles explained what the dilemma was. Then, to his surprise, they all started to ask him questions about the situation in London and what was needed. There was no hesitation about them going or taking any of the servants under them who would be useful. The questions and comments had to do with what material they had to take with them, which people, and how to do it.

Steves raised the question of how many people they could take with them. Could they count on changes of horses if they took many carriages and carts? Giles hadn't even thought of that problem as he rushed to get assistance to Daphne. They had to consult the stablemaster and Mr. Griffiths. Giles realized that there was no question in his servants' minds that they and those under them would help as much as they could. The only problems they could see were how to get the personnel to London. That would determine which servants they would take with them.

Steves sent for Fisher, the stablemaster for Dipton Hall's stables. At Giles's suggestion, a footman was also sent to ask Mr. Griffiths, the stablemaster for the hunter-stud enterprise, to come. His horses were not suitable for the task, but he had a great deal of knowledge about what horses could and could not do. The problem they had encountered was not primarily in the number of carriages and coaches they could use, but in the number of carriage horses, they could get on their way. London was too far away for a single team to make it all the way to London quickly. They had to have changes of horses. A single team could get to London at a measured pace and with adequate rest pauses. But realistically, the party from Dipton would have to travel more quickly to get there to be of use for the ball.

Mr. Griffiths, when presented with the problem, made two suggestions. Someone should go immediately to the Ameschester Arms to rent all the carriages, drivers, and horses they had on hand. His second was to send Walters, the dispatch rider, along the road to London to reserve as many carriage horses as possible at each posting inn. Giles recognized the wisdom of the second recommendation. He didn't want this venture to stall on the difficulty that had slowed his arrival at Ameschester. Giles approved both suggestions.

The meeting broke up, with everyone dispersing to start their tasks for getting ready for the journey. Mrs. Darling lingered a moment. "You must be starving as well as exhausted, my lord. Let me get you something. It will be ready in a few minutes. I'll get Mr. Steves to serve it in the small dining room just as soon as you have had a chance to wash up after your journey."

As he finished the simple meal and washed down with some excellent red wine, Giles realized he was dead tired. There was nothing more he could do today. Indeed, much of what needed to be done to get away to London would probably have to wait for daylight tomorrow. He might as well get a good night's sleep. His servants would be more efficient if he were not distracting them. Tomorrow promised to be another very long day!

Chapter X

Daphne was at her wit's end with the problems of preparing for the ball that would be held in three days, like it or not. Nothing was going right. Her servants were simply not up to the task: the house would not be adequately prepared, and they could not serve the guests smartly and unobtrusively or cooperate with each other. The footmen were poorly trained, and the butler, who was just a bumped-up footman, seemed to have no idea of how to get them to provide good service in the way that seemed so effortless and unintrusive with a well-trained crew.

There was nothing she could do now to rectify the situation. The ball would be a disaster, and she would be the laughingstock of all those horrible, supercilious society ladies who resented the arrival of a new star in their tight-knit world. It would be even worse if she canceled it. And she hated to let Giles down: he always had such confidence in her abilities.

She had just returned from seeing Madame St. Claire, her dressmaker. She had left ordering her ball gown until the last minute in the hope that new fabrics and patterns might arrive from Paris. A shipment was supposed to come before the ball, and there was still time for as good a patron as Lady Camshire to get the latest patterns and fabrics from Paris made into a stunning gown. However, to add to Daphne's misery, the news was terrible. No shipment had yet been received. Anyway, the modiste had learned that one of Daphne's rivals for putting on the most brilliant of balls, Lady Strangway, had somehow commandeered all of the next shipment to be smuggled in from France. It had not yet arrived, but what was clear was that there would be no innovations in style or cloth for Daphne's ball gown.

Daphne had had to order a new one from the now very common designs and fabrics already seen at several other balls this Season. At least, the dressmaker had promised that the new gown would be ready in time for the ball, provided that Daphne could arrive promptly for the fittings when needed.

Daphne turned into Camshire Square with Betsey trailing along behind her. The square looked a bit bleak as it waited for spring to bring it back to life, and there was no traffic to prevent it from seeming abandoned. But was that a carriage in front of Camshire House? Indeed, it looked very much like the carriage that Giles had taken to Portsmouth. Surely, he couldn't be back. How wonderful that would be, even though there wasn't anything he could do about the pickle she had got herself into. At least he would be a sympathetic shoulder to cry on, and she could tell him her feelings: he was the only person she could confide in.

Daphne dashed around the square to the carriage with Betsey following behind her, wishing that her mistress would act in a more dignified way. But Giles's carriage wasn't there because Giles had returned. Instead, it was filled chock-a-block with bundles, like some tradesman's cart. What in the world was Giles up to now?

It took several moments before Daphne discovered from the somewhat incoherent explanations of the coachman about what he was doing in London with a carriage full of parcels. In fact, it only became apparent when the coachman pulled out a hastily scribbled note from Giles. Somehow, Daphne's husband had intercepted the cargo smuggled from France that her rival had arranged to buy as a way to put Daphne down. Now, the note made it clear that the patterns and the cloth were hers, hers exclusively, hers legally. Lady Strangway had no claim on them; her claiming that they were hers would open the way for prosecuting her for attempted smuggling. Everyone bought smuggled goods, but no one would admit that they had arranged for the smuggling in the first place. With this shipment, there was no need to pretend that the goods were not smuggled; they had paid their duty. Daphne could flaunt the acquisition all over London if she wished. She could let her friends access the latest fashions and fabrics, if she wished, and withhold them to spite the snooty ladies who resented the newcomer to their ranks.

Of course, his note did not mention the implications of what Giles's intercepting the shipment could have for Daphne's feud with other ladies. Those arose in Daphne's wave of glee that occurred with the vastly altered situation about one of her main worries ever since she learned that the date of the ball was being changed. However, the remaining time before the ball was horribly short to take advantage of this windfall.

"Harrison," Daphne asked the coachman, "can you drive us with your cargo to Bond Street right now?"

"I suppose so, my lady, but there is no room for you and Miss Betsey in the coach."

"No matter. We can ride with you on the coachman's bench."

Daphne's servants had already learned that it was useless to protest that what she wanted to do was not considered proper for a noble lady. If she wanted to ride on the driver's bench, she would. Harrison would not even be surprised if Lady Giles wanted to drive the horses herself.

Betsey was not happy about making a display of herself scrambling up to the bench in her long skirt, but at least Daphne had not suggested that she could ride on the footman's step*; occupying that position was suddenly the job of Harrison's assistant coachman. At least no one would see her as she scrambled up. Somehow, she had not realized that she would have to climb down when they reached their destination and that there would be plenty of onlookers to observe her awkward descent in the middle of Bond Street.

Madame St. Claire had just finished closing her shop when Daphne's carriage pulled up in front of it, but she wasn't about to tell a countess that the establishment was closed and to come back the next day. She was as astounded as Daphne had been about the windfall that had come into Lady Camshire's possession. All her staff worked overtime to get all the material into the shop. Madame St. Clair, who had been born plain Susan Fisher, would make a tidy profit out of Lady Camshire's windfall, as would Lord Camshire himself.

Of course, as soon as the carriage had been emptied, Daphne and Mme. St. Claire had to examine their acquisitions, choose a pattern from the latest Parisian fashions, and select the fabrics needed to make it. They would have a fitting the next afternoon; Mme. St. Clair's seamstresses would have to work overtime to get it ready on time.

It was fully dark before Daphne was ready to leave the dress-making shop. In the carriage riding back to Camshire House, she discovered that a couple of packages had not been transferred to the shop. They were papers. When she got them inside her residence, Daphne realized that they were music — scores for the latest dance music from the Continent. She would waste no time: one of the footmen could immediately take a note to the orchestra leader who was scheduled to play at her ball, asking him to call on her the next day. Things were definitely looking up,

Daphne thought. Then she remembered all the other problems that had not been solved and promised to make her ball, if not quite the disaster she had faced earlier in the day, still far less than she had hoped for and an event to be ridiculed by her enemies.

What in the world did Giles think he was doing going off to Dipton? Was he trying to evade the disaster that the ball would be, leaving her to face the music by herself? She needed him here, not at Dipton, to show that he supported her fully even when things went wrong.

The following day, Daphne found herself on edge. It was partly because she had had morning sickness for the second day in a row. Daphne was glad to be pregnant. Indeed, she had worried a little about not being pregnant since Giles had been home for a good, long time, and they had enjoyed many intimate occasions together, which were likely to lead to another pregnancy. The only hitch was with this wretched ball hanging over her head; she wouldn't be able to daydream about the implications of having another child and what he or she might be like. But she couldn't stop thinking about the wretched ball, even though there was nothing constructive she could do about it now. Trying to get her rotten servants to be more efficient and to produce that particular effect, evident only when skilled and dedicated servants looked after a mansion, had turned out to be hopeless. Well, at least she had the fitting for her gown to look forward to, though that was in the afternoon. And, hopefully, that man Brown, the orchestra leader, would be calling to see the new music scores. She had almost forgotten them. She could spend her time looking at the new music rather than fretting about something she could do nothing more to rescue.

Mr. Brown arrived somewhat earlier than would usually be considered appropriate for a tradesman visiting a lady for whom they were doing some work. He was enthusiastic about her plan to include some new music from the Continent that had never been heard in London. Nothing radical, of course. People had to be able to dance to the new music without difficulty, so new rhythms requiring significantly different dance steps were out of the question until the dancing masters had found out what the steps of the dance should be and had a chance to demonstrate them to the more daring of society's dancers and instructions printed in the appropriate broadsheets.

Mr. Brown scanned the new scores and realized that Daphne had come up with a goldmine. As far as the dancing was concerned, Daphne's ball would be a great success, with every tongue wagging about the new, different, lively, and danceable music. The suppliers had sent more complete copies of the music than Mr. Brown required. Since Daphne could read music, she should have one copy to review in preparation for leading the elaborate dances.

When the musician had left, Daphne went over the music. It was delightful, covering most of the dances they had agreed should be included in the ball. She was particularly taken by one cotillion, with a catchy main tune and variations that would be very suitable for the opening dance. She and Giles could lead the first dance to that music unless the Prince Regent decided to attend, in which case he would lead the dance, but that was unlikely to happen. Even if he did put in an appearance, it was unlikely to be before the dancing had started. Things were certainly looking up!

A crash in the hallway as some inept parlor maid dropped something brought Daphne back to reality. If the service were unacceptable, or the food inedible, fine music and a new ballgown would not rescue the fiasco that was going to occur. It was too late to get a new butler who could train the footmen, a new housekeeper and well-trained maids, or even a different cook, and they were central to the success of the ball.

More bad news arrived with the information that the cook had come down with a high temperature and vomiting. The doctor had been sent for, but at least today and maybe tomorrow, she would not be doing any preparations for the supper that was originally Daphne had intended to be one of the main features of the ball. Well, that was just one more disappointment. They would have to make do with whatever the senior kitchen maid could produce on her own for the supper that always accompanied these balls.

When afternoon came, Daphne went to Mme. St. Claire's establishment for the next fitting of the ballgown. At least, this aspect of the ball was developing into a feature that exceeded Daphne's hopes. She would be the most stunning woman at the ball! It was a pity that Giles would not witness that one triumph that would be better than Daphne had expected.

Daphne dawdled at the dress shop. Returning to Camshire House had little appeal to her this afternoon. The sun was setting when she arrived again at Camshire Square. Just as on the previous day, a carriage was in front of her residence. In fact, several carriages and people were milling around and taking things into the mansion. As she got closer, Daphne saw that two carriages had coats of arms on their doors. She knew exactly what they were, for one was her own, and the other was her mother-in-law's. Steves, the butler at Dipton Hall, seemed to be directing traffic into the house.

It took Daphne only a moment to realize what must be happening. Instead of avoiding the problems of the ball, Giles had brought several carriages of servants from Dipton. There wasn't much time, of course, but the chances of having a satisfactory event had just shot up incredibly. Before moving to Dipton, Steves had been the butler at Camshire House before Giles's father had closed the establishment, and his skills had been honed by the Dipton Hunt Balls that Daphne and Giles had hosted. If Giles had also persuaded Mrs. Darling to come, the last of Daphne's worries would be ended. Daphne couldn't wait to get to Camshire House. She pulled up her skirt and broke into a run to get her to the other side of the square as quickly as possible. Betsey followed, as always, but, for once, she was not wishing that her mistress would show more decorum and act more as a countess should.

Inside, Daphne found Giles busy directing traffic and answering questions from people who did not know Camshire House. He greeted Daphne with a big embrace, of the sort married nobles were not supposed to perform in the presence of servants, and told her how all the servants at Dipton Hall, from the most senior staff to the humblest kitchen boy, had been willing to come to London to help out. All the senior staff were here and would soon be working furiously to prepare for the ball. But first, Giles told Daphne, space had to be found for the visiting servants to sleep comfortably. If the servants' quarters were full, they could sleep in the many empty guest bedrooms in Camshire House. That suggestion would normally be unheard of, but such a restriction did not apply to the Earl and Countess of Camshire.

Mrs. Darling insisted that she prepare and that the usual servants serve dinner for Daphne and Giles. Daphne had not expected to have much of a dinner when she returned from the modiste's shop, and Giles had intended that they should visit the nearby pub with acceptable food. But it was quite clear that Mrs. Darling was determined that *her* Earl and Countess should have a proper dinner, despite the strange location and the urgency to take the myriad steps that would ensure that the supper at the ball was the success Daphne craved. And though the servants were bustling about in all the public rooms, lit almost as brightly as they would be when the ball was held, Daphne and Giles retired to their bedroom early. It would never do for them to look tired at their own ball; the fiction was that it was no effort to host a magnificent ball.

Giles and Daphne had much catching up to do, but the most significant and happiest news was that Daphne was pregnant again. Nothing would do, but they made sure that they continued to be in good practice, just in case they were called upon unexpectedly to try to have another baby; after all, early miscarriages were not unheard of, Daphne explained to Giles, whose ignorance of the details of pregnancy and childbirth was still extensive despite already being the father of three children.

Giles and Daphne slept very soundly that night. They awoke, realizing that they had nothing more that was urgent to do to get ready for the ball. Mme. St. Claire would come to the house in the late afternoon with the new gown for Daphne. She would also bring seamstresses to make any adjustments long before the first guests were to arrive. Until then, Daphne was at a loose end. She decided to use the time to catch up on reviewing the accounts for some of their properties, which she had been neglecting due to her concerns about holding the ball. Giles went to his room to play his violin, which was his way of passing the time when *Glaucus* was approaching another ship for combat because until they were close, he had nothing to do.

Daphne heard Giles tuning his violin. She had not guessed how much he had been frazzled by the pressures and uncertainties of the last few days. His fiddle would calm him. However, she was next surprised at what he started to play. Usually, he played Mozart, which was unquestionably his favorite, usually the first violin part of one of the violin quartets. This time, however, he was playing dance music, Not very demanding music, indeed. She recognized that he was playing one of the new dances she had heard played by the orchestra leader just the previous day. She was surprised that he was playing it at all and how good his sight-reading was. To her ear, it sounded better than the professional's playing. It was happy music, she thought. Indeed, she was much happier than she had been for many days. Maybe Giles was, too. He went through much of the new music before taking a break, often playing a piece several times or reviewing what he found tricky bits.

The day dragged, but finally, it was time to dress for the ball and to have a light, early dinner. The orchestra members arrived and were given dinner. Daphne checked the ballroom and the supper room to make sure that they were perfect and that the flowers were fresh and well-placed.

The first guests arrived early, but everything was ready for them. Steves announced them, and Daphne and Giles welcomed them. After that, a steady flow of the cream of society kept the three busy. The adults were often accompanied by their daughters. Those young ladies were present to find a suitor or to consolidate their acquaintance with ones found at earlier balls. Dancing would, of course, occur and be enjoyed, but that was not why many of the young ladies made sure to attend. Their fathers were supposed to support and accompany their mothers, but most of them would gravitate quickly to the card room, many of them losing money that should be used to further their daughters' marriage chances.

The young gentlemen would come a little later, trying hard to disguise the reason that most of them were there: to improve their fortunes by winning a well-dowered young lady. Nevertheless, most of those looking for brides would arrive before the dancing began, hoping to get favorable places on the young ladies' dance cards and to arrange to take the most charming of them, either in looks or in dowry, to supper.

At a quarter past ten, the musicians appeared on their platform, tuned up, and the first dance commenced. There happened to be no royalty at the ball, at least not yet, nor any duke of dancing age. It was unusual, but not inappropriate, for Daphne to lead the first dance with Giles. She had thought of starting the ball with a waltz, her favorite dance, but it was also the one where the dancers were paired together, touching the whole time. Though it had been a common dance in England for many years, and versions were often played at private parties where young ladies could demonstrate their proficiency at the pianoforte, it was still thought to be inappropriate, indeed lascivious, by many of the more staid matrons who would be at her ball to be a waltz. Nevertheless, she chose to lead the ball with Giles, but with a more proper and more complicated minuet. It was, in her opinion, the most magnificent of courting dances, even though she had never had the chance to dance it with a serious suitor.

The minuet would rapidly sort out the young men who had paid attention to the dancing masters from those who thought they were so important that they could stumble through dances with women who were lucky to have gotten their attention. Most young men made sure to have the first dance on the card of women they were seriously interested in. That included the son of Daphne's enemy, Lady Strangway, an arrogant and self-satisfied lad who, Daphne thought, had inherited all his mother's worst tendencies. Daphne pitied anyone who won him in the marriage stakes. She was secretly delighted to witness the shambles he made of the elegant, intricate dance, though she felt for his partner, who did seem to know the dance well.

The ball was off to a splendid start. A cotillion followed the minuet, and then there was a gavotte. The first two were from the music that Giles had found on *The Ruddy Fox*; the third was not. Daphne thought it dragged and might even be missing one of the parts of the music. As the orchestra struggled to keep the dance going, Giles noted that Steves was on the side of the ballroom, signaling with his eyebrows that Giles was needed.

Steves had some very disturbing news for Giles. The leader of the orchestra had been sick to his stomach. He couldn't keep going. Their second violin was a stand-in for their regular one, and he was not very good, as no doubt Giles had noted. They had sent for another orchestra, not as good as the one Daphne had chosen but more adequate than what was now playing. Possibly, their leader would recover, but that would not happen until after supper.

Giles was furious, but he did not lose his temper even though the present orchestra was unacceptable. Daphne would be so disappointed, especially as the music was supposed to be the highlight of the ball. And now this! Good heavens, even he was a better musician than the man now trying to lead the orchestra; indeed, he was better than the leader who was now sick. However, he had never played in an orchestra, though he and Daphne had become quite proficient in playing violin-piano duets together, and leading was Giles's specialty, though not in music.

Daphne had been expecting a waltz to be the next dance, one of the ones in the bundle of new music. She had been looking forward to hearing it and presumed she would dance it with Giles. She now had wondered if they should take the floor if the orchestra were going to make as much a hash of the waltz as it had of the previous offering. As the orchestra started, Daphne noted that they had a firm, pronounced rhythm and a lovely tone, ideal for the waltz. They had found a solution to the problem that had ruined their previous offering. But where was Giles, who should be leading her out onto the dance floor even if they had not been there for the beginning of the waltz? How infuriating could he be?

She looked at the orchestra more carefully. The leader had his back to her as he sawed rhythmically at the instrument tucked under his chin. He must be the orchestra leader she had employed. Whatever had happened to him in the previous dance that had been such a shambles, now he sounded better than ever. Somehow, however, the man did not look right. Even though the period in which musicians were expected to wear the livery of their employers, like servants, was long past, they were not expected to look like the guests, and this man had very fine clothes. Of course, he did: the musician was her husband! He had saved the musical aspect of the ball, but how would she be able to live down his taking a role in it that was so utterly inappropriate for an earl, let alone the host of the ball?

The ball continued with several more dances played, with Giles leading the orchestra. Then they broke for supper. Giles reappeared in the ballroom to take Daphne to the refreshment. As they led the way to the dining room, they could hear whispers about the orchestra and Giles' outrageous behavior. Giles didn't seem to care while Daphne listened eagerly to snippets of conversation. Her known detractors commented on how inappropriate Giles's action had been. Her friends and admirers disagreed. It showed what a marvelously thoughtful, though unconventional, man Daphne's husband was. But, as far as she could tell, many of the guests had not even been aware of the change in the orchestra's composition.

When the orchestra returned after supper, it was back to full strength with professional musicians. If they were not as good as what went before — Daphne's firm opinion — they were more than adequate. Daphne got to dance her waltz with Giles, in fact, three of them, as the dance most suitable for courting couples interested in more than a business transaction now was danced more frequently and attracted especially those who took more spontaneously to the floor than had been the case in the earlier, formal arrangements whose purpose was to find marriage partners, not dancing ones.

The winter dawn was already breaking when the last guests left Camshire House so that Steves could finally lock the front door, and Daphne and Giles could fall into bed, exhausted. However, they did not fall asleep immediately; they too much enjoyed gloating over the triumph of Daphne's first ball given in London. But, soon, the strain of the last few days took over, and they fell into a deep sleep.

Giles and Daphne woke in time for a very late lunch. The early newspapers were already out with news of the ball; indeed, they contained long and full descriptions. Daphne lapped the columns up and had Steves send a footman to get all the other accounts, even though some were known to be most uncomplimentary about such events. All the reports agreed it was the best ball of the Season, even papers that usually showed themselves as part of the Strangway set. All also agreed that the music featured some new scores that were very welcome. All also commented on the erratic nature of the performance of the music, but none of them condemned Giles, as Daphne had expected, for taking part and leading the orchestra. An earl taking the leading role in a dance band was highly unusual and would have received condemnation from many for lowering the standards of the nobility. Still, Giles was a war hero who apparently could do no wrong. The newspapers treated his leading the orchestra as something worth noting but not dwelling on or commenting on extensively or critically.

Giles had been equally interested in the newspaper reports. But after a while, he tossed aside the newspaper he had been reading. "Enjoy it while you can, Daphne," he said.

"What do you mean?" asked his wife.

"Tomorrow, you will be inundated by a swarm of high-place ladies, all eager to discuss the marvelous ball you gave under the guise of a visit to thank you. I imagine that you will have to endure a lot of snide comments, even from your supposed friends. They will be jealous that a first-timer has received such notices."

"I'm not a first-timer. I have given very good balls at Dipton."

"Of course, you have, my dear, but they don't count. Only balls that are part of the Season are worth consideration in many of their minds."

"I suppose you may be right. I hadn't thought about what happens after the ball."

"Well, that's for tomorrow or later."

Giles returned to his paper but switched to the pages reporting on Parliament and other political matters. Though she returned to the society pages, Daphne was thinking about other things rather than absorbing yet another report on her triumph. She was also frowning a bit.

After a while, Daphne set down her paper. "Giles," she announced, "I don't think I will want to host another ball, at least not until our girls are coming out."

"You can't do that. We are committed to the Ameschester Hunt Ball in a couple of weeks."

"Oh, not that one, of course. I was thinking of these London Balls. It is a lot of bother for something to entertain many people I don't like. And I don't like the fuss everyone seems to make of them — well, not everyone. Many who don't pay much attention to the balls are more interesting. Preparing for our ball, I missed some opera performances I wanted to attend and some lectures. I know we have to be in London for your duties in the Lords. I would miss many of our activities here if we were in Dipton all the time, but I think I would be just as happy if I never attended one of the big Society events ever again, and I know that you would be too."

"Well, I would happily go along with your idea, but it doesn't become important until that group of old harpies gets together to plan the next Season. Then you can decide if you want to give a ball again, and we only need to go to the ones you feel like attending. I enjoy dancing with you, but there are many other activities we can indulge in. I might even like to attend some of your high-brow lectures.

Chapter XI

Camshire House became very busy on the second morning after the ball. The servants had been allowed to sleep late on the morning following the event, and some of the standard chores for that day had been delayed to the next one. Daphne didn't notice the extra cleaning and straightening that was required. All she noticed was that these servants were much less intrusive than the ones she had had before the Dipton contingent arrived.

As both Giles and Daphne expected, the first caller arrived just as soon as it could possibly be considered proper to visit the houses of the aristocracy. Daphne was ready for the onslaught and settled in the drawing room, which was larger than the morning room, while Giles went to the library to ride out the storm, as he called it.

Giles had hardly settled into the book he was reading, a tome on how to preserve hay and other such crops during the winter so that they would neither rot nor go sour when one of the footmen entered with a visiting card on a silver platter.

"My lord," said the footman, "The Baron Strangway wonders whether you are at home."

"Surely he wants to see Lady Camshire, Edgar," Giles said.

"No, my lord, he asked for you specifically. He is in a bit of a tizzy."

"I wonder why he wants to see me. Well, Edgar, the only way to find out is to ask him. Show him in."

Giles didn't know Lord Strangway and couldn't remember having him pointed out in the House of Lords.

The man striding into the library was short, hardly five and a half feet, and his face revealed that he was furious. The visitor was well dressed and tailored, with a figure best described as chubby and the red face of a man who frequently indulged in the bottle rather than one who was frequently outdoors. He carried a cane, though he showed no signs of needing one for walking. Looking at the cane carefully, Giles realized it was a sword cane and stood up in case the angry man might think of using more than harsh words.

"Lord Strangway," Giles started the conversation, "I don't believe we have been introduced. No matter, would you care for some refreshment?"

"What the Hell do you think you are playing at Camshire," the Baron replied. "Stealing those goddamn silks and patterns that I had obtained with great effort and cost to please my wife."

"Stealing? I have done nothing of the sort. Take your accusation back immediately!" Giles did not raise his voice, but the steely way he spoke should have warned his visitor that he did not take the accusation lightly.

"Don't play the innocent with me, Camshire! I paid above market to be sure to get the latest styles and fabrics in ball gowns from France. Exclusively! And then I don't receive the frigging shipment because of your interference, God damn it! Lady Strangway was counting on getting the bloody stuff exclusively so that she could have a unique and stunning gown in the newest pattern that no one could rival. It would make sure, she claimed, that she would be the most important person at the ball and would impress everyone. Then, with the best material owned by her exclusively, she could dole it out to her friends for a very healthy price so they would get the second-best ball gowns, thanks to her. And everyone else would have to put up with dowdy old dresses. It would put her at the head of the ton, she claimed, and do down all the rest of Society who think that we were second-rate people because of my origins, even though I am truly as high-born as anyone, you included, you lousy cur. She wanted to have all the fabrics to make new gowns in her possession, so she got me to purchase all the best materials and patterns available so that she could sell them only to her closest friends so that everyone else ends up wearing the same old dresses that have been seen before to your wife's ruddy ball. Now she looks stupid, and I am out of pocket, all because of you! I discovered that you obtained the shipment, and your bloody wife used it for her goddamned dress at her frigging ball."

Giles surged to his feet and seized Lord Strangway by his coat lapels.

"So it was you behind that shipment, was it, you moldy toad? I should have known, based on your sleazy reputation in the House of Lords, but I still find it hard to believe. And now you come and insult me in my own library, complaining because I prevented you from committing a hanging offense! Let me tell you what happened, you lousy pimp, and I'll only say this once."

Giles did not yell at the nobleman. Instead, he spoke in a normal voice, but ice cold, "I'll tell you exactly what happened. The lugger on which your parcels were being transported had the misfortune of being captured by a French vessel. The frigate that I have the honor to command rescued the ship. It turned out that the cargo was contraband material that would need a special permit to be landed in England and on which duty had to be paid. Captain Creasey was expecting the documents to be produced before he landed the merchandise.

"*I* was on the scene. *I* rescued Captain Creasey from the French. *I* learned that the owner of the parcels, who turned out to be *you,* had not given him the promised permission to import the material or the receipt for the customs duty that had been paid on the goods. For Captain Creasey to dock anywhere but at the Customs wharf would involve him in criminal charges of the most serious sort. However, without the proof of permission, even though the customs officer recognized that he might have broken the law quite innocently in bringing the French goods to England, without the document, the official had no choice but to confiscate the goods. The Customs Office is not in the business of trading in women's dresses or their materials. So if no one buys the goods at a reasonable sum from the Customs Office and pays the duty on the shipment, they would have to destroy the material.

"I know how important the best ball gowns to wear during the Season are to the ladies, and I knew that my wife would appreciate having a new gown for the ball she was about to hold. Indeed, she had been frustrated because someone — did I understand you to say that it was you? — had bought up all the supplies and was hoarding them. To solve that problem, I bought the cloth and papers on the spot in Portsmouth and sent them up to Lady Camshire in London. I regret that your incompetence inconvenienced your wife, and I also regret that you were not caught red-handed in what sounds like a deliberate attempt by you to evade the law on imports and duties. Next time you try it, you'll probably get caught and hung, which will be a good thing, too.

"Now get out of here, you whoremongering excuse for a nobleman!"

"Steves," Giles called, knowing that the butler was sure to be standing guard outside the reading room in case he was needed. "Lord Strangway is leaving now. Please, show him out. Lord Strangway, if you come calling again, I will not be at home."

Steves escorted Lord Strangway to the front door. On the way, they passed the open door to the morning room where Daphne was receiving visitors. Lord Strangway rushed into the morning room before Steves could stop him.

"There you are! The wife of the thief who stole my cloth so my wife couldn't have the ballgown she wanted while ensuring that no one would have a better one. Now you think you can lord it over us, You trollop! You daughter of a man whose money comes from a gun shop! Aping the manners of your betters. You whore…"

Steves had taken the man by the lapels of his coat to stem his torrent of abuse. Daphne took an equally good method: she slapped him in the face. It was no mere tap, either, but one that snapped his head sideways and left a rapidly reddening mark.

"Lord Strangway, are you drunk?" asked Daphne. It was not really a question, just a comment on Lord Strangway's outrageous behavior.

"Steves, Edgar," Daphne called even though the two servants were already standing by, fearing trouble with Lord Strangway, and Steves had him almost in a chokehold. "Throw this man out of my house."

"This way, my lord," Steves declared as he and the footman each took an elbow and frog-marched the nobleman to the front door, where they left him on the portico. Two ladies, with their maids trailing behind them, had just entered Camshire Square to call on Daphne and witnessed the rough treatment of the nobleman. They would tell the tale to everyone they met in the next few days, never giving the nobleman any benefit of the doubt.

Giles had settled back in his chair and was again absorbed in his book when Edgar again entered with his silver platter. The card read, 'Dr. Joseph Standish, Professor of Astronomical Physics, St. Simons College, Oxford University.'

Giles rose to his feet to greet the distinguished visitor. "Professor Standish, Lady Camshire and I greatly enjoyed your lecture the other afternoon."

"Glad you enjoyed it, my lord. You and Lady Camshire asked some of the most intelligent questions. You seem to know a lot about celestial matters."

"Well, that's truer of her ladyship than of me. I only know enough to use the stars for navigation, and I sometimes like to use my telescope on a clear night to see the planets. But I am sure you didn't come today to get my opinions on astronomy."

"True, my lord, though I think you underestimate how far your curiosity has taken you. But I have come to sound you out on an earthlier topic."

"Oh?"

"Yes. A number of us are not happy with the Royal Society either as a place for informal gatherings or for providing other features of a gentleman's club, and how it refuses membership to several individuals we would like to associate with. It is also hostile to women and will not admit them either as club members or as guests. And, of course, they provide no overnight accommodation for ladies, even though some of the more able scientists or philosophers are women, though they are not largely recognized as such. We would like to start a club more in tune with our ideas."

"I would support your effort, though I doubt I would qualify for membership. Lady Camshire certainly would, and she has teased me about the men's clubs, which she says are afraid of women. But I don't see why you have come to me."

"We heard that you might own a building that is suitable for a club."

"Yes, I suppose I do. Green's Club had become too disreputable for me to support it in any way, so I closed it down. I am unable to sell the property because of an entail my father put on it in his will. It's up for rent, but if I remember correctly, the building can only be for a gentleman's club. I'll have to talk to my lawyer about it. I think the premises would be very suitable for the sort of club you described. It even has a separate wing, which could be made into an exclusive section open only to ladies, which might deal with the problem of how they can stay at a club respectably.

"Now, Professor, I must ask how you would fund this club. I cannot sell the building to you, even at a discount, because of the entail. Even without rent, clubs are expensive organizations to run when they have their own premises."

"I don't think we had really got that far in considering the subject, though several of our prospective members are very well off."

"But many are not? It seems a pity to exclude many lively minds because they are not wealthy. This is what I can do. I'll talk to Lady Camshire about your inquiry, and then I'll talk to my agent, who is also my lawyer. I'll be in town for the next few days. Let's have luncheon at my club, White's, the day after tomorrow, at one o'clock, by which time I should have some answers so you can plan and see if your idea using the old Green's Club building is feasible."

"That's very good of you, my lord. Thank you for your time and consideration."

"I hope you do not have to rush off, Professor. There are one or two points about your lecture that I would like to discuss with you."

Giles and Professor Standish spent a pleasant hour talking about astronomy. Giles learned a great deal, and he asked several questions to which the Professor did not know the answers and which gave him subjects for further thought, calculations, and examination of the night sky. Daphne was still busy with the seemingly endless stream of visitors who wanted to discuss the ball, so Giles asked Steves to ask Mrs. Darling and Mrs. Wilson to join them in the reading room.

The meeting was going to be tricky, Giles knew. In principle, he could simply command them what to do, but they knew far more about running a house than he ever would. The same was true of Daphne. The trick would be to get and take their advice while making them think that they had only confirmed his intentions. Dealing with the petty officers on the ships on which he had sailed required the same skill, but he suspected that the master and petty officers on *Glaucus* had long ago realized what he was doing and were happy to go along with the pretense.

"I have asked you to come here," he began when the butler, housekeeper, and cook had gathered, "first to thank you for coming to London with no notice, together with the people who work under you, to save the first ball that Lady Daphne and I have put on in London. The ball was a tremendous success, and the newspapers all agree. Several said that it was the best ball of the Season up to now and would likely be the one most warmly remembered when it was over. One account went so far as to express the opinion that it was the best ball ever.

"Now, you all know that this would not have happened had it not been for the very hard work that you and all the other servants from Dipton Manor put in, and with some inconvenience both to you three and the others.

"There are two other matters I would like to discuss with you. First, Lady Camshire and I think all the servants who came to London should get three days off to explore London. The servants already working at this house can manage in the interim. Everyone will get extra pay of one guinea to enjoy London or to add to their savings for any use they want. We will not do any major entertainment in the period, so there will be plenty of London servants to do whatever is needed here in the interim."

"Oh, my lord, that is far too much."

"I don't think so. We have completely disrupted all your lives. It's only fair that we reward all of you. Incidentally, each of you will find an extra two guineas in your pay package next time."

"That is very generous of you, my lord," said Steves, and the others murmured their concurrence.

"You certainly deserve it. You can put it with your retirement funds if you don't spend it on something special immediately.

"Now, there is something else I want to talk with you about. As you know, the senior staff here at Camshire House have proved unsatisfactory. The butler we hired was useless, and the senior footman we asked to fill in was hardly any better. The housekeeper could not hire a suitable number of servants to keep the house properly maintained and was seriously lacking in getting people or directing them to prepare for the ball. The cook has been sick. However, before that, her menus were not excellent.

"That leaves us with a problem concerning servants for Camshire House. As you know, we did not do a good job finding servants for Camshire House when we reopened it."

"Yes, my lord, we noticed, but what do you want us to do?" asked Steves.

"I just want your advice on what we should do. You will undoubtedly have noticed some of the shortcomings here, and you are far more able than Lady Camshire and myself to suggest what remedies we should follow."

The servants were very hesitant about giving Giles advice. The people being served were supposed to know everything about what servants could and should do and would not solicit or appreciate the opinions of those who carried out the work. Asking for their advice, or even their opinions, was extremely inappropriate. Doing so went against all the rules of the proper rankings in Society. Indeed, Society held to a rigid status even more than did the Navy. Giles remembered vividly the surprised awkwardness he had met on his first command, asking the sailmaker for advice on the best shape for the sails of his ship. Luckily, the three senior servants of Dipton Hall quickly lost their shyness about offering advice on request and turned out to have very useful suggestions. It appeared that they recognized that not only did they know far more than either Daphne or Giles about how to make a comfortable house, but also that their employers recognized their greater knowledge and had no trouble acknowledging it.

By the time Giles released the senior staff because Mrs. Wilson needed to check on how the preparations for dinner were getting on, he had received very useful, well-thought-out advice, which he was determined to follow after talking to Daphne.

The meeting broke up when Edgar came to inform Steves that the last of Lady Camshire's visitors had finally left. Giles and Daphne went to change for dinner, even though they were the only people dining at Camshire House that evening.

"What a day!" Daphne exclaimed when they were alone. "The number of women who came and wanted to discuss the ball, over and over again, and exchange barbs with each other, was amazing. Even Lady Strangway showed up complete with her embittered tongue. And she remained even after Edgar and Steves had to be summoned to throw Lord Strangway out."

"What?" Giles responded. "Lord Strangway intruded on you when you were having your visits from ladies of Society? He stormed into my room, making wild accusations about how I obtained the material for the ball gowns. I thought he was going to challenge me to a duel after implicitly confessing to trying to commit all sorts of crimes. Luckily, it didn't come to that! I had no idea that he bothered you then. He must have crashed into your morning room when he was leaving me, having got no satisfaction at all from me. That behavior is intolerable. The man is a boor, not fit for good society."

"What else did you do, Giles, while I was suffering fools gladly — or not so gladly?" Daphne changed the subject.

"I had one interesting visitor." Giles went on to tell Daphne about Professor Standish and the possibility of founding a club catering more for the intelligentsia than for the gentlemen-about-town.

"This club would take women members?

"Yes, as full members. We would also provide separate facilities for them to stay in London when they visit."

"What a marvelous idea. Oh, Giles, you must support it! I would certainly join such an endeavor."

"The Green's Club building is really a white elephant for us. We can't sell it or give it away because of the entail. I would be inclined to let Professor Standish use it as a club, only paying us rent as the club prospers and expands. It is ideal as a place for ladies to stay because it has that separate building that can be used as the ladies' quarters."

"Oh, that brothel you told me about. We'll just have to keep quiet about why it exists. Certainly, Giles, let's go look at it tomorrow."

"All right. And then we can visit our lawyer to see what the entail says about such a use."

"You have had a less busy but more productive day than me, though I am not sure that finding out about Lord Strangway can be called productive. — No, I can't. There is bound to be a second day of visitors. Ones who are thoughtful enough to remember that there will be too many visitors today, so they will come tomorrow. But I cannot be absent until the day after tomorrow. You can have another day sitting by yourself, ignoring all the visitors."

"No, I can't, but I did more than that today."

"Oh/"

"Yes," Giles declared firmly. "I put some effort into solving the servant situation."

"How did you do that?"

"First, I met with Steves to tell him about the rewards we planned for the servants who came from Dipton to help out. Then I sounded out the three senior servants concerning what to do about the servant situation here. They had some very useful suggestions. They knew more about the servant inadequacies here than we did, and, more importantly, they knew how to start to fix them."

"Oh, what were their suggestions?"

"The resolution for difficulties revolved around getting excellent senior servants to manage the critical parts of the operation and involve them in choosing who should work under them. They all said they would be willing to help evaluate the job applications, but it might be a bit difficult with them at Dipton and the jobs here in London.

"Then Steves broached the idea that the best solution might be to use the senior servants at Dipton Hall. I should have known that Edgar and Maisie were ready to assume larger duties, but I didn't. Anyway, both think that they would, and should, start looking for other jobs because they have gone as far as they can with us since Steves and Mrs. Darling are not about to retire. It would solve our problem if they were appointed as butler and housekeeper at Camshire House and allowed to choose their own staff. It struck me as a splendid idea because they both know our habits, and we like them."

"I agree. That would be an excellent development. I suppose we should call them by their last names when they are appointed."

"Yes, my Lord. Edgar's last name is Rowling, and Maisie's is Smith,"

"Rowling and Mrs. Smith. Excellent. That solves two of our problems. What about the cook?"

"Well, there, the situation is rather different. The cook here —what is her name?"

"Mrs. Jenkins," replied Daphne in a tone that indicated that Giles really should know the names of their servants.

"Yes, Mrs. Jenkins, who has been ill, would be an adequate cook, but they felt that she was about to give in her notice."

"Why?"

"The illness reminded her that she is no longer young and that if she is to get married, the time is now. She is intending to give us her notice so that she can marry a saddler in Soho. They have apparently been walking out together for some time."

"So, we'll have to change our cook, I suppose."

"Yes. Mrs. Wilson, as you know, is a Londoner. She wants to move back here and claims that her assistant at Dipton, Martha, is ready to take charge of her own kitchen, or rather the kitchen at Dipton Hall."

"That's a very good idea. I know some of the best dishes served at Dipton Hall were produced by Martha, though Mrs. Wilson kept an eye on her to make sure that the result was perfect. It sounds as if you have solved all our servant problems, at least for now. Let's go to dinner and tell the servants what we have decided."

After dinner and telling the servants of their decisions, Daphne and Giles retired to bed for an early night.

"Giles," murmured Daphne, half asleep, "I'm glad the servants seem happy. Without what you did, the ball would have been a disaster, and it would still have been if our Dipton servants had not risen to the occasion. And getting the dresses and the music was icing on the cake, turning it into the best ball ever. I'm just sorry that Lord Strangway was such a nuisance."

"He was more than a menace. He actually threatened me and was extremely rude to you. I have to see Titus Emery tomorrow at the club — something about the upcoming Russian trip — and I'll talk to him about how to get back at Strangway. He is a disgrace to the House of Lords, and I wouldn't be surprised if there is some way his wings can be clipped because of the way he has been behaving, trying to avoid customs and illegally importing goods."

"I hope that works out for us. I'd love to see Lady Strangway's feathers clipped for once!" Daphne said sleepily. "But it's not like you to seek revenge."

"Isn't it? I don't think anyone has ever threatened you before and got away with it."

"Well, don't do anything foolish. I don't want you to run any risk over this silly matter," Daphne declared before falling into a well-earned, deep sleep.

Chapter XII

"Giles, there you are!" Sir Titus Emery was waiting in the lobby of Giles's club.

"Sir Titus, I hope I haven't kept you waiting." Giles knew he was only a few minutes late for his luncheon meeting with Sir Titus, but convention required the mock apology.

"Not at all. I suggest we proceed to lunch immediately, for I have some things that are best discussed where we can see that we are not being overheard."

When the two men had ordered and were taking their first sips of wine, Sir Titus opened the conversation: "That must have been quite a ball that Lady Camshire held."

"So you heard about it?"

"Of course, one could hardly fail to see how the newspapers treated it. I also heard about how you obtained the fancy material for the gowns. You have to realize that we do keep track of illegal activities and contact with the enemy, even by lords."

"I suppose you do."

"That isn't what I wanted to discuss with you."

"Oh?"

"Yes. I have been asked to sound you out about changes to your trip to Russia. Circumstances have changed a bit since it was arranged."

"Have they? Do your masters want me to abandon the voyage?"

"Oh, no, nothing like that. What the ministers have in mind is for you to go earlier and spend some time in the Baltic Sea before proceeding to St. Petersburg. That's why I wanted to meet with you today, Giles, at such short notice. Let me explain their thinking:

"As you know, the war has not been going well for our allies. Some developments in Eastern Europe may affect your mission to St. Petersburg."

"Oh? Is it called off?"

"No, but it may be enlarged. And we may want you to leave earlier on the voyage. You will recall that Napoleon pretty well cooked Prussia's goose at the battles of Jena and Auerstedt last fall."

"Yes."

"Well, Napoleon has continued his winning ways against our allies further east. Our dispatches are, of course, out of date by the time they reach us, but we know that the emperor is not content with the gains he has made so far. He is still advancing his control despite it being winter. The most recent reports say that Napoleon has Danzig under siege and will likely take it soon. That development and the likely French occupation of much of the Baltic coast present our shipping with a problem."

"Oh?"

"Privateers and piracy. Piracy has not been a serious problem in the Baltic recently. Still, with Napoleon's wanting to prevent us from trading with European countries, it may become more of a problem. He may have no inclination to stop piracy that is focused on our trade. More serious is the prospect of privateering. Privateers commissioned by Napoleon or his new 'allies' could raid British shipping without the interference of the Swedes and Russians, who have had some success suppressing piracy in those waters. Those countries would likely not interfere with privateers with papers from Napoleon or his lackeys operating against us. Our government is not yet ready to dispatch a squadron to protect our ships in the Baltic. However, they believe it would be a good idea if you spent some time along the south Baltic Coast — Pomerania, I believe it is called – on your way to Russia, and also visit Stockholm to demonstrate our friendliness to the Swedes. You can indicate that we can dispatch a squadron to harass the privateers and protect their and our shipping if there are serious privateering problems."

"Yes, I can see the virtue in what you have in mind. Are you considering sending some other ships with me to suppress the privateers?"

"No. Not yet. The Admiralty wants you to evaluate the situation before the government takes further action. They seem to have a complimentary view of how you get yourself out of jams without assistance!"

"I think that is a mistake. I have heard that those waters are shallow in many places, and only shallow draft vessels could catch privateers and pirates. Of course, from my experience there, most merchant ships keep closer to Sweden than to the southern part of the Baltic.

"I cannot go earlier than three weeks from now. I have commitments in Dipton that I am not prepared to sacrifice. After that, things became clear for me to go. Nothing is coming before the Lords that is contentions, I believe, or where my vote or comments would be valuable. A detour to Stockholm would be quite possible, and I would enjoy seeing that city and getting to meet some Swedish sailors."

"I think you are correct about the situation in the House of Lords, though I wish more members of the Lords were as conscientious in performing their duties without special favors as you are. Strangway, for example. You certainly put a crimp in his activities. Congratulations, Giles."

"You know about that, do you, Emery?"

"Oh, yes. We keep an eye on members of the House of Lords who abuse their positions illegally or in ways that could make them subject to blackmail. Strangway has had our attention for some time, though we had no idea how elaborate his smuggling attempt had been. Incidentally, congratulations on getting your hands on his illegal material."

"You probably haven't heard what happened as a result of that."

Giles went on to describe Lord Strangway's invasion of Camshire House the previous day.

"I can hardly believe you," said Sir Titus. "I knew that Strangway is a nasty piece of work and had financial troubles, but his attack on you sounds like more than anger about your diverting his cargo to your uses.

"I have heard that he has financial troubles," Sir Titus continued, "but they must be even more serious than I was aware of. Strangway went through a lot of his wealth one way and another, and his expenses are high. Lady Strangway likes to keep up with a racier crowd than they can really afford. That's how he came to our attention, for he might conspire to change our laws because he might be bought by some of the shadiest of special interests to do just that. I know that he will likely soon be in deep water financially unless he can find a way to stave off his creditors. Some may be willing to keep him afloat in exchange for the favors that Barons can dispense on things like divorce bills and canal licenses. Some lords still make a pretty penny over enclosures, as well.

"I know that some of my fellow lords leave much to be desired in the ethical domain, just as my father did," Giles replied, "but I don't see how Strangway's failures are relevant to clipping his wings and being revenged for his shocking rudeness to Daphne."

"One of the reasons why Strangway was so keen to make money from those ballgowns was that he is in a very precarious financial situation due to some extremely unwise contracts he made which, if nothing changes, will put him very deeply in debt quite soon. You may want to consider making sure that he can't wriggle off that hook. That would get him out of your hair, once and for good."

"How do I do that?" asked Giles.

"It goes back to the passage of the Anti-Slave-Trading Act. Part of the claim of those who were against it was that, without slaves, the price of sugar would reach great heights right away. This was nonsense, of course, but quite a few people who should have known better believed it. The crunch is coming up soon.

"Many contracts were made to accept delivery of sugar at a very high price in a few weeks based on the mistaken notion that stopping the slave trade would mean that there would be no workers to harvest the sugar crop," Sir Titus continued. "Of course, nothing of the sort happened in Jamaica or the other sugar islands. One person who invested very heavily was Strangway. While many of the over-enthusiastic speculators had the good sense to mitigate some of the effects of their contracts, Strangway did not. Instead of using what money he could raise to buy back his commitments when they could be had at a discount, he gambled that he could make enough money elsewhere to pay off the debt when it came due and sell the sugar for whatever it would bring. His grand scheme was to use what money he had to corner the market on ball gowns, or rather on the cloth to make them, and on new plans for dressmakers to follow. That is what brought him to our attention when we heard that an Englishman was paying exorbitant prices to buy up the supplies in France, as well as in England.

"That contract for the delivery of sugar is about to come due. You can buy Strangway's commitment from the current holder for very little since he is not interested in trying to get the money from Strangway through the debtors' prison and the law. For someone who is not of the nobility, that is a pretty hopeless task. Then, all you would have to do is buy the sugar and deliver it to Strangway with the contract. Bring a bailiff as well. When Strangway cannot pay to settle the contract, have the bailiff throw him in debtors' prison. You can let him rot there as long as you want or buy up the many debts he secured by putting up his London mansion as backing for unpaid bills and require him to sign it over to you in forgiveness of all his debts, which are then owed to you.

"Strangway would have to move to his estate in Northumberland, which he can't sell because it is entailed, and we have enough evidence against him to prevent him from improperly using his position in the Lords to make money. Indeed, while we certainly do not want a trial in the House of Lords, we would hold the threat of one over his head to make him stop abusing his position. He is sufficiently unpopular with his cronies in the Lords and, especially, with their wives following the ballgown fiasco that the House of Lords would probably sentence him to have his head chopped off, even though we have ceased doing that long ago."

"This has been very informative, Emery. I'll mull over what you have told me and talk to my agent about arranging it. Thank you."

"You're welcome. Incidentally, this is completely confidential, but the Cabinet has agreed that Blenkinsop should be hanged from his yardarm*, though I am not sure that any of them know what a yardarm is."

"First hanging of a senior naval officer in a long time, isn't it?"

"Yes. Very unusual. The hanging will be before all the fleet at Spithead since *Cicero* is anchored there."

"Well, if you ask me, Blenkinsop deserves it."

Giles's next stop was at the office of his agent-solicitor, Mr. Snodgravel. Following the usual greeting, the lawyer began by remarking, "I see from the papers that Lady Camshire's ball was a great success. And rumor has it that she completely bested Lady Strangway in the area of ballgowns."

"That she did, and Lord Strangway was most annoyed by what had happened. That's partly why I have come to see you today, Mr. Snodgravel."

Giles told the tale of Baron Strangway's behavior the previous day and how it followed the conspiracy between his wife and him to ruin Daphne's ball.

"That sounds awful, my lord," Mr. Snodgravel responded. "How can I be of assistance?"

Giles described what he had learned from Sir Titus about Lord Strangway's finances.

"I'd heard that Strangway was in trouble, but I had no idea it was so serious," said Mr. Snodgravel. "I can buy up that paper for very little if you want. No one thinks it is worth anything since Strangway is already deep in debt."

"Yes. A lengthy stay in debtors' prison would do him a lot of good, and it would make me feel better about the way he insulted Lady Camshire," Giles agreed. "Please arrange the purchase of these obligations as well as the purchase and delivery of the sugar on the appropriate day."

"Very good, my lord. I'll also make sure to have the bailiffs available to cart Lord Strangway off to gaol. Unfortunately, we can't arrange for Lady Strangway to accompany him, even though she undoubtedly plays a large part in his reckless and obnoxious behavior."

"Oh, she'll suffer when their credit is cut off, and she can't participate in the spending competitions among ladies of high society," Giles replied. "While you are at it, Mr. Snodgravel, you might see what liens exist against Strangway's house in Marylebone.

"Now, there is one other thing."

"Yes."

"The Green's Club property. Do you know what activities are permitted under my father's entail?" Giles asked.

"I'd have to check the exact wording, but essentially, it restricts use to a reputable gentleman's club."

"Are you sure that it limits it to housing a club for Gentlemen only?"

"What do you have in mind."

"A club that would accept lady members, but only in the most proper ways."

Giles went on to recount his discussion with Professor Standish.

"Do you think these people would have the resources to start a club of that sort?" Mr. Snodgravel asked skeptically.

"Probably not. Once it's running properly, the membership should be able to make it into a financially going concern. And yes, to your next question, Lady Camshire and I support the type of club they envision enough to finance it until it can survive on its own."

"It is a praiseworthy endeavor, my lord. I wish we had something like it for solicitors and other professionals. The barristers, of course, have their inns of court, but that is very different from the sort of thing you have in mind. The Masons also offer a very different sort of society, but that has never appealed to me."

"Nor to me. Well, Mr. Snodgravel, if you think there is support for such a facility, talk to Lady Camshire. She has much better judgment than I do about business matters.

"What condition is the old Green's Club building in, do you know?" Giles asked.

"Not really, my lord. You have been paying someone to keep the exterior and the grounds tidy and to report anything that needs to be done, but I don't think anyone has been inside since we cleaned the place up and removed any perishables after you closed the Club down."

"Well, Lady Camshire wants to see it before we go further with the possibility of using it. Meet us there at ten o'clock tomorrow morning."

The following morning, Giles and Daphne met with Mr. Snodgravel and Professor Standish in front of the old Green's Club. The street facade looked as good as ever, maybe better because Giles had approved of Mr. Snodgravel having necessary repairs and improvements done when he took possession of the building. The mews were equally well cared for. Indeed, for the first time ever, Green's Club building was reputed to be an excellent neighbor for all the others on the street. The inside of the building turned out to be not in such good shape. Dust was everywhere, and the furnishings were worn and quite out of date. However, both Daphne and Mr. Snodgravel agreed that it would not be very expensive to bring it up to date as a club with the latest fashions, and Daphne thought that that might be necessary to attract female members.

The group proceeded to examine the part of the former club that had been known as the 'Special Members' Smoking Room.' Rather ornate double doors closed off this area, but they were not locked. The doors opened onto a small vestibule, after which the four investigators entered a large room set up with chairs and tables and paintings on the wall, as one might expect in the smoking room of a gentlemen's club. What might not be expected was the subjects of the paintings. They all featured ladies in various degrees of undress and many in lascivious poses, quite unlike the innocent portrayals of nude and semi-nude figures from classical mythology that adorned public galleries. Mr. Snodgravel did not know where to look. He was highly curious about the portrayals but did not want his companions to know of his fascination. Professor Standish had an equally difficult time. There were no such paintings anywhere in his Oxford College, though off-color jokes were common. He was torn between a desire to examine the paintings more carefully and his belief that he should appear to be indifferent to such non-intellectual matters. Giles had seen such pictures before and was not interested in examining this art again.

Only Daphne showed a keen interest in the pictures. She had never been to Green's Club, not even when Giles had terminated its activities, but she was aware that such pictures existed and of the effect such poses had on men. Daphne had indeed presented herself in such poses for Giles's pleasure, not in pictures but solely in the privacy of their bedroom. She had been highly pleased by his reaction to her presentations. On this occasion, however, her interest was focused on one of the individuals portrayed in positions they would be ashamed to admit they had ever adopted, let alone using it for a portrait. Several of these paintings portrayed well-known ladies of Society, some of whom in polite society acted horrified at even the most indirect reference to the pleasures of the bedroom. Other pictures were of notorious flirts, so their existence was less of a surprise. For Daphne, the most interesting portrait was one of Lady Strangway, who was portrayed lounging provocatively on a chaise longue completely uncovered except for a whispy piece of cloth that concealed nothing. Could she, Daphne wondered, persuade Giles that this painting be given to an art dealer for display and offered for sale at a high price? That would put the hussy in her place!

When the shock of the paintings wore off, the group discussed how the large area could be used by a club whose members would have very different interests from those of the previous club's members. Then the trio went upstairs to the part of the building that had been a very exclusive house of ill-repute operated by a celebrated bawd, who went by the name of Mrs. Marsden, a whoremonger whom Daphne had bested her in an earlier encounter in which Daphne had learned far more about brothels than she had ever wanted to know. This area of the club turned out to be very extensive, occupying two floors of the building, mostly with good-sized, well-lit rooms that could easily be used as bedrooms where the ladies of the prospective club could be comfortable. There were even some small rooms that could be used for the ladies' maids. All the rooms had been stripped of furniture, and the special equipment that Daphne had learned was part of the furnishings of Mrs. Marsden's brothels.

"Well, Daphne, Professor Standish, what do you think?" Giles asked when they returned to the main foyer of the building.

"I think the building could house a very viable club," Daphne replied, "without, of course, the former special activities that were to be had in the 'Special Members Smoking Club.'"

"And you, Professor Standish, what do you think?" Giles continued. "Would this be suitable for what you have in mind?"

"It would be excellent, my lord," replied the scientist, "though I am not sure that we can afford it."

"Don't worry about that, provided that you can attract enough members to make it viable at membership charges similar to other clubs. Lady Camshire and I will finance the renovation and set the rents once the club becomes operative. We think your ideas for the club are good, and we will be happy to sponsor the venture.

"Mr. Snodgravel, please work up some estimates of the costs of running the club for various numbers of male and female members, supposing that the special wing becomes the ladies' part of the club, not open to the men.

"Now, Lady Camshire and I have to go to Dipton for the Ameschester Hunt and Hunt Ball. We will be back in three weeks. We can meet again then. Mr. Snodgravel, following my previous order, please arrange with our architect to survey the building and suggest the changes needed to bring it up to present standards. We don't want it to appear out-of-date or run down when our club opens."

"Yes, my lord," that agent replied. "Uh ... What should we do with the special paintings?"

"Oh, dear. I suppose we own them now, don't we? What do you think, Daphne?"

"Some are really quite good paintings. The trouble is that I know that several of the subjects are leaders of Society and would be highly embarrassed to have their provocative portraits exhibited for sale or even sold privately. Other models may be by professionals, and they might bring a pretty penny from some of the lecherous men of society. However, we often can't be sure which paintings are in which category. I suppose that we should have them all destroyed."

"I believe that you are right," Giles agreed. "Please see to it, Mr. Snodgravel."

"I would make one exception," Daphne declared. "That hussy, Lady Strangway, tried very deliberately to embarrass me and ruin our ball. I know just the place for it to be shown as being for sale at auction. A very good gallery, and once the news gets around about that indecent portrait of her, the ladies who think of themselves as being of the very best society will flock to see the picture and persuade their husbands to attend it so that they will know who bought Lady Strangway. One of their husbands might even buy her picture and allow his wife to hang it where her friends could gloat over it. That should pay the hussy back!"

Three weeks later, Giles and Daphne returned to London. They had had a very satisfactory time at Dipton, where they hosted the Ameschester Hunt's last meeting of the season and Hunt Ball. They also attended several other events connected with these festivities.

Things were even more hectic in London than at Dipton. Giles had to get fitted for the new robes associated with his more elevated status since those of an earl would never do for a marquess, attend the ceremony making him a marquess, and give a maiden speech in his new role. He also had to visit the Admiralty to confirm what they expected him to do on his forthcoming trip to St. Petersburg and be informed about what was happening in

Russia and other Baltic countries relevant to his mission to St. Petersburg.

The meeting with the Admiralty dragged on for a considerable time because the Admiralty was having second thoughts about the wisdom of hanging Captain Blenkinsop and wanted Giles's participation in the debate. He thought that, while Blenkinsop's behavior had been unconscionable, hanging him from his own yardarm would not be good for discipline, especially as few people observing the execution, whether officers or crew members, would understand the nature of his offenses. Better to hang him in private, but that was not allowed. So Giles recommended, in an argument that carried the day after much discussion, that the Admiralty commute Blenkinsop's sentence to transportation to Australia for the maximum period the law allowed. Blenkinsop would be unlikely to do much harm to the penal colony.

The meeting then proceeded to discuss Giles's forthcoming voyage to Russia. The strategic situation remained the same as when Sir Titus had raised the subject with Giles at their earlier lunch. But the worries must have intensified. *Glaucus* now would be accompanied by two other ships: one another frigate and the other a brig of war. The decision had only just been made, and Giles realized that he could have quashed it if he wanted to. But he thought it might be a good idea if the waters should be considered hostile, and he had no objection to having company on lengthy voyages, which could be tedious if nothing much happened while his ship went from one place to another. He was assured that he would be the senior captain; indeed, with other ships under his command, he could call himself 'Commodore,' which might enhance his status with the Russian officials.

Giles asked if the ships had been chosen and who their captains were. After an uncomfortable pause while the

Admiralty officials consulted each other in whispers, the First Lord, who was chairing the meeting, said, while still consulting a paper that the Second Secretary had passed to him, "The brig of war will be *Stoat*, commanded by Commander Etienne Marceau. I believe you know him, Captain Giles."

"Yes, indeed. He was, until recently, my first lieutenant. And the frigate?"

"Is that decided for sure, Newsome?" the First Lord asked the Second Secretary."

"Yes, my Lord"

"But not the captain?"

"No, my lord. As you know, that is on the agenda of the Cabinet Meeting this evening."

"Yes, I suppose it is. Damn interest! What a way to run a Navy!"

Giles thought that this was all supposed to be whispered, but since the First Lord was deaf, it was carried on at a volume that everyone in the room could hear. Nevertheless, the First Lord turned to Giles and declared. "The frigate will be *Cicero*. She is apparently the only one in harbor right now which can leave immediately. Her captain will be named this evening. I am afraid, Captain Giles, that you will not be consulted on the appointment. It will be made for entirely political reasons. I apologize."

Giles was not happy about this decision, but there was nothing he could do about it. If he objected, he wouldn't put it past some of the Cabinet to suggest that *Cicero* go by herself to St. Petersburg, forgetting that the original purpose was for him to accept an honor from the Tsar of Russia.

All this activity was on top of the events that the couple really wanted to attend, including visits to the theatre, a concert, and some dinner parties. However, they made sure to attend to the latest events in their feud with Lord and Lady Strangway. Daphne's morning callers were full of news of the reaction of much of the ton to the news that Lady Strangway's gentleman's picture was on display at Nipini's Gallery in Bond Street. That was where Daphne had taken the portrait when they left the Green's club building. The gallery was well attended by members of Society and had a special section where classical and not-so-classical paintings featuring nudity, or suggestive activities were displayed. Many of them were the work of well-regarded artists from earlier times, many portraying events of a biblical or classical nature, but others were more contemporary. Lady Strangway's picture will be offered for sale at an auction in a few weeks. Signor Nipini, the proprietor of the gallery, whose real name Daphne had discovered was Joseph Smith, had recommended this way of bringing the most attention to the exhibition since there would be healthy, or maybe unhealthy, speculation as to who would buy it. Of course, Lady Strangway could purchase the canvas at its healthy reserve price, but Lord Strangway had been reluctant to come up with the money. At Daphne's suggestion, Signor Nipini had arranged some special showings that could only be attended by ladies and their maids, events that had turned out to be very popular. Some of Daphne's morning callers speculated on how the artist might have embellished Lady Strangway's charms and wondered which rake might purchase it. Daphne was delighted to learn that Lady Strangway had not been at home to callers since it was discovered what sort of artistic treasure was now on display at Nipini's Gallery.

Mr. Snodgravel had also done his job preparing for the ultimate downfall of Lord and Lady Strangway. He had succeeded in buying up all the contracts for the delivery of the sugar which Lord Strangway had entered into in anticipation of the effects that halting the trade in slaves would have on sugar prices. Usually, when made for purely speculative reasons, such contracts were completed by the exchange of money before delivery had to be made unless one side or the other needed to deal with the physical materials on whose price the contract had been made. Giles was not interested in such a resolution of the contracts since he knew that Lord Strangway did not have the money to complete his side of the deal. Instead, Mr. Snodgravel had arranged for the sugar to be bought and seven carts loaded with it. They were due to appear in front of Lord Strangway's Marylebone mansion a little before two in the afternoon, the time specified for the delivery of the sugar. Before that, the carts were parked just out of sight of the Baron's windows.

As there was no possibility that Lord Strangway would be able to fulfill the contract, Mr. Snodgravel had arranged for a bailiff to be on hand and several thief-takers in case Lord Strangway tried to escape or avoid the contracted confrontation. The agent was very confident that Lord Strangway was headed toward the debtors' prison, where Giles and Daphne would be happy to let him rot for a while before offering him a way out.

A small crowd had gathered in front of Lord Strangway's house when Giles and Daphne appeared following the arrival of the carts containing the sugar. Mr. Snodgravel knocked on the door, which was promptly opened by the butler.

"I am here to see Lord Strangway," the agent declared, presenting his card, which listed his occupation as 'solicitor.'

"I will see if Lord Strangway is at home," was the response.

While the butler went to present the card to his master, the carts drew up in front of the mansion. Some of the thief-takers headed to the mews behind the building, while another one joined Mr. Snodgravel. Lord Strangway soon appeared at the door himself rather than telling his butler to show Mr. Snodgravel to the room where he was sitting.

"Your sugar has arrived, my lord," Mr. Snodgravel announced. "Here is the bill, payable today in any legal tender or other form of payment acceptable to the owner. As you know, the time stipulated for this transaction in the contract is two o'clock, *post meridian*. The church bell was starting to chime two in the afternoon when I knocked on your door."

"What are you blathering on about, sir? I cannot accept this shipment," the Baron huffed.

"Well, the contract states that the sugar must be delivered at this time and that payment will be made when it is. In case you have forgotten, though, I sent you a note two days ago reminding you that payment is due on delivery today. As you will recall, that is what your contract stipulates. I have been told to accept legal tender, other bank notes, or a bank draft provided that it is countersigned by the bank to verify that you have funds adequate to meet the total."

"I don't have access to such a sum right now. Just take your sugar away. I don't wish to purchase it."

"I am afraid that that would not satisfy my principal. Indeed, the Marquess of Dipton explicitly instructed me that if you do not pay as asked, then I should have you committed to the Fleet or some other debtors' prison."

"What? You cannot do that, you sniffling dog's body!"

"I most certainly can," Mr. Snodgravel replied calmly. "Bailiff!"

"Sir?"

"Take this man to the Fleet for failure to pay the debt owed to the Earl of Camshire, now also known as the Marquess of Dipton, and to take possession of this sugar."

Lord Strangway was unceremoniously seized and frog-walked off to the waiting bailiff's wagon to be carted away to the Fleet prison.

"What will happen to him now?" Daphne asked,

"We'll let him cool his heels for a few days," Giles replied. "Then we'll offer to take possession of this house — Strangway's London House — in exchange for forgiving his debt to us and for us paying his other contractual debts in London. He and Lady Strangway will have just enough to live quietly on their estate in Northumberland, far from London.

"Yes," added Mr. Snodgravel, "that estate is entailed to his next of kin, so he will have to make do with a quite modest income, or so I have discovered. I think you will see no more of Lady Strangway, my lady, even if she becomes the concubine of some wealthy rake. With the notoriety that her picture has produced, you will have turned a very healthy profit from Lord and Lady Strangway's trying to ruin your ball, and they certainly had it coming anyway! He has long been a disgrace to the House of Lords!"

That evening, Daphne and Giles attended the Haymarket Theatre, where Mozart's Don Giovanni was performed excellently.

"Giles," Daphne murmured as they snuggled together in bed, "I'm glad that you are no **Don** Giovanni."

"Really, Daphne?" Giles responded. "Don't you think that I could seduce a thousand and one women if I ever went to Spain?"

"I am sure you *could*. I just know you *wouldn't*. Do you think we were a little hard on Lord and Lady Strangway today? I feel a bit guilty about **trap**ping them that way."

"Do you? Would you like to have them go on and attack other people? Maybe wreck some other woman's ball who is less able to defend herself?"

"No, I suppose not."

"Turning the other cheek is fine if it is your cheek, though I don't entirely endorse the idea. But things are different when it is also some other person's cheek. After all, we didn't kill the Strangways. It was more like taking venom from a poisonous snake. I, for one, feel good about it, and so should you."

"I guess you are right, Giles. — As always."

Luckily, Giles had fallen asleep before Daphne whispered her final phrase. She was glad. She thought that it wasn't a very nice thing to say, especially as her husband did not *always* assume he was right.

Chapter XIII

"Mr. Lester," Giles greeted his first lieutenant at three bells of the morning watch. "I trust everything has gone smoothly in my absence."

"Yes, sir. We are ready to sail at a moment's notice for as long a cruise as needed."

"Excellent. As you know, we are going to Russia, though we are leaving a bit earlier than expected so that we can visit other places. We also have two other ships accompanying us."

"Two, sir? I know about *Stoat*. Commander Macreau brought the brig into Spithead a couple of days ago. He told me that he would be accompanying us. He had heard that there would also be another frigate."

"Indeed, there will be. It is your old ship, *Cicero*."

"Good Lord! That's something I never expected: to sail again with my old ship. I had hoped never to see her again. Who is in command."

"That is something I was only informed of just before I left London. He's … no, let me get it right." Giles pulled a piece of paper out of his pocket. "Yes, here it is. He's a Captain Archibald Lochlass, who has just been promoted at the age of twenty-three. My source in the Admiralty tells me that he was a commander for only three months and commanded no ship during that time. Before that, he served as a lieutenant on *Glenmore*, 64. He is part of the Scottish group in the Navy; he is the third son of Lord Machasley, a minor Scottish nobleman, but with close family ties with the most important members of the Scottish nobility. The Scottish group in the Navy spends a lot of effort scratching each other's backs, though some of them, like Lord Cochrane or Admiral Keith, are also outstanding officers. I am afraid that we will have to keep an eye on him and try to teach him how to be a frigate captain. It isn't fair to you, I know, but there is nothing I can do about it.

"Is that *Stoat* over there?"

"Yes, sir. Captain Macreau came over here after *Stoat* anchored. "

"Mr. Jenks," Giles turned to the signal midshipman who was close by, "As soon as there is enough light, signal to *Cicero* and *Stoat*, 'Captains report to *Glaucus* at eight bells.'"

Etienne Marceau arrived from *Stoat* several minutes before the ship's bell announced the specified time so that he could catch up on what had been happening with Giles since they had last seen each other and to give his reactions to his new command.

Eight bells came and went with no visible action on *Cicero*. Another quarter of an hour passed before activity could be observed on the anchored frigate's deck. Then her captain's barge was brought around to the entry port, the crew assembled, and a man in the uniform of a post-captain appeared on deck and descended into the boat.

"Mr. Lester," Giles ordered, "Prepare to welcome Captain Lochlass, even though I am tempted to ignore his barge for as long as he has kept us waiting."

A word to the bosun got the welcoming party together to greet the visiting captain at the entryway. A tall, young man with coppery hair, rather stout and with a permanent sneer on his lips, appeared at *Glaucus*'s entry port, stepped onto the deck, and came to Giles with his hand extended. He was smartly dressed in a fashionably tailored captain's uniform with a single epaulet on his right shoulder, indicating that he had less than three years' seniority in the rank of captain.

"Lord Camshire," this apparition announced, "it is good to meet you at last."

"Captain Lochlass, it is customary on this vessel for officers to salute the quarterdeck when they board her," Giles announced in a very frosty tone. "Furthermore, I do not use my title in the Navy, where I am known as 'Captain Giles.' I also expect subordinates to respond to orders promptly. 'At eight bells' means at eight bells, not at one bell of the following watch."

Captain Marceau and Lieutenant Stewart tried to hide grins at this dressing down. Giles always appeared to be easy-going, and so he was in ordinary times, but ignoring an order in flagrant fashion brought on the tone neither of them wanted to hear directed at them again.

"But I only returned late from celebrating with my friends my appointment to a frigate."

"**SIR,**" Giles roared."

"What?" asked Captain Lochlass.

"You address senior officers as 'sir' or by their rank. Now, is *Cicero* ready to sail?"

"I presume so, *sir*."

"You presume so?"

"Well, I didn't have a chance to ask my first lieutenant yesterday evening. I was in a hurry to meet my friends ashore."

"Then go and find out **now** and report back to me. If you are not ready, explain what needs to be done and how you will get ready as quickly as possible."

Cicero's new first lieutenant had little more experience than his captain. However, the ship's master, who had been on the frigate during Captain Blenkinsop's tenure, was well aware that a naval vessel should always be ready to sail, or, if it wasn't, the shortcoming should be dealt with immediately. When Captain Lochlass returned to her, he found that, indeed, she was ready to sail and signaled the news to *Glaucus*.

He was about to retire to his cabin, seeking some wine and a nap to soothe the headache that had intensified because of that arrogant, self-important Captain Giles had given him such an unfair dressing-down when the order came from *Glaucus* to set sail. The three ships worked their way out of the anchorage and proceeded east in line abreast, with *Glaucus* in the middle, well spread out so that they were likely to see as many other ships using that part of the English Channel as possible.

It was a sunny day with a light southwest wind blowing, quite warm for this time of year. The trio of ships proceeded eastward, but they saw nothing of interest, only a few fishing boats and many English cargo ships plying the northern waters of the English Channel. Nightfall came, and still, they continued eastward.

Dawn found them about halfway to Dover. The wind held for the rest of the day, and they made steady progress to the east. But, at nightfall, the wind backed into the east and became stronger so that the three ships had reduced their sails by full dark and were close hauled* on the starboard tack*, with furled topgallants and their other sails twice reefed. Giles had instructed all the ships to show lanterns so they could keep together, but it was not easy to keep the wicks burning in the choppy seas.

Not long after dark, the other two frigates lost sight of *Cicero*'s light. The conditions were such that it was not surprising. In any case, there was not much that the commanders of the other two ships could do about verifying where *Cicero* was in the dark.

The storm had blown itself out by sunrise, and the wind had settled into a cold southwesterly. There was no sign of *Cicero*. Captain Macreau came over to *Glaucus* with his ship's master to confer with Giles and Mr. Brooks. They were sure that *Cicero* could not have passed them in the night because, if anything, she was the slower ship, especially as *Cicero* could not have been sailing closer to the wind than they were. *Cicero* must have veered and continued on the course to the north-northwest that a master's mate thought he had seen *Cicero*'s light before she disappeared into the night. He had not mentioned seeing the frigate on another course because he had only seen it briefly and thought at the time that he must be mistaken.

"I'm afraid that we have no choice," Giles declared. "We will have to go back to see if there is any sign of her. Mr. Brooks, set the course to the west, going as close to the Godwin Sands as we dare. If she has passed us in the night, we will meet her at our meeting place at the entry to the Skagerrak*.

The two ships spread apart until only their topsails could be seen by each other. The wind allowed an easy course that would just let *Glaucus*, which was to the north of *Stoat,* skirt the southern end of the Godwin Sands. The morning dragged on until *Glaucus*'s masthead lookout finally called that he could just see a masthead directly ahead. As they got closer, it was evident that *Cicero* was hard aground. The tide was still ebbing, but Mr. Brooks thought it had only a little farther to go, and it would still leave a foot or so of water under *Cicero* at low tide. The central question was whether the frigate had been holed or else could resume her voyage when the water rose again as if nothing had happened.

Giles summoned *Stoat* to join him and ordered *Glaucus* to anchor as close to the stranded frigate as was safe. He set out with Mr. Brooks to see what needed to be done to save the grounded ship. On boarding *Cicero*, his first surprise was to receive no welcome appropriate to the arrival of the commodore in charge of the little fleet. Instead, he was met by two young midshipmen, who seemed to be no more than fifteen years old, and all the ship's petty officers except for her master.

The basic story of what had happened was quickly told. Captain Lochlass had decided to reef the topsails and had ordered a change of course. One of the blocks controlling the driver*'s sheet had given way. Mistakenly thinking that this meant that the frigate would turn downwind with disastrous effects, Captain Lochlass must have miscalculated the effect of this fiasco and ordered, "Starboard your helm," emphasized by, "Hard over." The result was that *Cicero* spun into the wind and followed through rather than missing stays, as might be expected. Chaos reigned above the deck as the sails were backed, holding *Cicero* on the wrong tack. It took some time before the crew could straighten out the mess they had produced in the ship's rigging. Then, just before they were ready to proceed, *Cicero* ran aground. Apparently, Captain Lochlass had neglected to take soundings and had been unaware that places in the Dogger Bank were too shallow for the safe passage of a frigate.

Cicero thumped several times on the ground before she came to rest as the breaking waves lifted her and set her down violently. As soon as the frigate was stable, Captain Lochlass sounded the well and found more water in the bilge than there should be. A second sounding showed even more water there; it was rising rapidly. A combination of Captain Lochlass, *Cicero*'s first lieutenant, and her master got all the sails furled properly. By then, the ship was resting rigidly on the bottom and would stay that way until the next high tide; indeed, the next time that the tide was at least as high as when she went aground, which would not be until the next night.

When the chaos created by *Cicero*'s running aground had been straightened out, the officers proceeded to explore what damage had been done to the frigate. In this task, they were severely hindered by knowing little about their command and the circumstance that many of the petty officers who did know her and her quirks had not sailed with on this voyage. Most of the senior petty officers on *Cicero* under Captain Blenkinsop had joined the ship long before the incident that had led to Captain Blenkinsop's being made her captain. Most of them resigned their warrants when they reached harbor again following his last voyage, knowing that they would be forever tarred with the failures of that voyage, even though the shortcomings had been entirely the captain's responsibility. Other petty officers who had stayed, including the bosun and the master, had decided that their health did not allow them to join Captain Lochlass's command when they learned who *Cicero*'s new captain would be. As a result, when Captain Lochlass wanted petty officers to inspect the damage caused by the grounding, the most experienced ones he could find were her new master, who had been a master's mate on a sloop of war until recently and a bosun's mate who had joined the ship just a few days before she sailed.

The informants told Giles that the storm waves were still grinding the frigate against the sand most ominously, so the situation might be becoming more dangerous. Captain Lochlass sent the carpenter's and the bosun's mates, the most senior of the remaining petty officers, to examine the hull from the inside. Their report was not good. There were several staves* that were broken. That was where the water was pouring in. The waves were still working the ship against some rocks. If she thumped upon them much more, the situation would be hopeless. Even if the grinding against the rocks ceased because the tide fell farther, the ship would still be done for since the damage would resume when the tide rose again. No, they didn't think they could make a repair, though the bosun's mate thought they had heard that somehow you could get a sail around the bottom of a ship to stop leaks. Nobody on board had any experience doing so.

Such was the story that Giles was able to put together from the excited and not entirely coherent stories of the midshipmen who had been left in command of the stranded frigate. But what, Giles asked mildly, had happened to Captain Lochlass?

Captain Lochlass was afraid, reported the older midshipman, that the ship would break up before help arrived. There were not enough boats to take everyone off. He would go ashore in his barge with the other officers to get help. They would be back soon, long before the rest of the crew would be in danger. All the officers would go because it might require the co-opting of several boats, and they would be needed. They would be back with help before there was any danger from the tide rising again.

On reflection, the midshipman conceded Captain Lochlass's plans didn't make much sense. Still, they seemed reasonable at the time, and, anyway, he wasn't about to challenge his captain in such grim circumstances.

By this point, the high tide had passed, and the water level was dropping. However, the captain's barge and other boats were still afloat. Captain Lochlass and the other officers rapidly descended into the boats and rowed away, leaving most of *Cicero*'s crew on board the stranded frigate. Those remaining did not fail to notice that those whom Captain Lochlass had chosen to accompany him were Scotsmen appointed to *Cicero* through the captain's influence.

There was nothing Giles could do about the departure of *Cicero*'s officers, at least not at the moment. But he wasn't going to just leave the frigate in the hope that Captain Lochlass would return with help. He would first attempt to get her afloat again. He conferred with Mr. Lester and Mr. Brooks. First, they should pump the ship as dry as they could to see what damage had been done to the hull and whether they could patch her from the inside with some oakum*.

The pumps, which had been idle after the tide stopped rising and the water level in the hold had started to drain out, were put to work again. Giles, realizing that the crew members of *Cicero* were already tired, sent back to *Glaucus* for more men to help with the stranded ship. *Cicero* was not high and dry, but after a few shifts at the pumps, Mr. Brooks declared that they had now reached the level where no more water would be coming in. Examination from inside the ship of the place where *Cicero*'s bottom had been breached revealed some stove-in planks, surprising on a sandbank where large stones were few and far between normally. Mr. Brooks suggested that some other vessel must have gone aground in the same spot recently and had unloaded some of her ballast to get off again. Whatever the reason, several strakes* of *Cicero*'s hull had been forced into the ship before they splintered. Repair would be a task for a shipyard with a proper drydock. *Cicero*'s carpenter and her bosun agreed that fixing the problem from within the hull was impossible. It must be treated with some sort of temporary patch from the outside if the frigate was going to be saved.

Giles and Mr. Brooks realized that they couldn't fother* the hole in the damaged part of the hull in the usual fashion, which involved hauling a well-tarred sail under a ship to cover a hole and then relying on the lines holding the sail in place to prevent it from tearing away from the hull to expose the hole again. Instead, since they could not get the lines under the ship, they would have to find another way to cover the hole in the hull while they were still hard aground. They decided that they would have to get their improvised patch over the hole and securely fasten it to the hull before work on it became impossible because water reached the hole while the ship was still firmly aground.

The tide would soon be rising, so they would only have a short period of time to effect the repair before the rising water level made it impossible until the tide had fallen again. If they didn't plug it quickly, all the work they had done to pump *Cicero* dry would be wasted.

A flurry of activity broke out. A mizzen topsail was deemed to be the best-sized piece of canvas to go over the damaged part of the hull. First, though, the sail had to be tarred, with the unraveled and shredded ends of some ropes mixed with the tar to make the patch more waterproof. The tide was rising, and it had almost reached the lowest part of the damage to the hull. The treated sail was almost ready to be put in place. A little more work might make it even better, but there was no time to do that: it was now or wait for the next low tide to complete the work, and anything might happen in the interim. The bottom of the hold had not yet disappeared under the rising water. The patch was fastened securely in place. Now, they would have to wait for news of how well they had stopped the leak. The water kept rising, now infuriatingly slowly, for there was still quite a bit to go before *Cicero* would be afloat. Everyone onboard the frigate wanted to see if the patch would hold and get the stranded frigate underway again. Night was falling, and still, the frigate was hard aground.

Giles had had the anchor rowed astern and dropped so they could pull the frigate away from the shallows before trying to sail her to safety. Finally, Mr. Brooks signaled that they could start trying to pull the ship to safety. The first clanks of the capstan sounded as the crew took up the slack. Then *Cicero* moved, grinding a bit on gravel as she struggled to get loose from the sand into which she had dug a shallow trough. Then she was free. The clanks of the capstan speeded up as the crew worked to make sure that she wouldn't be stranded again.

The news from the depths of the hull was good. The patch was holding, and only a small trickle of water was getting past it. At this rate, there would be no problem getting *Cicero* to a dockyard; a short period of pumping when the watches changed should be enough to keep her from sinking.

Giles now faced a dilemma. Usually, when disaster struck one of several ships sailing together that required the vessel to find a port, the damaged ship would be sailed by her own officers, and the other ships would carry on with their mission. That could not happen here.

The problem was that Captain Lochlass had left no responsible officers on board *Cicero* to sail her now that she was floating again. Conversely, when Giles captured a valuable prize, he would have one of his junior officers sail her to a suitable port to turn her over to the proper authorities. However, he did not want to lose any of his junior officers at the start of his cruise. He was also afraid that they might be side swiped by the attempts of Captain Lochlass and his cronies in the Scottish peerage and the Admiralty to limit the effect on his career of the Scottish captain's actions. As a result, Giles decided to go to Chatham in *Glaucus,* accompanied by *Stoat*.

Mr. Lester had no desire to command *Cicero* on the short trip to Chatham dockyard. He knew that any association with his former ship when it was in trouble again would likely damage his career. Giles did not agree with this difficulty, but he had his own reasons for agreeing with his first lieutenant. He felt that Mr. Stewart richly deserved promotion to commander but was held back by his youth. It could only be countered by additional experience in roles of command. Giles, therefore, was happy to have his second lieutenant take command for the short trip. The more experience Mr. Stewart could demonstrate, the sooner Giles would get him promoted to the rank of commander. If Archibald Lochlass could be elevated to the rank of post-captain with no proven readiness to assume command, then Mr. Stewart certainly deserved to be made a commander.

Giles had heard that there were often quite long waits at the Nore to get a pilot to take ships up the Medway to Chatham. There was no knowing how long the patch on *Cicero* would hold.so Giles allowed his second lieutenant to take *Cicero* directly to the dockyard without waiting for a pilot, a tricky passage that many ships required a tow to accomplish, even with a pilot. Giles did lend Mr. Brooks to *Cicero* for the trip: the master's knowledge was as good as any pilot's, Giles felt. In keeping with calling attention to Mr. Stewert's expected accomplishment, Giles anchored *Glaucus* at the Nore while he took his barge up the river. If carrying out this plan didn't demonstrate his lieutenant's ability to handle a frigate, nothing would!

Giles was amused when he reached the dockyard to find that Mr. Stewart had even succeeded in getting *Cicero* placed in a drydock ahead of the queue of vessels awaiting repair, apparently by shamelessly invoking the name of the Marquess of Dipton as being behind the need to repair the frigate immediately. Giles, himself, was now aware of the influence he had in naval matters but was still hesitant to invoke it for his own benefit. Mr. Stewart was certainly showing his ability to assume command of one of his majesty's ships: one of the unwritten qualifications of a successful captain was how to maneuver in the face of shore-bound recalcitrance in keeping the fleet at sea. If all went as he expected, when he returned from the Baltic, Giles would use his interest to advance the career of his second lieutenant, and there was no reason not to demand that Commander Macreau be raised to post-captain.

The Port Admiral at Chatham had had no warning that *Cicero* would require repair. Whatever else Captain Lochlass might have done when he went ashore, warning Chatham of the plight of his command, was not among them. In fact, the Port Admiral first heard of the trouble when *Cicero* appeared in the river demanding help as soon as possible. He reacted promptly, somewhat to Giles's surprise, whose experience with admirals had not always been favorable. *Cicero* would be repaired immediately. A drydock could be cleared immediately because the work on its occupant could be completed while she was afloat.

Repairing *Cicero* would be a major undertaking, and she would not be ready to sail for some time. Captain Lochlass and the rest of his band of officers had not yet appeared in Chatham. What had happened to them was unknown. Giles could wait for the Admiralty to assign another frigate to his little squadron or proceed immediately to the Baltic.

The mystery of what had happened to Captain Lochlass and the other officers from *Cicero* was solved later that day while Giles and his officers were having dinner at an inn near the dockyard. A ruckus broke out at the hotel's entrance where they were eating. Glancing towards the noise, Giles spotted a somewhat bedraggled Captain Lochlass arguing with the innkeeper. Behind the captain were the other officers from *Cicero*. Captain Lochlass's uniform no longer had the tailored perfection that he had demonstrated when visiting *Glaucus*. It had not survived the boat trip and subsequent land travel in pristine condition; now, it was good for the rag box only. Captain Lochlass had demanded lodgings and dinner from the innkeeper, who had been skeptical of the bedraggled group's ability to pay.

Giles left the table and went to the lobby of the hotel. "Captain Lochlass, what seems to be the problem?"

"Captain Giles. I didn't expect you to be here. Shouldn't you be on your way to Russia?"

"I should, but I had to deal with *Cicero*."

"*Cicero*? So, you know how she was lost through the incompetence of the petty officers left over from the time of Captain Blenkinsop?"

"No. She wasn't lost, though she seems to have been abandoned by her captain."

"What? Not lost?"

"No. *Cicero* is now in drydock here, waiting to be repaired. Of course, you will have to stand court-martial for abandoning her irresponsibly."

"What? Don't be nonsensical!"

The outside door of the hotel lobby opened at that moment to admit the Port Admiral, followed by his flag lieutenant and some sailors.

"Ah, Captain Giles. Is this the Captain Lochlass you told me about?"

"It is, sir," Giles replied, wondering how the Port Admiral had been informed so quickly of the appearance of *Cicero*'s captain.

"Captain Lochlass," declared the Port Admiral, "I hereby place you under arrest on the charge of abandoning the vessel under your command without good reason and without ensuring the safety of her crew. Mr. Lanks," the Admiral addressed his Flag Lieutenant. "See that they are confined to the brig until I can convene a court martial. You had better take the rest of this rabble to the gaol with you to keep them there until we can sort out their role in the disgraceful abandonment of their vessel.

"Captain Giles, you didn't actually witness the abandonment of *Cicero* on the Godwin Sands, did you?" asked the Port Admiral.

"No, sir."

"Then, you didn't observe Captain Lochlass abandon his personally, did you?"

"No, sir," Giles replied, wondering where this was going. Surely, Captain Lochlass's grip on the interest system didn't extend to his evading his responsibility for *Cicero*'s fiasco.

"Then, Captain Giles, I think that your providing me with a full, written, witnessed description of what happened will suffice for the court martial I have to convene about this incident. After providing it, you can then proceed to the Baltic according to your orders. Of course, if you wish to stay, I am sure that the court will appreciate your presence."

Giles was relieved. He had no desire to wait in Chatham until the Admiral had assembled a court-martial. He would much rather continue his voyage to the Baltic as soon as possible. He was also pleased not to be accompanied by Captain Lochlass. That officer promised to be as much of a burden as the diplomat he had taken to Russia on his previous trip to St. Petersburg.

Chapter XIV

"Mr. Lester," Giles ordered, "Signal Captain Macreau to come here."

"You know, Captain Giles," remarked Mr. Lester after transmitting the order, "I've learned more about the rest of the world in this cruse than I ever knew before. I was never anywhere except the English Channel and off Brest in all my previous time in the Navy."

"Well, it is good to be in new waters," Giles replied, "but we all learned something when *Cicero* went aground. That was certainly in home waters. Though, I am afraid that some of that lesson was more about what not to do when you command a ship of your own.

"I am sure you also learned something when we went by Copenhagen. Hopefully, we can learn some more as our journey continues. Even Mr. Brooks told me he is looking forward to finding out more about this coast, even though it is supposed to be uninteresting.

"Now, let's welcome Captain Macreau on board. He's not a post-captain, of course, but he is a good friend of much of our crew who want to give him a bit of a formal welcome."

Mr. Lester was happy to lay on an appropriate welcome with the aid of the bosun. The first lieutenant had observed and wondered at Etienne's qualities when his previous ship, *Cicero*, had been recaptured. He also recognized that the crew members of *Glaucus* were fond of him, remarkably since first lieutenants were often not liked by the crews of their ships. Deviating from the standard way of welcoming a ship's captain who only had the rank of commander was a good idea, in Mr. Lester's opinion. Another lesson learned, *Glaucus*'s first lieutenant thought, as he issued the appropriate orders.

"We now may be in enemy waters, from what we were told," Giles said as soon as Captain Macreau joined the three officers from *Glaucus*. "Though they may not be. No one in London knew for sure exactly who our enemies are or much else about our situation. I am not clear which country has administrative control of the area; it might be France or one of its satellites like Prussia, or some country that may or may not still be on our side, like Sweden or Russia. Sweden is one of our allies and, I am told, is willing to act as our agent or prize manager if we capture ships sailing under a hostile flag or from a country subservient to Napoleon. What I do know is that we are coming up to Danzig, an important port at the mouth of a large river whose name escapes me.

"River Vistula, Captain," Mr. Brooks stated sotto voce.

"Thank you, Mr. Brooks," Giles continued. "We can spend up to ten days along this coast to see what we can find or go to Stockholm to get news. I certainly would like to know where things stand before going to Russia.

"The land here is pretty bleak, and the Navy doesn't seem to know much about it. There are some big bays, flat islands, and mud banks. According to Mr. Brooks, there are no reliable charts, and he couldn't find out much about the currents except he says that there are no tidal currents. All the Navy and the private masters he talked to knew little of this coast. Apparently, their knowledge of the islands near Sweden is much greater. While we are off this coast, we will have to be sounding all the time and recording the results so that we can get an idea of what is below. That applies to *Stoat* even more than *Glaucus*, Captain Macreau.

You draw less water than we do and look less dangerous, so you will cruise nearer the coast than us. The people who ply these waters regularly may have a better idea of what and where the dangers are, so be cautious if you close on one of their ships. You will proceed only under jibs, mainsail, and driver. Signal us immediately when you spot anything so we can help to catch whatever suspicious ship you encounter.

"Some distance ahead of us is Danzig, a port that may attract privateers or pirates. We will presume that the French have captured it unless we find out otherwise. Our first task is to find out what the situation is. If we find a fishing boat – there have been surprisingly few so far – we may learn the state of affairs here but presume that any vessels leaving or entering the port are trading with the enemy. Captain Macreau, take *Stoat* along the coast. *Glaucus* will follow you about two miles off your larboard quarter. That way, vessels leaving Danzig are less likely to turn around when they spot you, and we will have a better chance of catching them, while *Glaucus* will be better positioned to capture any ships approaching the port from the north."

The two warships separated to go hunting for vulnerable merchant ships. The wind was moderate from the northwest, and visibility was good, ideal conditions for their endeavor provided there were any ships at sea going to or coming from Danzig. Time wore on as they sailed slowly eastward.

Glaucus was the first to spot a ship. She was northeast of the frigate and headed in a southerly direction when sighted by the masthead lookout. Giles decided to go aloft himself, but halfway up, he realized that he should do this more often as he was already somewhat out of breath. He also cheated by going through the lubber's hole* rather than taking the topman's route up the mast. He settled at the masthead, embarrassed to have the lookout see him so out of breath. Of course, the seaman, a sharp-eyed man from Somerset with a ready grin, paid no attention to the state of his captain, though he waited a minute or so before pointing out the ship that had induced Giles's climb.

It was indeed a strange-looking craft. She was still hull down, and all that could be seen were the tops of two gaff-rigged sails whose gaffs were almost parallel with the horizon and came almost to the tops of the masts, so there was no provision for topsails. No sign of jibs, either, though they might not be of much use on the course the strange ship was sailing. The ships were on converging courses, though Giles figured that if both ships held their present courses, the stranger would pass ahead of *Glaucus* by half a mile.

There was no point in Giles staying at the masthead as the two ships converged. He descended to the main deck, where he gave the officer of the watch the change of course needed to intercept the stranger. Then, leaving orders to summon him again when the unknown ship was hull-up* from the masthead, he went to his cabin. As usual in such a situation, he got out his violin and played while, on deck; there was no unusual activity as the day wore on. When word came that the stranger's hull was now in sight, Giles returned to the masthead. It was a very strange craft in terms of the ships he had seen up to this time. On his previous trip to Saint Petersburg, he had heard of such ships, but he had not seen one. He had been informed that they were mainly to be found in the Gulf of Finland. Besides the two large, gaffed-rigged sails, the strange ship's main features were piercings for five oars on the side he could see and gunports for two guns, maybe ten-pounders.

Giles returned to the deck to tell the officer of the watch what he had seen. Then he continued, "Mr. Lester,

Mr. Brooks, we want to intercept that strange ship. Set the course to do so and adjust it as needed."

Then Giles retreated to his cabin to take up the violin again and work on some tricky, extended passages for the violin of the sonata he was practicing. Daphne had been working on the same piece, and she was much smoother while traversing it than her husband. Giles did not want it to be a stumbling block the next time they tried the duet; he knew that Daphne was keen to perform it before guests at the next musical soirée they held. Giles had the passage under fine control and was about to get onto the next tricky bit of the sonata when Mr. Lester sent a midshipman to tell him that they were about to meet the strange ship.

"What do you make of her, Mr. Brooks?"

"She is a fully loaded merchant ship, I would guess, Captain Giles," the Master replied succinctly. "Swedish from her flag and not alarmed by meeting us: no changing course, or adjusting sail, nor, especially, trying to row upwind in the hope that we couldn't catch her."

"Good. Signal her to heave to, Mr. Lester," Giles asked when he came on deck.

The first lieutenant promptly ordered a shot across the approaching ship's bow from one of the bow chasers. She must have expected it because she immediately let fly her sheets as she turned into the wind. Mr. Lester ordered the main topsail backed, and the two ships drifted downwind near each other. Before Giles could order that his boat be brought to the entryway, he saw that the Swedish captain was ahead of him. He should have expected that maneuver, he thought. When he had been patrolling the English Channel and stopping merchant ships to get news, they often tried to meet him on his ship rather than having him visit theirs. He knew the action was to try to prevent his searching for contraband, which they all carried, though, on most ships, they carried only small amounts. It was also done to prevent any light-fingered members of Giles's crew from walking off with things that did not belong to them. In British waters, the desire to be the visitor rather than the visited might also be based on a forlorn hope of preventing the naval captain from deciding to impress some of the ship's sailors. Giles was sure that that reason did not apply here.

"Oscar Svensson, captain of *Sainte Anne*," the visitor announced in a thick accent when he came on deck.

"Richard Giles, His Majesty's frigate, *Glaucus*," Giles responded.

"Why you stop me?"

"To get news and information on your cargo and destination."

"Cargo steel for Danzig."

"Who controls Danzig now?"

"Gdansk? Franska."

Giles took that to mean 'France.'

"Do they let you land your cargo?"

"Ja. They need. Not legal, but no one care."

"Are there any pirates near here?"

"Ne. Nearer Stockholm. Not here."

"Thank you, Captain Svensson. You have been very helpful. Don't mention this meeting to the French."

"You think I stupid? Only trouble if tell."

Captain Svenson took his leave. When he had gone, Giles turned to Mr. Brooks. "It sounds to me that we are in the wrong place to catch the pirates. Set a course for Stockholm, and let's see what we can find."

The wind had backed into the northwest, so to reach Stockholm, a tack would be needed, indeed several tacks to guard against the wind veering into the north. Soon, ship-handling activity ceased on *Glaucus* again as she waited for new situations to present themselves; just the usual periodic shipboard activities, such as changing watches and piping for dinner, interrupted the tranquil scene. Giles returned to his cabin after pacing up and down the windward side of the quarterdeck to get his daily exercise, settled into his armchair, and took up the book on crop rotations he had been re-reading.

The wind held steady, and *Glaucus* kept sailing towards Stockholm, changing tack at every second turn of the glass. They saw many small merchant ships but nothing to interest them. The day wore on, and night fell. *Glaucus* reduced her canvas to prevent missing too many possibilities during the night.

The sail limitation turned out to be wise, for in the very early dawn of Nordic waters in the summertime, a cry came from the masthead, "Sail in sight, maybe four miles away off the starboard bow." The cry woke Giles, and he went on deck immediately. What sails he could see from the deck were the tops of two gaff-rigged ones of a size that indicated that the strange sails were powering a ship that was larger than *Sainte Anne*. The two sails appeared to be the same size, with masts the same length; maybe that was the popular rig in these waters.

"Stay close-hauled on the larboard tack," Giles ordered. "We want to get well to windward of her before she is aware of us. She can undoubtedly sail closer to the wind than us, but we should be faster."

"I agree with you, Captain," stated Mr. Brooks, who had come on deck with the cry from the masthead. "Might I suggest that we station a lookout with a telescope at the mainmast fighting top to report when he can see the target's sails? That is when they are likely to become aware of us, and at that time, we can raise our topsails and topgallants to try to catch her."

"Quite right, Mr. Brooks," Giles responded. "Mr. Dunsmuir, make it so," Giles addressed his recently promoted third lieutenant.

On this course, *Glaucus* was rapidly closing in on her target, for within half an hour, Mr. Dunsmuir stated that he could spot the top of her mast. There was no change in the other ship's course. Did she not care about the frigate, or did she not have a safe place at her masthead for a lookout? Giles realized that he knew next to nothing about fore-and-aft sail rigs, even though he had sailed small gaff-rigged boats many times over the years, though not recently.

"Mr. Brooks, please calculate a course on which we can come up with her as soon as possible," Giles instructed. "Mr. Dunsmuir, signal to *Stoat* to parallel our course."

The chase continued. *Glaucus* was drawing closer to the unknown ship. She was now hull up, and Giles could see clearly through his telescope that she flew no flag indicating to which country she belonged. She seemed to be oblivious to the frigate, which was chasing her and held the weather gauge.

"Do you suppose that she hasn't noticed us?" Giles asked Mr. Brooks.

"Possibly," replied the Master. "You know that these pirate crews are not the best-trained and obedient of sailors. They tend only to look ahead where prey may be found. But she is bound to see us soon. Not that there is much she can do; she probably has all her sails set. We are catching up on her handsomely. Look, you can make out what's happening on her quarterdeck."

Giles trained his telescope on the ship they were following. He was in time to see a large man, who was standing beside the wheel, turn to look astern. A look of horror appeared on the man's face as he stared at *Glaucus* catching up with his ship. The hypothesis that no one on the other ship had been aware of *Glaucus* was confirmed when hectic activity broke out on her deck as her course was changed and her sails were adjusted for the change in course. The ship turned slightly to have her stern pointing straight at Glaucus. That point of sailing would make *Glaucus* sail the longest distance before coming up with her prey.

The chase continued. *Glaucus* was clearly gaining on the other ship. Soon, she was close enough that Giles could read her name as written on her stern: 'METSASTAJA.' Giles had no idea what that meant or even how to pronounce it. She is called 'Metsa' – something," he announced. I have no idea what that means nor what language it is in."

"Deck there," came a call from the masthead. "I can see into what we thought might be rowers' benches. They are not. They are cannon."

"Get aloft, Mr. Bunting. See what you can make of what they are doing," Giles ordered. The youngster dashed to the shrouds* and started to climb much faster than Giles had been able to when he had visited the masthead earlier. Soon, the midshipman was at the top and had his telescope trained on the ship ahead.

"Deck, there," he cried, "they are guns. Ten-pounders, I guess. Six a side. They are being loaded right now."

"I guessed that they were ports for galley sweeps," muttered Mr. Brooks. "Just as well to learn that they are something else."

"I am sure that that is what they expected us to think," replied Giles. "They might also be used for oars." He raised his voice to cry, "On which side are they being readied, Mr. Bunting?"

"Starboard, sir," came the reply from the masthead.

"Mr. Stewart," Giles called to his second lieutenant, who was commanding the unusually powerful bow chasers that *Glaucus* carried, "Open fire."

Giles knew that the large splinters sent everywhere across a ship's deck when a cannonball hit her railings, decks, or masts were the leading cause of serious wounds and confusion in a naval battle. It might be brutal, but there was no better way to disrupt an enemy and make them yield before boarding, a development that was often very bloody for both sides.

Technically, the first shot from the larboard bow chaser was very poor. The pulling of the larboard gun's lanyard to fire the cannon was mistimed, and the ball went low rather than slicing across the deck or hitting the taffrail to produce the maximum number of splinters. However, though not aimed that way, the ball skimmed off the water and hit the rudder just above the waterline. The force of the impact tore the wheel from the helmsman's hands, and the enemy ship turned sharply to larboard.

The starboard bow chaser was fired hardly more nearly according to plan. The ball went high and a bit wide. It did no damage except to sever part of the mizzen mast's starboard shrouds. That would not have mattered except for the unintentional success of the other bow chaser. The violent change in the rudder made the ship spin to larboard. Through the eye of the wind, she went, and the mizzen sail was violently caught and blown to the larboard side of the ship. Its progress, however, was stopped when the sheets came taught again. That put pressure on the mizzen mast, which, in theory, would be handled by the starboard shrouds. Because of the injury produced by the misdirected bow chaser, those shrouds could not take the strain. They snapped, and the mizzen mast went by the board, falling to larboard.

Metsastaja slewed to larboard, dragged off course by the mast and sails in the water. *Glaucus* slid across the exposed stern, grappled with it, and hauled tight. *Metsastaja*'s stern chasers had been loaded and run out, but, in the chaos, no one was manning them, and the first of *Glaucus*'s boarders took possession of the cannon. *Metsastaja*'s crew had been so distracted that they had prepared no defense against their enemy's grappling onto her stern, and a man, who was slightly better dressed than the others and had a sword, pulled it from its scabbard and presented the hilt to Giles, who was leading the boarders.

Glaucus's crew was well-schooled in what to do as soon as an enemy surrendered. In fact, Giles had held some drills on the way from England to refresh the memories of officers and crews about the steps to be taken, and Mr. Lester had found out in those sessions what his duties would be when the time came. Now, the training has come into use. Members of the crew turned to use their opponents' rigging tools and axes to cut away the fallen mast and secure the rigging so that the main sail could be lowered, the jibs furled, and the main mast could stand safely alone. Meanwhile, the Marines rounded up *Metsastaja*'s officers and crew. Most of this work was done with a minimum of orders from *Glaucus*'s officers and petty officers. Mr. Lester was again amazed at the difference between *Glaucus* and *Cicero,* where no planning had been done on what to do if she ever secured a prize.

Giles encountered one major problem following the capture of *Metsastaja*. Everyone on that ship seemed to speak some extraordinary language of which he could not understand a word. Nor could any of his officers, and apparently, no one on board the captured ship spoke English or French. Mr. Brooks confirmed Giles's impression that it did not sound like German, Russian, Danish, or Swedish and the captives clearly were not speaking French.

"What do you suggest we do, Mr. Brooks?" Giles asked the person on board most likely to have encountered a similar situation.

"Better head for Stockholm with this ship: what a name she has! We'd better call her *Metsa*. There will be someone there who understands the situation. They can also deal with the crew and officers if she is a pirate ship. I wouldn't be surprised if they execute them as we do with pirates. I doubt we will get any prize money for her, but we can't send her home at this point in our trip or keep her with us."

"Very good, Mr. Brooks. Mr. Macualey," Giles addressed his lieutenant of marines, "Confine this ship's crew and officers in the foc's'le and set a good guard over them. Mr. Brooks, calculate a course to take us to Stockholm. Mr. Lester," Giles turned to his first lieutenant, "Take charge of *Metsa*. Get the course from Mr. Brooks, but keep close to us. *Glaucus* will adjust her speed to accommodate you. It won't be easy to sail her without her mizzen mast. You can have Mr. Bunting as your other watch-stander. It should only be overnight before we reach Stockholm, but you will still need two watches."

It took less than an hour from the time at which *Metsa* lost her mast for the ships to set off for Stockholm. *Glaucus* once again was on the lookout for strange ships but matched her pace to what *Metsa* could manage with only one mast. They would reach Stockholm sometime during the next day if the wind held, and there was no point in Giles worrying about how he might be greeted in the capital. He retreated to his cabin for a solitary meal, during which he read some more of his book.

Giles did, of course, write his nightly letter to Daphne, an unusually long one since he could tell her about the capture of *Meta* and how the new officers were performing in action. He also mentioned his worry that he knew little about Sweden and where she stood in relations with Britain. He realized it was somewhat strange to be telling Daphne his worries since they would be resolved one way or another the next day. His letters usually arrived at Dipton Hall in bundles. Daphne always read them immediately, in sequence, so she would read about his worries and about what would happen in Stockholm one after the other almost at the same time while he would have to wait till the next day to see what would occur. Nothing would happen before dawn, though that would arrive very early in these northern summer waters. When the letter was finished, Giles got to bed for a good night's sleep before he was called before dawn.

As the sky lightened, land was revealed ahead. Mr. Brooks said that they were looking at a series of islands lying in the approach to Stockholm. Soon, they spotted a small boat under oars coming towards them. Through his telescope, Giles saw that it had a man in the stern sheets wearing what might be a civilian uniform of some sort. Undoubtedly, he was a pilot who would take over the nerve-wracking job of finding a safe passage among the islands to Stockholm.

The pilot climbed aboard *Glaucus* and announced himself as "Jensen, pilot," though to everyone on board the frigate, it sounded like "Yensen, peelout." That was about the limit of intelligible conversation that anyone on board *Glaucus* could hold with the man who also knew no French, while *Glaucus* had no one who spoke any other languages. Nevertheless, communication by sign language worked, they hoped, as the pilot gestured for them to proceed with the other two ships following the frigate. The pilot instructed the helmsmen and sail handlers by gestures while he directed them through passages between some islands before the waterfront of a major city came into sight. Various hand signals directed them to dock along a quay where several idlers stood ready to take and cleat their lines. The pilot's final set of gestures instructed them to remain on board while he went away.

They did not have long to wait. Soon after they had stowed everything, two men appeared on the quay, walking rapidly towards *Glaucus*. By their dress, one was unmistakably a government official, probably from the Swedish equivalent of the Foreign Office, and the other was a high-ranking naval official. This time, there was less of a language problem. The naval officer, whose name was Karlsson and whose position, Giles reckoned, was as a captain reporting to the port admiral or maybe to the Admiralty, spoke broken but intelligible English. In contrast, the official, whose exact position Giles couldn't understand, spoke French fluently, though he seemed to have no understanding of English. Captain Macreau, whose native language was French, was on *Stoat,* tied up to the quay, while he waited for permission to land. Luckily, Giles found that his many conversations with Etienne while he was his lieutenant meant he could communicate quite easily with the official. Giles showed him the letter of introduction given to him in London. The result was a profuse welcome from the Swedish official, who assured him that some sort of official welcome would soon occur.

The naval officer was equally friendly. Even before asking what *Glaucus* was doing in Stockholm, his main interest was with the prize. Where and why had Giles captured her, and what was he expecting to do with her? Giles started to explain the circumstances that led to his capture of the vessel. He had only got started when he mentioned the name of his prize, *Metsästäjä.*

"What you say?" demanded the naval officer. Giles repeated his version of the name. This still did not enlighten the official, but the matter was resolved when Mr. Brooks pointed to the name he had chalked on the slate,

"Ah," said the Swede, "*Metsästäjä.* You catch her. Jolly good! She big problem for us. Finnish pirate. Thank you. She have cargo, prisoners?"

"No. She was empty."

"Starting new raid, maybe."

"What will happen to her?"

"Don't know. Herre Nilsson maybe know." The naval officer started an extended discussion with the official, during which Giles heard the word captain, which was used when the civilian addressed the naval officer.

"That ship you captured is now your property, Captain Giles," the official announced in French. "You can take her with you, or you can sell her, or we can give you the value that our experts set."

"That last offer is very attractive to me," Giles replied in French. The conversations he had been having regularly with Captain Macreau while the commander was one of his lieutenants were certainly paying off. "What will happen to our prisoners?"

"Since they are pirates now on Swedish territory, we will try them. You don't need to be involved in their trials; we have plenty of evidence against them. In fact, you didn't witness the piracy, so you won't have to wait here for the trial."

"What will happen to these pirates?"

"They'll hang, except for some who may be condemned to the galleys. We still have many galleys; some use condemned men to row them," Herre Nilsson replied.

At that point, a well-dressed man came up the gangplank. "Sir Bromley Harvey," he announced. "British Ambassador. Welcome to Stockholm, Captain. I want to help you in your visit here in any way I can."

"Thank you, Sir Bromley. I have a letter for you and one to pass on to the Swedish Government. Mr. Bunting," Giles addressed the midshipman, "go to my cabin and bring the two envelopes that are on my table."

"These letters," Giles resumed, addressing the visitors as the midshipman scurried off, "should explain fully why I have come to visit Sweden. It was not, I can assure you, to find a place to dispose of a prize."

Giles's visit to Stockholm had only been planned as a possibility depending on what political situation he found when he arrived at St. Petersburg. Still, he knew that the letters were worded vaguely enough that they would serve to get special treatment on this visit as well.

When Mr. Bunting delivered the envelopes, Giles handed both to Sir Bromley. The ambassador broke the seal on the one addressed to him and scanned the words quickly. Then he handed the other letter to Herre Nilsson, saying something in French too rapidly for Giles to understand. The Swedish official did not open it. Instead, he turned to Giles and addressed him again in French, but at a slow enough speed and with such clear enunciation that Giles had no trouble following what he said.

"Welcome again to Stockholm, M. le Marquis de Dipton. We are honored to have you visit us. I believe that King Gustav will wish to meet you. I hope that you can remain in Stockholm for a few days so that we can arrange proper hospitality. We will coordinate with Sir Bromley about official meetings."

"Do not forget Navy," said Captain Karlsson. "We want also to entertain Captain Giles. Admiral Lindgren want give dinner for him."

This produced many remarks among the two Swedes and Sir Bromley. Sir Bromley conveyed the result, "Captain Giles, there will be a naval banquet for you and the officers of your two ships. The Swedish fleet is mainly at Karlskrona, south of here, so the banquet will be at the Admiralty. Then there will be a banquet at our embassy – really my house – tomorrow for the English residents of Stockholm and some of our good Swedish friends. Finally, a state dinner with King Gustav IV Adolph will be held at the palace the following night. The Swedes are good friends of ours, and they have not forgotten the contributions of Sir Sydney Smith in their war with Russia. They seem to be very pleased that we have sent them a war hero with no selfish purpose."

"I am surprised that they and you are making such a fuss about my visit."

Sir Bromley laughed, "Sweden has been enthralled by the news of our country's war with Napoleon. Our great naval victories, of course, are the main focus, but your own remarkable exploits have been the subject of much conversation here, especially on our long winter night. For gossip, your exploits have the advantage of happening much more often than battles like Trafalgar. Incidentally, I should congratulate you on being made a marquess. That will also be of great interest to both our English residents and the Swedish admirers of Britain. I might add that my wife would also be irate if I did not arrange for us to entertain Lady Camshire's husband; she is a great admirer of your wife based on what the papers write about her.

"Now, on more practical matters. The Swedes have given permission for you and your crew to go ashore whenever you want. For my sake, I hope your men will not be too rowdy. The district near the harbor can supply whatever your sailors want."

Giles went ashore to give the news to the other ships. Mr. Lester was first. He was visibly grateful that his assignment of guarding the prisoners would soon be over. He wouldn't admit it, but he had been afraid that the few seamen and marines with which he guarded the prisoners would not prevent the captives from trying to retake their ship. He was glad that the Swedes would soon take over.

Captain Macreau had anticipated that his crew would have a run ashore and that his officers would receive some sort of entertainment. He spoke English and French fluently, and he could make a respectable stab at German. He expected to enjoy the sudden social swirl.

Giles returned to *Glaucus*. He would also be giving his men time ashore, but first, he had to address them. He ordered the crew to assemble at the waist of the ship, and when they had gathered, he gave a very practical, short speech. The crew members were not to antagonize the local men or get into fights in the taverns. They should respect the local citizens and not act provocatively. Those who had not been with him when they visited St. Petersburg some years ago should ask those who had been there what the consequences of getting out of line in a foreign port were. Finally, he reminded them of the instructions they had been given about how to avoid venereal disease. The first warning Giles hoped would be effective. He had had to flog some men when they ran amok in the Russian capital, and he would not hesitate to use what was virtually an unknown punishment on his ships for serious rowdiness or getting into fights in another foreign city. He trusted that his convoluted way of threatening the punishment would convince all the crew that he would use that punishment here if necessary. He had less hope that their sailing from Stockholm would not be followed by many members of the crew visiting the surgeon in the hope of finding relief from the pox or the clap contracted in fleeting moments of pleasure with the local whores.

That chore completed, Giles left *Glaucus* to take a solitary walk through the town. He had already spotted a striking, large building, which he suspected must be the royal palace, and had seen church steeples that might repay investigation. And the streets of the city would have their own wonders to explore. He had developed these interests from Daphne when she first went with him to London and subsequent visits to the capital. He realized that before he knew her, he had noticed very little about the features of the places he visited and that he had been all too typical of most aristocrats who were unaware of their surroundings other than their own estates. Their limited interests were reflected in their conversation. Giles realized as he walked along how he was gathering observations and thoughts to share with Daphne as well as to reflect on during the long, empty, and lonely periods that plagued the captain of a vessel at sea. He certainly needed this break before having to endure the three dinners the Swedish functionaries had so enthusiastically planned.

Well, he would just make the best of the situation; at least, he could tell Daphne all about his thoughts and activities when he wrote his nightly letter to her. There was no one else he could confide in as he could with his lifetime companion.

Chapter XV

Daphne had returned to London from Dipton. She wasn't happy about being in the city. She had wanted more time at home. When she had made her plans before her ball, two weeks at Dipton, starting a day or two after her ball, before returning to the capital, seemed plenty. But then the need to give the servants from Dipton time in London and for her to deal with the ruination of Baron Strangway and his intolerable wife delayed her return to her country home and her children. So, she had made a commitment to meet the architect who would be making plans to renovate the old Green's Club and another one to attend a lecture by Professor Milner, her friend from Cambridge. She could, of course, break the appointments, but she did not want to. It was important to get the club functioning as quickly as possible since opening it in the fall would be best. She had learned by comparing her treatment with the reports of many members of the aristocracy that those who kept their appointments and paid their bills on time got much better service from professional men than ones who thought it was their right to be unreliable and slow to pay. Arbitrarily postponing the meeting about transforming Green's Club would undoubtedly lead to considerable delays in completing the renovation and the opening of the new club.

To add to her reasons for being in London, there was a concert that evening that she had promised her aunt-in-law, Lady Struthers, to attend with her. Lord Struthers did not want to miss the session of the House of Lords, where various matters were coming to a head, and Daphne did not want to disappoint her aunt, who hated going to concerts by herself. Anyway, she had lots of work to do catching up with various accounts that she had been neglecting, and she could get more of it done away from the distractions of Dipton.

Daphne's reverie was interrupted by her new butler, Edgar – no, now he was called Rowling since he had been promoted from his position as first footman – bearing a visiting card on a silver platter.

"A Mrs. Marsden wants to know if you are at home, my lady," Rowling announced.

"Mrs. Marsden?" said Daphne, examining the card. "Mrs. Marsden? Do I know a Mrs. Marsden?"

"She is dressed in the height of fashion, my lady, more so than usual for a morning call and not quite in the best taste," the butler remarked.

"Ah, of course, the whore monger." Daphne declared. Mrs. Marsden had run a 'house of ill repute' near the men's clubs in the St. James district. Giles had inherited the premises when his older brother died, together with a contract supporting the madam. With the aid of her brother-in-law, Lord David, Daphne had outwitted the brothel keeper while winning her respect. What in the world could the madam want? There was only one way to find out.

"Rowling, show Mrs. Marsden into the morning room and say that I will be with her in a few minutes."

Daphne waited five minutes before bustling into the room.

"Mrs. Marsden," she said in a harried voice. I'm so sorry to keep you waiting. There is so much to do when one returns to London, isn't there? What can I do for you?"

"Lady Dipton," replied Mrs. Marsden, who Daphne realized was dressed in excessively elaborate clothing for a morning visit, "I wanted to come and thank you for putting that marvelous painting of Lady Strangway up for sale."

"Why thank me? And why is it any business of yours?"

"Hadn't you heard? I bought it. At Green's Club, it was by all odds the picture most likely to induce the members to visit one of my ladies. It will do the same at my new establishment. Indeed, it already is stimulating business."

"That will serve Lady Strangway right! So, you are running another knocking shop, are you?"

"Please, my lady, I prefer to call it a house of leisure."

"Well, it doesn't matter what you name it; it is still the same business."

"Not really. Many of my present customers are content just to laugh and drink with my ladies and not to visit the bedrooms at all. I provide what they don't get at home. There is more to satisfying interactions between a lady and a gentleman than just making the creature with two backs."

"So you say, but still Lady Strangway's painting excites men, you say, enough for them to break their marriage vows."

"True enough, though I can assure you that, in most cases, the vows have been broken long before they visit my house of leisure. Speaking of Lady Strangway, you will be interested to know that she has joined my establishment."

"What? She is not in Northumberland or wherever Strangway's estate is located?"

"No," responded the bawd, "She found society there very limited, especially since Strangway has no money.

Lady Strangway prefers to be in London, even if she has to earn her keep. Indeed, she seems happier as a member of the demi-monde rather than of the ton. That picture has helped her to command very superior fees."

"No doubt that is very good for you, too," Daphne said sarcastically.

"Of course, I am a businesswoman. But I also came to give you some free advice." Mrs. Marsden continued.

"Yes?"

"You relative – niece, half-niece, I don't know what – Mrs. Catherine Bolton – may be getting herself into a lot of trouble that could end with her joining my establishment."

"What? How can that be possible? She is happily married and spends most of her time at their residence near Dipton. She sometimes visits London to keep up with the art world. While in London, she usually stays with our aunt, Lady Struthers. Now that this house is finished, she is always welcome to stay here whenever she wants, whether we are present or not."

"It's not quite that simple, I am afraid. Things are not all that good in her marriage, and she is getting fed up with her husband. She knows that he visits my type of lady, both when he is in foreign ports and when he is in London. He has graced my house on more than one occasion, though recently, I have barred him for refusing to wear a condom even though he had the pox. Your niece has refused his advances for that reason and has been looking for other lovers among the artists of London."

"How do you know such things? Why should I believe you?" Daphne asked.

"How do I know? Servants. They talk about their masters and mistresses more than any other subject when they get together. I pay mine to tell me any good gossip they get about the ton. Why should I tell you? Because I know how much trouble you can cause those who cross you, and not telling you when I know something you should be warned about is asking for trouble since all sorts of people know that I know everything that goes on among the 'better' sort of people. I also have seen how ruthless you can be when someone crosses you. I am simply playing it safe."

"I'm glad to hear it. And that Lady Strangway has found her true calling."

After Mrs. Marsden left, Daphne remained sitting for a while, reflecting on what the bawd had told her. It was alarming to hear her news about Catherine. Though undoubtedly it was said to upset Daphne and provide her with the worrying conundrum she now faced, Daphne had no doubt that the information was correct. But what could she do about it? If Catherine were in London, she would be staying with Lady Struthers. And Lady Struthers often knew far more than anyone would guess. Daphne should call on Lady Struthers anyway, especially as she hadn't done so in the days following her ball. In fact, she should do it right now. Dealing with Mrs. Marsden's allegations was more important than anything she would be doing otherwise.

Lady Struthers was at home and had no other callers with her. "Daphne," she greeted her niece-in-law. "I hear that your ball was a smashing success."

"It was. I am sorry that I didn't visit you right after to tell you all about it."

"Don't worry. I remember from my days of giving balls that the days after are hectic.

"They were, especially with the servant problem I ran into, but it all worked out well in the end, thanks to Giles and the servants from Dipton."

"I'm not surprised about that. I also heard about how you ruined Lord and Lady Strangway. In fact, I have heard so many conflicting reports that I am glad to have a chance to find out what really happened."

Daphne obliged by giving a succinct report on how Lord and Lady Strangway had attempted to ruin Daphne's ball and how she and Giles had evaded their nefarious schemes.

"Good lord," Lady Struthers exclaimed when she had finished. "I knew that you and Richard are brilliant, but I had no idea how effective you two could be. Now tell me, what happened to that scandalous picture of Lady Strangway? Who bought it?"

"I just found that out today. Mrs. Marsden, the brothel keeper, visited me and said that she had bought it. She also told me that Lady Strangway was now working at her house of ill repute."

"Oh, my! I am not surprised. What little I have seen of that lady did not impress me, and I know that Struthers loathes Lord Strangway. Oh, thank you, Daphne! I never have juicy tidbits to throw into the cesspool of gossip that passes for conversation among the ladies of the ton, and this is wonderful stuff.

"Glad to provide you with ammunition, Aunt," Daphne said sarcastically.

"Now, now, Daphne," responded Lady Struthers. "But that is surely not what you came to tell me."

"You know me too well, Aunt Gillian. I also came to see if there is any truth in another story Mrs. Marsden told me."

"Oh, do tell me, dear."

"Yes. Mrs. Marsden claimed that Catherine's marriage is having a rough time, and that Catherine is in with a very scandalous set when she is in London. I am sure that if there is any truth to the rumors, you would know, though I don't believe for a moment that you would have spread them."

"Well, of course, I haven't, but I am not completely surprised that rumors are out there, even though Catherine is not prominent enough to be much of a prime target for scurrilous gossip. It is quite true that there are problems in her marriage, though I don't know what either of us can do to help."

"I had no idea that Catherine and Bolton were having difficulties," Daphne declared. "She could have come to me, surely."

"I doubt that she would want to confide in you, my dear. You and your husband are so remarkably successful and compatible. She is about your age, and she envies you."

"She does?"

"Yes, she does. After all, she has a noble background, and you don't, yet you are the talk of the ton: positive and envious talk; they don't even know she exists. Your husband is rich; her husband, though also a post captain, is not. To add insult to injury, the only time Captain Bolton earned a significant amount of prize money was when he was sailing in a group with Richard. And you and Richard do not disguise how genuinely in love you are, a very remarkable aspect of any marriage among the better class of people."

"I never realized how she might feel, though I had noticed that she seemed to be getting colder towards me. What can I do about it?" Daphne asked.

"I don't know," replied Lady Struthers. "It really should be up to her mother to straighten her out, but that is not likely to happen. Maybe you could have a word with Catherine."

"I suppose I'd better. Maybe tomorrow for luncheon."

"I think dinner might be better. Catherine is always busy about noon, it seems, and might not come."

"All right. Tomorrow evening, I think. I have a lecture to attend this evening, and then you and I are going to the concert a couple of evenings later. If you can let me have a pen and paper, I'll write her a note inviting her."

"I can, of course, provide the writing materials. But Catherine is not staying here. She is visiting a friend in Bloomsbury, a Mrs. Higgins. I have the address here and can have the note delivered for you."

Daphne left Struthers House quite contented. If Mrs. Marsden was right, she had taken positive steps to set things right. Now, she could fill her afternoon with seeing the architect and builder for the renovation of Green's Club before a light dinner and the lecture she was looking forward to.

All went as planned. Catherine Bolton showed up a few minutes before the appointed time, and the two women chatted about inconsequential matters until dinner was served in the small dining room. Remembering Mrs. Marsden's mention of her source for gossip, Daphne steered the subject to uncontroversial subjects such as the plays and operas that were on. Catherine was delighted to tell Daphne about the paintings displayed in various galleries. She was clearly up to date with the artistic world. She also sounded quite forlorn about not being able to participate in any of the special activities of the London season since she didn't feel comfortable asking Lord and Lady Struthers to take her to balls when they had quite firmly withdrawn from those activities.

Since there were no others at the dinner, Daphne suggested that they remain in the dining room when the meal was over to enjoy whatever they wanted to drink as the men did. She was not surprised when Catherine agreed and wanted to drink port, a wine that was never on hand in the drawing room when the ladies had retired there after dinner. Daphne herself thought that a bit of port might give her a bit of Dutch courage to tackle the difficult conversation ahead.

Daphne decided to take the bull by the horns and not try to dance around the subject, which she wanted to discuss with Catherine after Rowling had left the wines and glasses and would retire to the butler's pantry to enjoy the left-over dinner wine that was the butler's perk, so there was little likelihood that any of the servants would be listening. She had not forgotten Mrs. Marsden's comments about servants and gossip.

"I had a very disturbing visit from Mrs. Marsden yesterday. She is the proprietor of a house of ill repute catering to the gentry," Daphne introduced the subject which had induced her to have Catherine to dinner."

"How in the world do you know such a bawd?" replied Catherine, showing that she at least had some worldly knowledge about brothels.

"That's a long story," Daphne replied. "Suffice it to say your uncle David and I had dealings with her after your other two uncles died. She came to gloat that she had bought the gentlemen's painting of Lady Strangway and would be displaying it to encourage business at her establishment. She also came to tell me that she had heard some disturbing rumors which she thought I should be aware of."

"What were they about?" Catherine asked, though the sudden droop of her previously smiling face indicated that she could form a pretty good guess about the subject of this part of their conversation.

"It concerted you and the stories that are spreading about your bohemian doings."

"What? But I'm not doing anything improper. It is all completely innocent. I have been visiting my good friend, Mrs. Higgins, and I have been taking art lessons from a prominent painter, Michael Findley. You know him, I believe."

"Well, the rumor is that you are more than just a pupil to him."

"That's nonsense!" Catherine declared, but the expression and the vehemence with which her denial was made suggested that it was not nonsense.

"Is it?" Daphne asked rhetorically. "Your reaction indicates that it is not."

"Well, we have attended some gatherings of artists together. They can be a bit unconventional, but I have done nothing improper. I *am* married, you know."

"Of course I know," Daphne responded. "Mrs. Marsden also said that the rumor is that you and Captain Bolton have been having difficulties that are causing you to wander."

This remark prompted a flood of tears from Catherine. Daphne let her cry uninterrupted, except to offer a handkerchief that she kept in her sleeve.

"Oh, Daphne, you don't know how it has been for me, how lonely, how unhappy I am, especially as I have no one to confide in. My Friendship with Helen – Mrs. Higgins – is not that close. My mother says that is the way marriage can be, and I just have to bow to fate and accept the situation, but surely that can't be true."

"Is it really so awful?" Daphne asked.

"It wasn't, to begin with. Bolton was always very loving and exciting to talk to. I even enjoyed it when he came to my room to exercise his marital rights, though I know many women don't.

"All this changed after that cruise with Uncle Giles. He got more prize money than he had ever earned before. He had to be in London to try to get orders that would be favorable for him to continue getting more prize money. He didn't want to stay with Aunt Gillian, so he was at some hotel. Unfortunately, he started to drink and gamble to celebrate his good fortune. He gambled in games like whist, where the result was not pure luck but also required experience and skill, neither of which he had. He lost steadily and drank heavily until he had run through all his money. I think he also visited brothels when he started to lose; some of his remarks suggested he had sought relief in such places. He returned to Dipton only when he had no more money left, with some debts he couldn't pay, and in a very foul mood."

"That sounds awful for you, Catherine. I am so sorry," Daphne stated.

"That is not the worst of it. Bolton continued to drink excessively when he came home. He ceased to be able to perform in the marital bed. It couldn't get stiff, if you know what I mean, or keep it that way to complete the marital act. He blamed me for not knowing how to serve him or do disgusting things to get him ready. He said I should learn from prostitutes how to service a man properly. He stormed out of my bedroom and has never been back. He is at sea now, east of Gibraltar, and you know what Nelson said* about that."

"So, you came to London after he went to sea again?" Daphne's declaration was more like a question requiring an extended answer.

"Yes. I needed some distraction and wanted to pursue my interest in drawing and painting. I've been taking lessons from Mr. Findlay. You know, he's the man who did some paintings for you and who painted my gentleman's picture that hangs in Bolton's dressing room. I've learned a lot from him. He's also taken me to some gatherings of artists and their friends. Much more interesting than the tea parties at Aunt Gillian's, though these people also gossip a lot about each other and about prominent members of society whose portraits many of them paint.

"That's how I met Helen. She is a successful artist, a widow with a house in Bloomsbury. She asked me to stay with her since we got on well, and she could provide me with studio space and friendly criticism.

"But aren't their gatherings very immoral?" Daphne protested. "Won't everyone presume that your morals are very low and you must be having affairs with all sorts of men?"

"I don't see why they should. These people are not as stuffy as Aunt Gillian's friends, but affairs are just as blatant among the ton and not any more frequent."

"Well, your friendship with Mr. Findlay must be very hard on your reputation, surely?"

Catherine laughed. "Anyone who knows him knows that he prefers men to women for intimacy. Women are perfectly safe with him; he is a fine conversationalist and a good teacher. That's why I enjoy seeing him, quite apart from the art lessons."

"Yes," Daphne agreed, "but no one else knows that do they? At least no one in the ton will likely know his strong preferences. I know that he is sufficiently good at flattering his feminine subjects, so his apparent interest would lead people to guess that this would lead to an intimate relationship if a woman indicated it was possible. You don't have to do anything for society to guess that you are misbehaving and spread the rumor that that is so. Catherine, having that story widely broadcast would make re-establishing your intimacy with your husband much more difficult if the stories came to his ears. Do you want to restore your marriage to be more than a formality?"

"I don't know. I still love the man I married. The man he has become, I don't think so."

"Then I think we should take steps to try to improve your reputation. If he is like most men, Bolton won't want you if he thinks you are spoiled goods."

"What do you suggest, Daphne?"

"Well, to start with, you should stop seeing Mr. Findlay for now and certainly not go out with him. Instead, I suggest that you attend a couple of events with me. Maybe you could come to the concert with Aunt Gillian and me. And then we could attend Lady Throgmorton's Ball this Saturday."

"A ball?" Catherine asked dubiously. "I've never been to a ball except at Dipton, certainly not a Society Ball."

"It is high time you had that experience. Just don't dance with the same man more than twice, and don't flirt with them. Remember, we are trying to improve your image among the gossip mongers."

"But Daphne, I don't have a ball gown."

"That's easily fixed. My modiste owes me some favors. If we go tomorrow morning, I am sure she can make something in time. Then you can return to Dipton in my carriage the following day."

"Yes. That might be a good idea. I think I may be getting on Helen's nerves. She likes her privacy, especially when she is working, and having a break from me might do her good, but I can't pay for a ball gown. Not on the pittance that Bolton allows me."

"Consider it my gift. Giles will approve if he even notices the charge. You are his niece, and he takes supporting family very seriously."

Everything proceeded according to plan. The modiste created a stunning gown for the ball that took Catherine's breath away and made her eyes sparkle. The concert opened her eyes to how wonderful music could be when played properly. The ball was also a success for her. Her gown and the wedding ring on her finger made it clear that she was not one of the young debutants whose courting rituals were the excuse for the lavish entertainment. That didn't stop several men from asking her to dance and to show considerable interest in her, but she turned aside their more personal remarks with aplomb and made sure not to dance with any of them more than once. Daphne also had a full dance card, but her partners were older, and often, they were seeking a closer acquaintanceship with the woman who was known to be handling and controlling the growing investments and businesses that the Marquess of Dipton owned. The contempt they felt for people in trade did not extend to members of the nobility who were shrewd investors. Most of them, but not all, had not ruined the dance with her by indicating that they knew she had control of Giles's burgeoning wealth; they were more subtle than that. Even the supper, which could be awkward with so many of the men ensconced in the card room and unwilling to move to the dining hall for the break, was fine. Catherine went in with Sir Geoffry Wilder, a well-known Italian Renaissance art expert. Daphne had been paired with Viscount Ardendale, who was heavily involved with canals in the midlands and was eager to hear about Daphne's canal business and the purchase she had made of the canal their barge company used, which he presumed meant Daphne would be making most of the decisions about any expansions or improvements without waiting for Giles to come back.

Daphne's only regret about her efforts to save Catherine's reputation was that it had required two extra days in London, which she would rather have spent in Dipton. She liked being in London, but she couldn't stay there long without missing Dipton, especially when her children had not accompanied her to the capital. Only two things bothered her as she contemplated leaving the capital: how would Catherine adjust to being in unexciting Dipton again, and would Giles be able to be home for the birth of her baby, who was beginning to show signs of life with hearty kicks that were most uncomfortable for its mother.

Chapter XVI

Giles was woken at six bells of the morning watch, which the people ashore called seven a.m. It was a half hour before the pilot would come to guide *Glaucus* and *Stoat* out of Stockholm. The move had been arranged the previous afternoon before the reception given by King Gustav IV Adolph, as the Swedes strangely called their ruler. Giles had heard inuendoes at the two earlier receptions that the king was unreliable and not very respected, but he could not judge from the previous night's revelry. When the ladies had left the table, and the cloth had been drawn, the Swedes, including the king, got down to serious drinking. On most toasts, one could just sip in agreement, but on toasts made directly to a person, including to Giles, the recipient was expected to empty his glass with the man proposing a toast. Many toasts were drunk to the prowess of the Royal Navy or to King George III, and each time, Giles had to down his glass.

The tipple in which the toasts were made, and the only one that seemed to be available, was something that the Swedes called brainwine, or so it sounded to Giles, and it was just as strong as the vodka he had encountered in St. Petersburg. It left him with a terrible headache, blurred vision, and the need to drink a large amount of water. He wanted to roll over and go back to sleep when his servant woke him, but duty called. Because his first lieutenant was not yet very familiar with dealing with foreigners, Giles had to get out of bed and dress.

The official reception had been much more of a trial for Giles than had been the evening at the British Embassy that had preceded it. There, the purpose had been to meet the English families who were living in Stockholm who all wanted news of home and his opinion on many matters, especially on the war with Napoleon and how it affected the trade with Sweden, which was the reason for most of them being in Stockholm. There was quite a crowd of people, and the event was held in the ballroom of the embassy.

After being led around to be introduced to the most important members of the community by Sir Bromley Harvey, Giles was abandoned to hold court to the many people who wanted to talk to him and be seen in the presence of a marquess of their own country who was also and a celebrated war hero. They were also worried about the conduct of the war and the safety of their positions in Sweden, and they treated him as an expert on how the war was going. Giles had no alternative but to try to deal with their worries optimistically but also honestly.

Giles presented the story that, unfortunately, Napoleon was a very uncouth general who was having substantial but limited success on the continent but was bound to be brought down because England and her allies, such as Sweden, would control the oceans and wear him down on land. It was bound to take a long time, but there should be no doubt about the outcome. Giles could only hope privately that this was not a lot of nonsense.

While the conversations continued, music started to be played. As Giles expected, most of the men drifted off to the card room. At that point, Giles found a large number of women still surrounded him. They were not much interested in the war or what the government was thinking. Letters and newspapers from London had preceded Giles's arrival, and these sources of information had, it would seem, been full of Daphne's ball and her triumphs over the shortage of materials for ball gowns. While Giles agreed that the ball had been a tremendous achievement, he remained mute on the subject of how the ballgowns had been obtained, only saying that it was all his wife's doing. That, however, did not allow him to escape the subject of his wife. Persistent questioning turned to the subject of Daphne's various adventures and her many endeavors, which had been the subject of articles in the papers for some time. In London, these matters would be considered old news that was not worth discussing. In Stockholm, however, further revelations about how unusual Daphne was were eagerly listened to, and Giles was pressed to reveal more. The ladies seemed to be in awe of his remarkable wife, and they got him to admit that the publicity had been accurate but only covered a fraction of her accomplishments.

When Giles began to fear that he would be spending the rest of the evening answering questions about Daphne and his family, the small orchestra, which was to provide music for the dancing, started tuning their instruments. As the crowd drifted over to the sides of the ballroom to give the dancers some room, Giles seized the opportunity to ask one of the more attractive, married ladies to dance.

Giles enjoyed dancing, and Daphne had made sure that he was fully proficient in both the traditional dances and the more modern ones. The scraps of not-very-serious conversation that took place on the dance floor were a great relief from the cross-examinations he had been suffering from the ladies. They had found it hard to believe that another woman could have had the accomplishments and adventures that Giles had been relating about Daphne and wanted to know more about them. Luckily, Giles had left out some of Daphne's most outrageous endeavors; otherwise, he could never have got free of them.

While answering his wife's admirers' questions, Giles had observed that Etienne Marceau had also not escaped having a number of the guests questioning him, and they had stayed even when most of the others had sought out the cards and liquor that drew them to the card room. His former first lieutenant seemed to have gained as much interest primarily among the gentlemen as Giles was experiencing with the ladies. What in the world could Etienne have been talking about? Giles should have realized that his former officer had served with him long enough to have acquired a large number of tales about his commander that fascinated listeners who lived more prosaic lives. Whatever had been going on, Giles suspected that Etienne was at least as glad as he had been to begin dancing as a pleasant way to avoid further questioning. His colleague certainly had wasted no time in asking a young lady to join him on the dance floor.

Giles also noted that Etienne seemed to have the same partner for many of the dances to an extent that indicated a serious interest in the woman. The subject of his attention was Sir Bromley Harvey's daughter, to whom Giles had been introduced when he arrived. Had his protégé developed an interest in women? He had always noticed that Etienne had been very reticent about his attraction to the opposite sex while he showed no interest in his own. Maybe Miss Higgins was getting him out of his shell.

The reception at the embassy broke up quite early, and Giles and Etienne walked back to the quay together. Giles was not surprised when Ettienne was very enthusiastic about Sir Bromley's daughter until Etienne realized that he was probably revealing more of his feelings than he wanted and changed the subject to some speculation about the reception they would get in St. Petersburg. Both had commented on how nice it was not to have to respond to every toast by drinking another slug of the Swedes' appalling liquor. They also groaned that the King's reception the next night would likely again plunge them into the need to consume far more of the brainwine than they wanted.

These reflections on how waking up on the preceding morning had been far more pleasant than what Giles was experiencing this morning did nothing to quell the headache and nauseous feeling he was experiencing. Why did men seem to think that downing excessive quantities of hard liquor was required as part of a special male banquet? Whatever the pleasure was in the alcohol, it was not worth the way one felt the following morning.

When Giles emerged from his cabin, it took only one glance by crew members who had been on *Glaucus* for some time to know that they should tread very lightly around him. Their captain rarely drank much. It was only after the official banquets in Russia that he had returned to the ship exceedingly drunk. They also wished that he had slept longer this morning.

To make the day worse, Giles was greeted when he came on deck with a bright, sunny summer morning accompanied by no wind at all. *Glaucus* and *Stoat* would not be sailing any time soon by the look of things. Giles might as well have stayed in bed until there was some hope of leaving Stockholm harbor. His only consolation was that Etienne Macreau had also had to drink a great deal of the raw alcohol, and Giles knew that Etienne was by nature abstemious and never drank hard liquor if he could avoid it.

After a quarter of an hour on deck, Giles gave up trying to appear attentive and happy, returned to his cabin, and lay down fully clothed. He wondered if Etienne Macreau felt as badly as he did. Etienne had been the only other British officer at the King's reception and had had to respond vigorously to all the toasts. As he had thought earlier, Etienne had always been a moderate drinker while he was on *Glaucus,* limiting his intake of brandy to the royal toast. He was likely in worse shape than Giles. That was Giles's last thought before dropping into a deep sleep.

Giles was awakened at noon with the news that Sir Bromley Harvey had arrived, in a very excited state, with a letter from the British government for him. Giles straightened his clothing and went on deck, still with a raging headache.

"Captain Giles," Sir Bromley broke out, not waiting for Giles's welcome, "I have received news, terrible news, from our government and a letter for you."

"What news, Sir Bromley? Do take it slowly before you give yourself apoplexy," Giles replied.

"There has been a great battle at a town named Friedland. It is somewhere in Poland, I believe. The French were commanded by that devil Napoleon, according to the message I received from the foreign office. Russia was decisively defeated. Peace talks were underway between Tsar Alexander and Napoleon, according to my letter, but the results of any treaty that they agreed to were unknown at the time of writing. In particular, they didn't know how much land Napoleon was acquiring in the treaty. In addition, the foreign office does not know whether the Russians will be forced to join Napoleon in the war against us or can be neutral, though pledging not to assist us militarily or continue to take bribes from us or to trade with us. In short, they have no idea of the extent to which Russia has become a vassal state with little or no control over its foreign policy or the use of its army and navy.

"I don't know how useful this information is. It is quite old, I know. I would expect the Swedish government to know more, but if they do, they are not telling me. This news certainly affects you, Captain Giles. You can't very well sail to St. Petersburg to get a medal and strengthen relations with Russia if we are at war with Russia. The Swedes may know more, but they haven't told me anything."

"There may be more information in my letter and orders on how to proceed," Giles suggested.

Giles broke the seal on his document and read the contents from beginning to end before making any comment.

"I am afraid," he stated after refolding the message, "that my letter does not give any more information, indeed less. It says that they have heard that the French defeated the Russians in battle. They don't yet know how severe the defeat of our ally was and whether the French will be able to force Russia to join them in the war against us. It is abundantly clear that the Admiralty knows little about the consequences of the battle.

"My orders," Giles continued, "are not very helpful. They state clearly that I should not go to St. Petersburg until I receive explicit orders, but also that I should not return home. They suggested I could liaise with the Swedish navy without any suggestion about how to do that or the reason for it."

"I believe," said Sir Bromley, "that you should let me approach the Swedish government. King Gustav can be very touchy about thinking that we are monitoring how he uses our subsidies to his government."

"You know best, Sir Bromley," Giles replied. "I'll just stay here until I hear from you. I'll also tell Captain Macreau on *Stoat* about what is happening."

It was well into the afternoon before Sir Bromley returned. He looked very harried. Of course, he had also been at dinner the previous night and had to drink more than was wise. Giles recognized the fraught look on the ambassador's face. "Let's go to my cabin to discuss the news, Sir Bromley. Possibly, a bit of the hair of the dog would be appropriate now."

When they were in Giles's cabin, he poured two bumpers of the French cognac that Captain Creasey had given him.

"What have you discovered, Sir Bromley?" Giles asked after they had each had a couple of sips in fast order.

"I am very angry about the post from our government," the ambassador replied. "They waited ten days after they learned about the battle to inform me, and they still didn't know the result of the talks between the French and the Russians, which was their excuse for not informing me sooner. It is equally annoying that the Swedish government knew all about the situation, but they weren't going to tell you or me until they learned the outcome of the talks. The question was whether the Tsar had joined Napoleon in war against us or whether Russia would stay independent, though possibly in agreement with the ban on trade with Britain. Though they wouldn't say it, I think the Swedes wanted us to join them in a war to regain Finland from the Tsar, but our government made no mention in their letter to me about sending the Swedes more money."

Giles thought that this was all very unsatisfactory. He was left with the need to liaise with the Swedish and Russian governments without any helpful instructions from the Admiralty or the Cabinet, and he faced the likelihood that he would be left twiddling his thumbs operationally while trying to prevent his crew from running amock in a foreign capital. This was not what he had envisioned when he agreed to take *Glaucus* to St. Petersburg so that he could receive an award.

Sir Bromley had anticipated Giles's problem and thought he had found a way to reduce it. "I talked with the Swedish officials about how to make your visit to Sweden more profitable to us both. We came up with a couple of suggestions that might interest you."

"Oh?" Giles couldn't help keeping his cynicism about governments out of his question.

"Yes. The Swedes offered interesting trips for your two ships. They suggest that you visit their fleets and go on an exercise with them. I believe that they want to strengthen our belief that they are a worthwhile ally, especially one who should keep on being subsidized. From our point of view, you would gain useful information about the state of their navy."

"Exactly what did they have in mind?"

"The first suggestion involves *Stoat*. The Swedes want to show off their galley fleet, which, as the name suggests, is largely made up of galleys. Did you know that the Swedes have two navies? I didn't until I had been here for a while."

"Do they? How does that work?"

"The first one is responsible for the group of islands off Stockholm and implicitly over to the coast of Finland, which, of course, is held by the Swedes. They are also responsible for naval action in the Gulf of Bothnia, which, you know, is the northern arm of the Baltic Sea. The fleet consists of smaller boats, without any of the ships of the line or large frigates that are the principal weapons of the deep-sea fleet. The chief features of this second fleet are that the army runs it and that many of their ships are types of galleys. Its ships are designed for shallower waters than the main battle fleet and have an amphibious element in their mandate, though the Swedes may deny that officially. The Swedes thought that Captain Macreau might be interested in having a cruise with some of these ships."

"Captain Macreau might well enjoy that," Giles replied. "Recently, when he was captaining *Glaucus* for me, he captured a frigate that the Berbers had transformed into a sort of galley and was most interested in its possibilities. I found that the vessel had some properties that our usual warships do not have, especially when there is no wind or it is foul.

"What are the Swedes' thoughts about what I should do, Sir Bromley?"

"The Swedish Navy intends to mount a venture to discover to what extent the French and their recent German friends have really taken possession of Swedish Pomerania and whether they have any naval forces to stop the trade which they now treat as smuggling, but which for the Swedes is a valuable trade in both directions."

"Yes, I would be happy to participate in an excursion with the Swedish Navy. I would certainly like to see their main battle fleet at its base and share some adventures with them. I was also given the task of finding out what is going on in that part of the world."

"Good," said Sir Bromley. "Now, I've had a very tiring day. I don't suppose you have any splendid brandy we enjoyed earlier."

"Yes, I do. Let's have a glass before getting on with our duties."

Giles was more than happy to accommodate the ambassador. He had delivered much better news than Giles had had any reason to hope for earlier in the day. Things looked much more promising for this expedition to the Baltic than they had at any point since he had agreed to undertake it. Giles sent Midshipman Hunter to *Stoat* to invite Captain Macreau to join him. Etienne came to *Glaucus* a few minutes later.

"Did you lose Midshipman Hunter?" Giles asked his former first lieutenant.

"No, sir. The lad asked if he could explore *Stoat*, and I allowed him to do so with one of my midshipmen. I learned from you, sir, that interest in ships other than their own is a good trait to encourage."

"Well, then, your next opportunity falls right into the same category. The Swedes have invited you to go to sea with their galleys and possibly accompany them on raids on smuggler bases. The most interesting feature of their suggestion is that that part of their fleet uses galleys extensively."

"I'll be more than happy to accept this opportunity. Not just for myself. My crew will also benefit from being engaged in a real operation."

"Good. We should hear the details of what is involved in meeting up with our hosts tomorrow."

"What will you be doing, sir, while I am learning about the Swedish galleys?"

"*Glaucus* will be joining ships of the Swedish deep-sea fleet in a trip to those waters off the islands of Pomerania where we were not long ago."

Etienne was delighted to hear that they would be spending another night in Stockholm before leaving. It would give him a chance to see more of Miss Harvey. Indeed, though it might seem presumptuous, he would call on her again as soon as he could get free of his mentor. If it raised eyebrows among her parents, he didn't care. Though it was late in the day to call on a young lady, such visits were not unheard of. He immediately took the first step necessary for his plan.

"Captain Giles, Sir Bromley, I should return to *Stoat* to tell my officers and crew that we will be spending another night in Stockholm. They behaved themselves very well yesterday, so I think they should be allowed ashore this evening as well."

"Yes," Sir Bromley said, anticipating Giles, "the Swedes remarked on how well your sailors behaved themselves. Only one small brawl in one of the most disreputable taverns. You could certainly let them go ashore again, Captain Macreau, except, of course, for the ones involved in the disturbance."

Etienne rapidly gave orders to his first lieutenant when he returned to *Stoat* and then hastened to the British embassy. The footman who opened the door accepted Etienne's card with the words that he would see if Miss Harvey was at home. Etienne was glad to hear it. On the way to the embassy, he had worried that maybe Miss Harvey would have been elsewhere. Now, he knew that at least she was not away; the footman would no doubt have informed him of the fact if it had been the case. He had forgotten that people could be 'not at home' when they didn't want to see a caller.

Miss Harvey was indeed at home. The footman ushered Etienne into the parlor where Miss Harvey was sitting on a settee. She greeted Etienne with a smile, "Good afternoon, Captain Macreau. I thought that you were sailing away today."

"No. It was decided that we should stay in Swedish waters for a while until the situation concerning Russia becomes clearer. I will be here at least one more night."

"Well then, you must stay for dinner with my family. I would hate to think of what might happen to you on your own in Stockholm," Miss Harvey teased him rather daringly.

Even though that was precisely what Etienne wanted, he thought he should demur for politeness's sake. After all, it surely was up to her mother or father to issue such an invitation, not Miss Harvey.

"No," replied Miss Harvey firmly. "You must come. Mother has arranged for a small soirée of the English community. They will come here after dinner. We usually have some music and dancing, though there are always more young ladies than gentlemen who want to dance. I know that my father thinks highly of you, Captain Macreau, and you charmed my mother when you came to the reception the other night. So please say that you will come."

"I will be delighted to, Miss Harvey, especially if you will hold one or two dances for me. Did your father invite Captain Giles?"

"I don't know, but Father was very impressed with your superior. He remarked to my mother how unpretentious he was despite being a Marquess and a very famous frigate captain. I have never known my father to be excited about meeting anyone, but you mustn't tell anyone I told you," Miss Harvey giggled.

"Captain Giles's wife is equally remarkable. They are very devoted to each other and their children," Etienne told her, hoping that that information might direct Miss Higgin's attention away from Giles as a possible match and towards himself.

"Oh," exclaimed Miss Harvey, "it is so good to hear about devoted family men when there are so many rakes around."

"Yes, I suppose it is," Etienne replied, wondering what he might be getting himself into when he only wanted to flirt.

The conversation luckily turned to other matters, and very pleasantly, too. When Etienne left after the suitable length of time for an afternoon call, he couldn't remember what topics they had discussed, just that it had been delightful.

When he returned to *Stoat*, Etienne took extra care in shaving and combing his hair. He got his servant to press and remove any stains or marks that had accumulated in the past few nights of being entertained at dinner with splendid cuisine with the appropriate sauces and too much hard liquor. Then he gave orders to allow most of his crew to go ashore, with firm warnings about what the fate would be of anyone who was late returning. Since he had galleys on his mind, he declared that the Swedes would condemn anyone who was not on board by dawn to the galleys. After that, it was time to set off for the British embassy again.

It turned out that the dinner would be a small, family affair, with the other guests arriving later, shortly after the dining room cloth was drawn. Etienne was the only person at the table who was not a member of the Harvey family: Miss Harvey's mother and father, her brother Anthony, and her younger sister Rebecca completed the party. They were all very interested in Etienne's story: how his parents had fled France, one step in front of the guillotine, how they had been taken in by a cousin who had a modest estate in Buckinghamshire, and how his cousin had secured a berth for Etienne as a midshipman, and, finally, how his career had developed after that.

Etienne, in turn, learned a great deal about the Harvey family and what it was like to be an ambassador in a not-very-important country. Sir Bromley's family estate was in Hertfordshire, a very modest one. He had been a minor official at the foreign office when the post of ambassador to Sweden became vacant. He had applied for the job and was accepted. Though not stated explicitly, the attraction of the posting was the stipend and allowance for expenses that accompanied the position rather than any strong desire to see Sweden.

The summers in Sweden, Lady Harvey informed Etienne, were endurable, but the winters were dreadful. Anthony Harvey was only home for a break after he graduated from Oxford before going to the Inns of Court to become a barrister. The two girls complained that the young Swedish men were very boring and did not speak much English.

The conversation then returned to Etienne. He found that he enjoyed talking about his adventures. This opportunity was the first time that anyone had been interested in his own story. He tried to seem modest even though he knew he was boasting about his successes. His boasting was constrained by Giles' unambiguous orders that their involvement in nipping the Scottish rebellion in the bud, including the adventures that he and Daniel Stewert had earlier in the year, were not to be mentioned. Even so, he somehow worked into the conversation that he had been very fortunate in the matter of prize money.

When the ladies had left the dining room and the cloth had been drawn, Etienne took the chair nearest to Sir Bromley. The ambassador did not beat about the bush: "You seem, Captain Macreau, to be a serious fellow. It would be best if you weren't under any illusions about Harriet's situation. She already has had her heart strained, if not broken, by apparent suitors who had presumed that she would have a large dowery. I know she is attracted to you, but I don't want you to lead her on, expecting that she will be the source of a handsome bit of money."

Etienne was stunned and speechless by this statement. He did find Miss Harvey attractive, but this was only the second time he had seen her; he didn't even know her first name. He certainly had not considered wooing her, but he didn't want to offend his host, so he would have to be careful. "Sir Bromley, I appreciate your informing me about Miss Bromley's dowery. I have only just met her, and she strikes me as a most attractive young lady. If we become more serious about each other, I shall, of course, call on you first. I can say now that I do not need a dowry to be able to marry. I have been fortunate in the matter of prize money, and I don't have any expensive habits like gambling. As a commander, I am now well paid, and even if I lose my command for some reason, I will still have an adequate pension. I also have every expectation that I will be posted to the rank of Captain quite soon if this war lasts. My family, I am afraid, is without interest, but I know that Captain Giles tends to use his very substantial influence to benefit people whom he thinks are deserving rather than ones who can help him. But as I said, I am not about to ask for Miss Harvey's hand now."

"I appreciate your frankness, Captain Macreau," responded Sir Bromley. "I confess that I only asked at my wife's urging; she is apprehensive that Harriet, my older daughter, is susceptible to having her heart broken, partly because she does not like living in Stockholm at all."

With that, the two men drank the last of their port and went to see how the preparations for the soirée were proceeding. It turned out that everything was ready for the guests who started to arrive. Harriet explained to Etienne that the small English community of gentlefolk met once a month at the British embassy for an evening among fellow countrymen, exchanging news from home and tips on how to survive in Stockholm. They also had some music to show off the young ladies' talents and to allow some dancing. She made it clear that dancing was her favorite part of the evenings.

Sir Bromley's encouragement induced Etienne to participate fully in the dancing. Although Etienne was usually shy among strangers, the ambassador's remarks made him search out Harriet Harvey and start asking her about life in Sweden. It turned out that what she really was interested in was returning to London and questioning Etienne about life in the capital. Somehow, the conversation turned from the fact that Etienne had spent little time in London to where he had lived in England and how he had come to live there when he was born in France to French parents. Harriet persuaded him to sing 'Au clair de la lune' for the group while she accompanied him on the piano. When the playing of music led to dancing among the younger members of the group, Etienne danced with Harriet Harvey more than with any of the other young ladies.

When the soirée broke up, Etienne walked back to *Stoat* with his brain working overtime. What a marvelous woman was Harriet Harvey! How he would like to see more of her! Had the time arrived when he could seriously contemplate marriage? As he had told Sir Bromley, his salary would be more than adequate to support a wife, even on half pay, and he had a sizable nest egg built up from prize money. Marriage now was not just a possible action; his thoughts were not focused on a particular woman.

Etienne's problem now was that he was about to leave Stockholm. Were *Glaucus* and *Stoat* likely to return to the Swedish capital? If not, how could he continue to woo Harriet? And yes, he realized, he did want to woo her. Nevertheless, despite the problem of how to see her again, Etienne continued to think about Harriet Harvey as he settled into his bed on *Stoat*. He really must find some way to see more of her.

In the interim, Etienne could write to Harriet. Would she write back? If she did, how long would it take him to get the letter if he was at sea? He was sure that when he fell asleep at last, he would dream of her all night. But, in fact, he did not.

XVII

Daphne found that she much preferred Dipton to London, even though she was much busier with routine chores in her country home. In town, while lectures, concerts, and the theatre kept her occupied, she spent a lot of time alone or with visits to and from other ladies, most of whom shared few real interests with Daphne. At Dipton, she had the children and all the activities on the estate in which she was pleasantly involved. Then there was the need to visit and talk with the local farmers, and if she wanted gossip, her friend Elsie, though only a publican's wife and her former lady's maid, was far more knowledgable about gossip concerning people whom Daphne knew than was usually true of the gossip in town.

Returning to her country estate always meant that Daphne had to catch up with many tasks. Her first concern was with the children. They were all happy and excited to see her; they also demanded her attention, including the youngest child. When Nanny Weaver came to announce that playtime was over, the two oldest children, her niece and nephew, Mary and Hugh, wanted desperately to take Daphne to the stables to see the progress that they had made in riding during the time she had been away. It took another hour to satisfy the children, and even then, it was only ended by the appearance of one of the footmen sent by Nanny Weaver to summon the children to their dinner.

As she walked back to the mansion with the children, Daphne realized that they changed a bit every time she was away, getting more interesting as they did so. They had both developed a great deal since they came to Dipton. She realized that she didn't want to miss too much of their development or that of her own children, who, she confessed to herself, were also becoming much more interesting than they had been as babies. Now, they were developing distinct personalities which were evolving steadily.

When they reached the Hall and the children went off to the nursery for their evening meal, Daphne decided to see if, before dinner was announced, she could make a beginning of the paperwork that always awaited her after she had been away from Dipton. On the top of the pile of mail that Steves had placed on her desk was a letter that must have been delivered just that morning before she arrived at Dipton Hall. It was from a Mrs. G. Matthews of some address that seemed familiar to her. She thought that the address must be in St. James or maybe Bloomsbury, even though the two were quite far from each other.

The letter was a begging and blackmail request. Mrs. Matthews claimed to have a long-term, ongoing relationship with Captain Horace Bolton of the Royal Navy, the husband of Daphne's husband's half-niece. Mrs. Matthews had been a successful milliner, she claimed, but Captain Bolton had been supporting her financially to add to her income, even when he was at sea. He had increased the amount provided to this Mrs. Matthews when she became pregnant with his baby and was no longer able to serve in the millinery shop, but he had recently stopped giving her money. Her position was now especially precarious because she had recently given birth to a baby and had no money to feed and clothe either the baby or herself. She could not return with the baby to the milliner's shop, so with Captain Bolton removing her support, she could not survive in her present situation. If she sought help elsewhere, Mrs. Matthews claimed, she would undoubtedly have to reveal the name of the father, and it would, she was sure, become widely known that the nephew-in-law of Captain Giles, Marquess of Dipton, had sired a child whom

Giles's relative refused to support. Since the baby was a member of Giles's family, even though it was conceived on the wrong side of the blanket, it was up to Giles to provide support so that the child could be brought up by its mother in a style befitting a relative of such an important nobleman. Mrs. Matthews stated that £250 in consols* would be the minimum needed for her to bring up the baby boy in dignity.

Daphne was horrified by what the letter implied about Captain Bolton's behavior and what it suggested, implicitly, about Catherine's marriage. Her first inclination was to tear up the letter and pay no attention to it, but reflection made her consider more deeply what the appropriate response should be.

The person with whom Daphne knew she should discuss the letter was Catherine Bolton. It was Catherine's husband who was alleged to have fathered the baby, and that relationship was the only reason that this 'Mrs.' Matthews thought she could extort some money from Giles. The timing of the letter's arrival was unfortunate because Daphne really should have raised the subject of Catherine's behavior before the letter arrived since her husband's shortcomings were likely also to be the subject of gossip and could not be ignored.

Daphne did not look forward to either conversation. Couldn't she just ignore the infidelities in the Bolton's marriage, leaving it for Giles to deal with the resulting problems when he returned? Daphne shook her head. No, she could not. The mess should be dealt with now before the situation becomes worse. At that point in Daphne's ruminations, the gong rang to tell those who were dining that it was time to get ready for dinner.

Only the two women were at the dining table, but they couldn't talk about the things that were on their minds until the servants had withdrawn. Daphne felt that she talked nonstop about unimportant matters while Catherine sat in troubled silence. Only when the cloth had been drawn, the servants had left, and the ladies settled in to enjoy their port did Daphne open the conversation that she had been dreading. "Giles received a letter from a Mrs. Matthews in London today. She claims that she knows your husband."

"Oh, I don't know any Mrs. Matthews. What was it about?"

"Mrs. Matthews wrote to Giles saying that she has borne your husband's child. She claims that he had been supporting her financially but has now stopped making the payments. She is asking Giles for the ridiculous sum of £250 in consols, which, of course, would provide that sum forever so that she can raise the child. Do you know anything about this, Catherine?"

"Not really," Catherine replied rather gloomily. "I know that my husband has not been faithful. He has also been unable to sire a child with me or even attempt it. I also know he has gone with other women with whom he has had intimate relationships. He boasted about how it was my fault that he couldn't succeed with me because he did very well with women who knew what they were about to get him ready to perform his duty. When I asked him to show me what he wanted, he claimed that my mother should have told me. Anyway, women were supposed to know what to do without instructions. It was up to me to find out how to act in bed. Of course, I asked my mother, but she refused to talk about such a difficult subject. She said that what Bolton suggested was nonsense, and the man always knew what was necessary. But I had no idea what he or she was talking about. It was so unfair. I have been terribly miserable!"

By this point, Catherine was sobbing in between series of words. Daphne came around the corner of the table to hold her and give comfort, but she wasn't prepared to end the discussion. It would be better, she thought, to get it all out at once rather than to wait for another time to pry further into these unpleasant matters.

"How awful for you! Of course, you are not supposed to know anything about the marriage bed until you are married. It is up to your husband to know what to do and show you. And it was up to your mother to tell you what to expect. It sounds as if neither of them did their duty, but that's not your fault. I was lucky that Giles knew all about what was involved and was very patient with me."

"No, neither of them did what you suggested," Catherine said between sobs, "and Bolton never cared to discover what was needed. I know he went to prostitutes who must have never shown him what a woman needs but were very proficient at getting a man ready. Anyway, though it is hard to believe, he never ... ugh ... entered me, and I only found out recently what is involved. He thought that having one of those gentlemen's paintings might get him ready to 'do his duty.' That's what he called it. That's why I posed for one. I had, of course, seen nude pictures before, or semi-nude ones, through my interest in art, but I had no idea at that time how they affected men."

"So that's why you sat for that picture. I happened to see it at the artist's studio but thought I shouldn't mention it to you."

"I would have been terribly embarrassed about it then if you had. Now, it doesn't matter anymore."

"Oh? Why not?" Daphne wondered.

"Because much worse things have happened. No, sitting for that painting doesn't count among the things I haven't been able to talk about, and that may come out now. While Bolton said that the picture got him ready, its effect disappeared as soon as he came into the bedroom, and he blamed me for that, too. Why, I don't know. That was the last time he came to me at night. And he doesn't come to Hillcrest Grange, either. Indeed, he told me that he wanted nothing to do with the Dipton area anymore, and he wasn't going to pay for the rent or the servants either. I don't know what to do. Bolton gives me a pittance. I was in London just now to see his agent in person and to look for any way I could find employment in the art world. I do know quite a lot about art, and Bolton did teach me some more until everything went wrong, and he started drinking and gambling at his club and, I suppose, visiting women of no virtue."

With that, Catherine dissolved into wrenching tears, indicating all too clearly that her husband had ruthlessly broken her heart. Daphne let her cry for several minutes before taking steps to stop their discussion for the evening.

"I did know that Bolton was behind in the rent on Hillcrest Grange," Daphne remarked, "but I had no idea that it represented anything more than poor instructions to his agent. I am appalled by what you are telling me. Still, I can assure you that Giles and I are not going to let you sink into penury or even financial difficulty just because the husband we thought was perfect for you turned out to be such a rotten, a rotten … well, you know what I mean.

"Now, it has been a very hard day for you, but Giles and I will help you make the best of this unfortunate situation. You look worn out. A good night's sleep should help to make things seem not quite so grim, and we can talk further and make plans tomorrow."

Catherine hurried from the room, and Daphne heard her clattering up the staircase, still weeping noisily. Daphne remained at the table for a long time after that. She poured herself another glass of the excellent port and sipped it as she tried to absorb all the new information that Catherine had given her. She had long prided herself on a very successful bit of match-making that had resulted in the wedding of her half-niece-in-law and Giles's good friend, the cultured and amusing Captain Bolton. How true it was that you didn't know what went on behind closed doors with married couples!

More to the point, what sort of help should she offer Catherine? Her niece certainly could stay at Hillcrest Grange as long as she wanted. Giles and Daphne didn't need the rent. But would Catherine truly wish to remain in the large residence that she had renovated so carefully in preparation for her marriage, which she had no reason to believe would become such a disaster? Catherine was welcome to live again at Dipton Hall, but wouldn't that seem to be a sad step backward? It was where she had lived before getting married. It would seem like a step backward, especially as her mother had since wed Major Stoner, left Dipton Hall, and seemed to be content with her husband while Catherine was retreating from an unhappy marriage.

Daphne suspected that after getting over all the ramifications of having a failed marriage, Catherine would like to be involved in the art world, and the best place for that would be London. Giles could easily buy her a house in Mayfair, Marylebone, or Bloomsbury. But then Daphne remembered Mrs. Marsdon's visit and warning about Catherine's recent inappropriate behavior, which became a more likely problem after what Daphne had just learned and still threatened her niece's reputation and her acceptance into gentile society. Men could get away with such behavior without much effect on the rest of their lives, but that was not the case for women, at least not if they didn't have an acquiescing husband. That behavior was something that Daphne had to take up with Catherine in the immediate future.

Daphne drained the last of her port. She wouldn't have another glass. She would go up to the bedroom she shared with Giles, where she always wrote her end-of-the-day letters to her husband. This letter wouldn't be easy. Captain Bolton was a good friend of Giles. Giles had been instrumental not only in getting Captain Bolton his command but also, more importantly, in introducing him to Catherine and facilitating their marriage. However, Daphne wasn't about to hide unpleasant matters from him, and telling him all about the situation would help her to focus her thoughts even though she could not expect a reply to her letter within a helpful amount of time.

Catherine did not appear until quite late the following morning. Daphne hoped that it meant that her niece had had a solid night's sleep now that some sort of solution to her problems was imminent. Daphne had no problem occupying her time until Catherine appeared with visits to the children and dealing with the correspondence and reports that had piled up in her absence in London. When Catherine poked her nose into the morning room to see if her hostess was busy, Daphne was quite happy to put aside the paper she had been examining to converse with her niece.

"Good morning," Daphne said as she greeted her visitor. "I trust you slept well."

"Better than I have for a long time. It was so good to be able to unburden myself to someone else. Now, I hope that you can tell Steeves to arrange for the carriage to take me to Hillcrest Grange."

"If you want to. You are, of course, very welcome to stay here."

"Thank you, but I have to start clearing our belongings out of Hillcrest Grange now that Bolton isn't paying the rent anymore to Giles."

"Don't worry about that. We don't need the money, and I am afraid that having to go through the house that you renovated so carefully and with such high expectations of its being your happy home with an adoring husband will be horribly painful for you now that that has fallen apart. You are always welcome to stay here for as long as you like, even forever, and I can help you plan on how best to go forward."

"I don't think you will want me here when I tell you the other awful news I have."

"I can't think of anything that awful, so you had better tell me and get it off your chest."

"I think I am in the family way."

"You are *what*?" Daphne exclaimed.

"I'm with child."

"Oh! And Bolton is not the father?"

"Yes, he is not. And he will know for sure because we have never been intimate in the way that produces babies. Anyway, he had already been at sea for two months when I … I … I got pregnant."

Daphne was horrified, but she tried not to express her feelings. Instead, she replied, "I see. That is not good news! Do you want to keep the child?"

"Yes, I do. I'd like to be a mother. I just don't think that Bolton would be much of a father. Not now that I have learned so much more about him and his weaknesses."

"Well. As I understand it, the law presumes that he is the father even when he isn't, and he can even take the baby away from you if he wants to and prevent you from seeing the child.."

"Oh, no. Surely he can't."

"Yes, he can, *that* I do know. I don't know if there is any chance of you getting divorced. It is almost impossible to obtain a divorce, even if your husband agrees. One way, I have heard, is to demonstrate that the woman has never been with a man, but that can't be done in your case."

"No. But it's not Bolton's child. Why should he have control of it?"

"I don't know. That is just the way the law is. Once we women are married, we have precious little say in anything unless our husbands want us to. How in the world did you allow yourself to get into this pickle?" Daphne asked.

"I had been exploring my interest in painting when I was in London," Catherine replied. "Seeing pictures, of course, but also seeking out artists in their studios to get ideas on how to improve my paintings. They were all very friendly when they realized that I was truly interested and wanted to learn, not just dabble but produce innovative works of art. I have a very good eye for art and made some suggestions about their work that some of the artists found to be helpful. A surprising number of them knew of successful female artists and encouraged me. Especially one man who is called Alexander, although his friends always call him Alex.

"Alex specializes in paintings with nude or, usually, very scantily clad women. You know, paintings like those classical ones where everything looks at first glance to be very improper, but on examination, nothing very private is actually being shown. When I mentioned how Bolton had stopped giving me enough money, he suggested that I pose for him. He would change or hide my face so no one but he and I would know that I was the model. He would pay me his standard model fee when he sold the picture.

"Well, I was flattered. No one had ever told me that I had a beautiful body. I am afraid that I had not thought out the implications of a suggestive painting that would be exhibited. I wouldn't be recognizable, but the art world is very gossipy, and if anyone were curious, it would be easy to find out who was serving as the model. I posed for Alex. I got quite excited while doing it, especially as Alex sometimes came over to rearrange my arms or make sure that the cloth draperies hid what they had to but still clearly suggested what lay behind."

"Surely that was not the end of it," Daphne asked in a puzzled voice.

"No. Of course not. That painting sold very quickly and over asking price, so he wanted to paint another one of me. This one was still perfectly decent – they all were – but this was more daring and more demanding of me as a model. As a result, he had to spend more time getting me in just the right pose. I got very excited as he did so, and I am sure he noticed, but he did nothing except praise my beauty, which excited me still more.

"Bolton never did anything like what Alex was doing to get me excited, and, frankly, I was enjoying it. Not just having a man paying attention to me but also him touching me illicitly. Wasn't this what Bolton was supposed to be doing to me? It felt delicious. I was certainly missing something in my marriage!"

"I think I can understand how you might enjoy that attention," said Daphne, though rather disapprovingly, "but was that the only time?"

"No. I knew I shouldn't have, but I felt so valued when he said I was beautiful, with fervor in his eyes, and with the extreme pleasure we enjoyed when he finally took me fully. Of course, I knew it was wrong, but in those moments, I did not care."

"So, what happened then? It is not still ongoing, is it?" Daphne asked.

"No. Alex suddenly lost interest in me. It was because he took up with another woman. I went to his house one day when he wasn't expecting me. His housekeeper wasn't around, so I went up to his studio and straight in. He had another model on his couch, but he wasn't painting her. He was … he was… he was having his way with her. Well, not that. She was being very active, too. I watched them, fascinated for several minutes. I had never seen anything like it … ever!

"After a few minutes, Alex noticed me. He became furious. I shouldn't have been there, and I was spying on them. I had to leave immediately. I turned around and rushed down the stairs and out the front door. I went back the next day, and he wasn't busy, but he made it clear that he was through with me. He would rather have a more experienced woman who knew how to please a man. I was mortified. I ran from the house and have never been back. He hasn't contacted me, not even to pay me my share of the last picture I posed for him. Even though he owes me money, I never went back there.

"I tried visiting another couple of artists and indicating that I was available to model in somewhat daring poses. They were eager and just as proficient as Alex, but for me, the satisfaction was mechanical. Not at all the same as with Alex. So, I stopped. But I don't know what to do."

"What do you mean?" Daphne broke in, having sat without comment as Catherine unburdened herself.

"I am in a loveless marriage to a man who pays no attention to me when he is in England. He would rather visit ladies of the night and waste his money on them or on gambling and on drink. He no longer gives me enough money to live on and isn't paying the rent on Hillcrest Grange, and the last time I was at the house, the servants complained that they hadn't been paid. I don't know what to do. To add to my troubles, I'm with child! I am going to have a baby! All because I have been so stupid."

"Well, you are not the first woman to yield to temptation when they were in an unsatisfactory marriage, nor will you be the last. It has happened. You now have to decide what to do about it."

"What can I do about it? I am trapped. Unless I die in childbirth, I am sure to be shunned by everyone."

"Not necessarily. I suppose there is no hope that Bolton will just presume that the child is his and be no more the wiser about it?"

"No. he has done nothing to produce a baby. I see no hope that he will not know that I have been unfaithful. I'm sure he will give me no support at all for the child. As you know, he has already left me on the brink of the poor house and is not paying the rent or the servants at Hillcrest Grange."

"Let's not worry about all that," Daphne replied. "Giles will make sure that you are taken care of financially. You are welcome to stay here as long as you want. I quite understand that you may not want to return to Hillcrest Grange.

"Now, let's talk about this baby. Do you want to keep the child after it is born?"

"Yes. I want a child, even though Bolton is such a poor husband, and I misjudged the child's true father so badly."

"Good. Then we won't have to try to hide that you are with child or have you give birth elsewhere, secretly. You do realize that the child will belong to Captain Bolton, even though he has had nothing to do with its creation."

"I hadn't thought about that. Could he take the child away from me?"

"I think so. Legally, at least. I don't see any reason why he should want to," Daphne replied.

"Spite! That would be the reason! Just spite. Bolton can be a very mean-minded man when his wishes are denied."

"Well, we'll cross that bridge when we come to it. Marquesses have a way of getting things done that they want.

"Now, I have neglected my own children long enough this morning. I'll send for Mr. Jackson to examine you to make sure everything is on a smooth track to deliver the baby. You will have to tell your mother before the baby's presence becomes very noticeable, you know."

Daphne spent a very satisfactory hour and a half with her children and then went with her brother's two offspring to see the stables. Mary insisted that Daphne pet her pony while Hugh wanted to demonstrate how he could leap into the saddle of his pony without using the stirrup, an accomplishment that Daphne felt she must praise enthusiastically even though she thought it was silly.

While the children were riding around the coral, the stable master, Mr. Griffiths, came over to chat with Daphne. Daphne also preferred it to having a formal meeting with the man. She was sure that she discovered much more when the stable master was not on his guard about revealing matters that were on his mind to which he had yet to make a firm decision. Standing in front of her desk seemed to rob him of any spontaneity or willingness to speculate about possibilities.

"My lady," Mr. Griffiths opened the conversation, "the children are progressing very rapidly on the ponies."

"They certainly are," Daphne agreed. "Have you thought more about our breeding children's ponies?"

No, I've been too busy with the hunters we are producing.

"How are the breeding mares doing?"

"Very well, generally, though I do have one problem."

"Yes?" Daphne would not be surprised if he were about to willingly make an important revelation that she would have to pry out of him otherwise.

"It's about Dolly, you know, one of our best breeding mares."

"Yes?"

"Well, she came into heat very late last fall, and that was missed by the stable boys, unfortunately, and of course by me."

"Well, don't blame yourself. You are very busy, and it is a condition that is easy for the stable boys to miss. What is the problem? Did she get pregnant by choosing her own cover?"

"Yes. So we don't know who the sire was. Knowing that usually raises the price of the foal that is born."

"But you can still get a good price for the pony, can't you?"

"Normally. Not, I am afraid, in this case. The most likely sire is Dark Paul."

Daphne laughed heartily. "Oh, that is marvelous! You are afraid that we can't, in good faith, sell a horse who may have inherited all of Dark Paul's most loveable properties? You are right, of course, but I think there is one possible way out of it, provided that the offspring looks to be a good horse otherwise."

"What is that."

"We stress to buyers that we are afraid he has inherited Dark Paul's more unpleasant properties. Stress that no one but Giles and one crazy stable boy can ride Dark Paul successfully. And me, of course, but that wasn't a real success, if you recall. There are a lot of well-heeled gentlemen who ride to hounds who are jealous of Giles for all sorts of reasons, one of which is his horsemanship. Being offered a horse that is like the one that only Giles can ride might well stir their competitive instincts to buy the colt just to show that they are as good as Giles."

"Oh, what a grand idea, Daphne! The very prospect of having such a challenge for some of our more disagreeable clients warms my heart.

"I would like to see you this afternoon to discuss a proposal I would like to present to you sometime soon," Mr. Griffiths continued

'Very good. Come at two o'clock."

"Yes, my lady."

Daphne turned back to watching the children riding their ponies. Did she really need to have so much of her time taken up managing Giles's properties? A steward could do it, not as well, perhaps, as she, but adequately. But she knew she wouldn't change. At least not until her coming baby was born. Then, she would think again about how she used her time.

Daphne returned to Dipton Hall just in time to catch Mr. Jackson leaving. Midwifery was high on the list of the apothecary's many talents.

"Have you seen Catherine, Mr. Jackson?" Daphne asked.

"Yes, I have just completed my examination. Both Mrs. Bolton and the baby are fine. She has an excellent frame for carrying and delivering babies. I don't expect any problems with the delivery if she stays active until the baby is ready to join us. You know the routine. Mrs. Bolton is as well-shaped to have babies as are you. She is about a month ahead of you. Do you have any problems?"

"No, not yet."

"She told me that the baby is illegitimate and that she intends to keep it. Is that going to be a problem?"

"I hope not. Bolton is bound to find out that the child is not his and could cause trouble. I hope he won't and that Giles can talk him out of it if he does."

"I hope so, too," Daphne responded. "If anyone can prevent him from taking the child, it is Giles, but hopefully, Bolton won't want to exercise his legal right to the child."

The rest of the day went uneventfully for Daphne. She gave Mr. Griffiths the go-ahead to start getting ponies for that extension of the business. At dinner, Catherine was far happier than she had been previously. She seemed to be convinced that, with Daphne and Giles on her side, there was no need to worry about the future. Daphne knew that her niece was far from being assured that there was smooth sailing ahead as Catherine tried to establish a respectable family. However, Daphne didn't feel that this was the time to bring up the likely difficulties that would remain even if

they could persuade Bolton to let her raise her child in peace. Instead, she waited
  until she retired for the night to express these worries. Then, she could tell Giles all about the developments of the day in her nightly letter to him. There was nothing he could do about them, of course, but just writing them down to share with him meant that they would be less likely to go through her mind all night. Indeed, she fell asleep immediately after snuffing her candle.

Chapter XVIII

On the morning following the soirée at the British Embassy, shortly after daybreak, Etienne was woken with the news that a Swedish Army Lieutenant had arrived with a pack and had asked for him. Etienne hurriedly pulled on his uniform and went on deck. There, he met a young man dressed in the uniform of a Swedish Army lieutenant who saluted him smartly.

"Lieutenant Adam Magnussen, reporting for duty, sir."

Etienne knew that naval lieutenants were considered to have the same status as army captains, so he outranked Lieutenant Magnussen. But he certainly would not pull rank on this officer until he found out what role the lieutenant was supposed to play. His response to the introduction was to say,

"Glad to have you aboard, Lieutenant. I am Commander Etienne Macreau. This is Mr. Hackney, my first lieutenant, and Mr. Phillips, my second. What are your orders?"

"I am to guide you to our base. You can meet our colonel there and join us in an expedition to put down some pirates in Finland."

"Don't we need a pilot?"

"No, sir. All officers of our force are qualified pilots for the Stockholm Archipelago. When we get to the base, Colonel Borg will welcome you to the fleet and discuss the possibilities."

"Very good. When can we leave? There is no wind now."

"That's why we have a galley fleet. In these waters, it is often too calm to sail."

"Well," said Etienne, "that seems to leave us stranded, doesn't it? We have no oars on *Stoat*."

"That's all right. I have arranged for rowboats from our military college to tow us out. It is not very far, and it is good for the cadets to experience serious rowing firsthand," Lieutenant Magnusson replied. "All our cadets have to do it, as I remember all too well from my days in our naval college."

"Then let's go," Etienne said enthusiastically. "When can you get the tow boats here?"

"They are standing by out there," said Lieutenant Magnussen, with a grin, pointing to four large rowing boats crewed by men in soldier's uniforms, "just waiting to be invited to start pulling. There are four boats which will take turns towing your ship, two at a time."

"Stand by to cast off," Etienne called out. "Bosun, prepare two tow ropes to pass to those boats waiting off our starboard bow. Mr. Wells," he addressed a midshipman, "prepare to pass the lines to the boats when instructed by Lieutenant Magnussen. Mr. Hackney, prepare to cast off."

A flurry of action broke out on *Stoat*'s main deck. Soon, all three officers reported that they were ready for the next step. Lieutenant Magnussen summoned the waiting row boats to approach. There was nothing subtle about how he gave his orders. He just went to the starboard rail and waved his arm in a come-hither gesture. Before long, the tow ropes were passed, *Stoat* cast off, and the row boats started to pull her away from her berth. There was no wind, and the current eased the rowers' task. Lieutenant

Magnussen gave directions to the helmsmen on *Stoat* to ease the job of the towboats.

They made steady progress away from Stockholm, with the tow boats trading places every half hour. Soon, Stockholm was hidden by a bend in the waterway. They then passed a string of islands, most of them inhabited. Prosperous-looking farms and healthy woodlands produced a placid scene, quite divorced from any military threat. The sky was a brilliant blue with puffy white clouds floating about them. There was not a breath of wind; if this was a typical summer day in these waters, Etienne could understand why galleys might be desirable. Sailing ships could not move in these conditions except by being towed when it was calm, and in the winding passages among islands, a ship relying on its sails would have great difficulty when the channels turned into whatever direction the wind was blowing. In either case, a galley could proceed easily. *Stoat* could only be moved along these channels by being towed by other craft on a day like this.

After a while, time dragged on boringly for those on *Stoat*. There was far less for the crew to do than if they had been under sail. When the watch changed at noon, and the master's mate was taking the noon sight, Etienne invited Lieutenant Magnussen to share a luncheon repast in his cabin. They got on famously, and their private talk made Etienne feel more comfortable about going on an expedition with a Swedish officer about whom he knew nothing. They sat long over their repast, exchanging information, at first about naval matters and then more personal ones. Lieutenant Magnussen was fascinated about how a French refugee boy of not very distinguished parentage had become a commander in the Royal Navy; Etienne was equally interested in how a Swedish youngster had picked up such a complete knowledge of English that he sounded to Etienne more like some pompous offspring of an English noble than a Swedish man with a thick Scandinavian accent.

They remained chatting until they were summoned on deck to see that after exiting one of the many channels between islands, a naval base had appeared. Indeed, there was an impressive group of naval vessels docked and anchored in front of them. In fact, at first glance, it seemed to Etienne that it looked like a fully equipped navy, though a small one, with craft ranging from small gigs to large frigates. Indeed, the fleet was also enhanced by some galleys equipped with substantial, forward-pointing cannons, much larger than the bow chasers on most of the British warships with which he was familiar. Only missing from the fleet were the large ships-of-the-line that were the pride of the naval anchorages with which he was familiar.

Further examination suggested to Etienne that the ships that appeared normal were very odd indeed. They were all equipped not only with gunports but had other openings for oars that, at first glance, were similar to gunports. That meant that they could perform well in any weather. The rowers towed *Stoat* to dock behind the largest of the galley-frigate. Lieutenant Magnussen indicated that it was the flagship of the Galley fleet. Lieutenant Magnussen had stated that it was the flagship of the Galley Fleet, commanded by Colonel Borg. Etienne and his first lieutenant studied the ship closely as they came nearer and nearer. How would the strange craft perform when used in battle, they wondered. As the towboats eased Stoat into her berth just behind the flagship

When *Stoat*'s mooring lines had been cleated to bolsters on the dock, Colonel Borg was the first to step on board. Even if he had not been introduced, Etienne would have been sure that this man was some sort of admiral by the confidence he exuded. Of course, he was not really an admiral. Probably, it was the equivalent of a brigadier or a colonel in the army. Colonel Borg spoke fluent English, though with a strong Swedish accent.

"Welcome to the Galley Fleet, Captain Macreau," Colonel Borg declared in a loud voice after introductions had been made. "I hope that you and your crew will enjoy visiting us here. You will find that our base, being on an island, makes it far harder for crew members to wander off unexpectedly. The island provides for all the wants of our soldiers or your sailors, provided that they have money, without disturbing more respectable citizens. I am sure that your crew will find a stay here enjoyable."

"But," said Etienne, "I understood that my brig, *Stoat*, would be joining you on a trip to Finish waters, chasing pirates."

"I am afraid that the people in Stockholm promised more than we can deliver, probably due to their thick-headedness about these waters. It is highly likely that your ship, excellent though she undoubtedly is in open waters, would be needlessly challenged here. We really can't tow her all through the archipelago, you must realize, and with only sails, you would likely spend your time becalmed or aground if you try to negotiate our channels under sail. No, what I suggest is that you, your first lieutenant, and your master accompany me on our next patrol over to the Finnish coast to try to keep the pirates at bay and hinder the Russians from encouraging the smugglers to bring contraband into our territory."

"That would be satisfactory for me, and I will take up your invitation enthusiastically," Etienne replied. "However, I think it would be wise to leave my other officers here. I have a rather inexperienced crew in terms of their knowledge of how to behave on land, and I would hate to return to find that your authorities found it necessary to throw them all in jail or to flog them, much as they might deserve it."

"I quite understand, though I think my officers would enjoy experiencing an outing with your men," replied the admiral. "However, all of your officers must come to dinner this evening, and then we will leave at dawn tomorrow."

The following day, Etienne was less enthusiastic about going on a voyage at the crack of dawn. The dinner in the wardroom of the galley-frigate had been a convivial affair with many toasts drunk in the Swedish version of vodka. Etienne had a more refined palate than most naval officers and a rather poor ability to absorb large amounts of raw spirit without getting a splitting headache the next day. Nevertheless, he forced himself to appear cheerful as he led his officers down the quay to where the galley-frigate, the flagship of the fleet that they were going to board, was moored. Etienne noticed that her name, as written in fancy capitals on her stern, was *JÄGARE*.

The flagship's first lieutenant, a man called Sven Mattsson, welcomed them aboard with the news that Colonel Borg had yet to appear that morning. While they waited, Mr. Mattsson showed Etienne and the others the vessel's features as they waited.

"What does *Jägere* mean?" Etienne asked their guide.

"Hunter," replied Mr. Mattsson. "I think it is a good name to describe what we do."

Colonel Borg had been among the most enthusiastic participants in the previous evening's proceedings, leaving no glass used to drink a toast with a single drop left when he put it down. Nevertheless, when he appeared, he seemed to be bursting with energy as he came aboard the ship.

"Captain Macreau, good to see you. Hope you slept well," Colonel Borg greeted Etienne. Without pausing to let Etienne answer, the officer ordered, "Mr. Mattsson, ready to cast off?"

"Excellent!" Colonel Borg continued without pausing to get an answer. "Let's get underway. It looks like a perfect day to go hunting pirates. Cast off, Mr. Mattsson."

A hive of activity broke out. Some of it involved taking in mooring lines, which Etienne found familiar. Some activities most definitely were not. No seaman went to the shrouds to climb aloft to loosen the sails. Instead, the crew members lined up in pairs to take long oars from where they were stowed down in the middle of the ship. Those on the landward side of the ship thrust them through the oar ports to push the ship away from the wharf before placing them in their thole pins while the men took their places on the rowing benches. Those on the other side simply put the oars, ready to row the ship when she was clear of the dock.

The sergeant in charge of the rowers transmitted the order to start to the corporal in charge, who called in a booming voice to start rowing. All the rowers bent forward at the same time, dipped their oars in the water, and started pulling on them in synchrony. The first stroke seemed to be the hardest, and the following ones became easier as the ship gained speed. A corporal beat the time on a small drum, just loudly enough that it could be heard over the noise of the oars working against their thole pins.

It was a perfect summer day: clear blue sky with only a few puffy, white clouds floating in it, a mild temperature, and absolutely not a breath of wind. The water ahead was so still that the shoreline was perfectly reflected in only a slightly darker tone. Their course took them through a series of islands well-spaced out, though there were rarely long straight stretches before they had to change course to clear another headland jutting out into the channel with no discernable pattern as to where the next obstructions might occur. 'Clearly,' Etienne thought, 'it would be challenging to navigate this route under sail. Indeed, it would be impossible.'

The rowers, there were thirty-two at a time, changed every hour, and there were three sets of them. The result was that the galley-frigate skimmed through the channels at a very rapid pace. Most of the islands were heavily treed, though even those featured places where the land was being cultivated. That was especially true on the large islands.

The galley-frigate came into a more open body of water as the afternoon started to change into the evening. *Jägure* turned to where a village hugged the shore. Soon, the ship docked at the main quay of the settlement. Once the mooring lines were secure, the officers from *Jägere* headed off for what Etienne figured must be the local pub, a low wooden building made of weathered wood, with a series of small windows down the side and a steep roof with generous overhangs. Inside was a large single room filled with long tables with wooden benches down both sides. It had no ceiling—instead, an intricate system of wooden beams held up the high-pitched roof. In the center of the room, a wood fire burned, with a large iron hood above it to capture the smoke and send it out of the building via a metal pipe through a hole in the roof. At the far end of the building, there was an open kitchen with a counter in front of it where the male and female servants went to transmit new orders and pick up finished ones.

Colonel Borg led his group straight to a long table in the middle of the room that was empty and took places close to its end near the fire but leaving the seats still closer to the blaze empty. The rest of the group took places beside and across from him while still leaving the seats across from their leader and closer to the fire empty.

Colonel Borg called to a waiter in a hearty voice. It was apparent what he had ordered since the serving people immediately came to the table with trays loaded with beer mugs. The beer was excellent. Etienne was pleasantly surprised, for his experience with brainwine had made him suspicious of Swedish drinks.

Etienne was about to ask Lieutenant Magnussen, who had joined the trip to serve as an interpreter for the English guest, about the unusual seating arrangement when a small party of men, seamen by their dress, entered and sat down in some of the spaces beside and across from Colonel Borg. The colonel called for a waiter. He must have ordered drinks for the newcomers because the waiter came back with glasses of what looked like brainwine.

A lively conversation broke out between the leader of the seamen and the colonel. Of course, Etienne could not understand a word of the rapid exchanges in Swedish. Lieutenant Magnussen lent over to Etienne to explain in a low voice that the newcomers had just returned from a trip to Finland, and Colonel Borg was asking them what they had seen over there. The newcomers said that they saw several well-known merchant ships, Lieutenant Magnussen told Etienne, but one or two of the others might be smugglers. They suspected another ship of being pirates, though it looked more like a small warship than was usual with pirates who usually wanted to masquerade as merchant ships.

The conversation that everyone was listening to took a turn to more general matters. Colonel Borg called for more liquor for his informants and ordered supper for his men. The management of the tavern must have been expecting the order, for almost at once, large bowls of a seafood stew arrived with an additional mug of beer. Etienne tasted his bowl very cautiously since he had had some nasty encounters with Swedish cuisine. However, the flavor was exquisite, the best he had encountered in Sweden so far: unpretentious but excellent cooking.

A couple of other parties of sailors sat down with Colonel Borg before his crew finished eating. The reports were similar, and so were the rewards to the informants. As for the group from *Jägure,* Etienne noted that none appeared to be intoxicated. They would all be alert in the morning, not suffering the effects of overindulgence. Though seemingly relaxed and happy-go-lucky, Colonel Borg was very serious about having his crew ready for whatever might arise the next morning.

Jägure wasted no time getting underway the next day. There was a bright, clear summer dawn with no wind. No time was wasted as the crew had their breakfasts and prepared to set off. They shoved away from the dock and started to row across the extensive span of water in an east southeast direction. Before long, a good wind from the south-southwest sprang up. The crew below was called on deck as pandemonium broke out. Some sailors sprang to the ratlines to release the square sails, and others raced to the fore-and-aft sails to unfurl them and haul on halyards and sheets to set them. Meanwhile, the rowers continued to propel *Jägure* forward until the sails were about to be sheeted home. Then, the rowers shipped their oars, stowed them, and slammed the oar ports shut.

Jägure proved to be very tender*. As Etienne observed, once the sails were set even in this light breeze, the galley frigate heeled well over. More wind, and they would have to start reefing, and Etienne suspected that their progress would not be what he was used to. *Stoat* was a very stiff ship, and *Glaucus* was even stiffer. *Jägure* could not spread anything like as much canvas relative to her size as either of the vessels that Etienne was familiar with, so she was losing a lot of speed in comparison with stiffer ships. Of course, he reflected, *Jägure* was tender primarily because she drew less water than the ships he knew. In shallow waters, it was preferable in all weathers to move forward rather than to be stuck on some sandbank.

Jägure made good speed across the open water as the wind strengthened somewhat. Soon, they could see the far shoreline, and its features became clearer as they approached. It looked very much the same as the coastline behind them: islands of various sizes with channels in between them, primarily wooded. As they neared the coast, its features became better defined, and more channels leading behind the foreshore could be distinguished.

When the waterline on the land they were approaching became clear, Colonel Borg ordered the Swedish flag to be lowered and a different one raised. Etienne was not familiar with the new one. It featured a raging, yellow, heraldic lion on its hind legs with a sword on a red field in one corner. The rest of the flag was a series of blue and white stripes.

"What is that flag?" Etienne asked Colonel Borg, who was far more approachable than most post-captains of the Royal Navy, let alone its admirals.

"It's the flag of the Dutchy of Finland. It's not really official, but it is used by Finnish ships whose captains don't much like us Swedes and by pirate ships pretending to be traders. Flying this flag does not have much effect on our activities, especially when we are using our oars, but when sailing, it may allow us to get closer before our target realizes who we are."

Jägure sailed on. As they neared the land, the wind dropped, and orders came to take in the sails and return to rowing. The galley frigate soon was close to land, probably a large island or headland. There was a channel that entered the broader stretch of water that *Jägure* was crossing. As the galley frigate rounded the headland, allowing them to see down the channel, they spotted a vessel that was becalmed a short distance ahead. She was sailing with the two large gaff-rigged sails and some jibs, a rig that seemed to be typical of these waters. She appeared to be heavily laden.

Colonel Borg let loose with a string of orders which had *Jägure* cleared for action while a group of soldiers took up muskets and cutlasses, clearly in preparation for boarding the ship. The becalmed ship obviously noted the preparations being made on *Jägure* to attack. She hauled down her flag, which had been hanging limp unrecognizably in the dead calm that prevailed. It turned out to be the same Finnish flag that *Jägure* was sailing under.

"Come along, Captain Macreau," called Colonel Borg as he was prepared to get into one of the ship's boats that had been trailing along behind *Jägure*. "Let's see what we have here."

Etienne joined the colonel in the boat, not even thinking of the incongruity of a Swedish colonel leading a routine boarding exercise accompanied by a commander of the Royal Navy. It was only the work of minutes to row across and board the target vessel. As Etienne followed Colonel Borg up the side of the merchant ship, the colonel was already introducing himself boisterously to the assembled officers of the merchantman. Etienne followed the colonel aboard, followed by Lieutenant Magnussen.

"The ship's captain has told Colonel Borg," Lieutenant Magnussen informed Etienne, "that he has a cargo of barrels of tar that he expects to sell for the British trade. Finland, you know, Captain Macreau, has a large trade in forest products with your country. The colonel has asked to see the bill of lading."

'Why would he want to see that? What else could the ship be carrying, and if he doubts it, why doesn't he search the hold?" Etienne asked.

"He is making sure that the ship is going to transship the tar at Stockholm. It is required for all exports from the Dutchy of Finland. With this record, that law will be enforced. If the ship does not proceed to Stockholm, she is liable to be seized next time she enters our waters for ignoring the requirement that everything must be transshipped in Sweden."

Colonel Borg had a lengthy conversation with the merchantman's captain before calling to his men and descending rapidly into the boat. His companions followed quickly, and the sailors pulled it rapidly towards *Jägure*. He surged up the boarding battens the minute the boat reached *Jägure* and started issuing orders. The galley frigate spun around and headed for more open water.

"What's going on?" Etienne demanded of lieutenant Magnussen.

"Colonel Borg learned that the ship we boarded had seen the other mysterious ship we had heard about last night going down the next channel out of the archipelago. It's an armed frigate sailing under the Finnish flag. She is almost certainly a pirate, and he wants to confront her as soon as possible.

Jägure spun around with the starboard oars pulling forward and the larboard ones pushing back. Then, the rowers all pulled together to get the galley moving rapidly so that *Jägure* could round the next headland as quickly as possible. As they neared the larger body of water, a breeze sprang up from the south, but *Jägure* continued on her course using oars. Soon, she rounded the headland on the south side of the inlet, and a sailing vessel came into sight.

The new ship was square-rigged, under sail, surging along, making the most of the wind. She was a two-masted brig with gun ports on both sides, somewhat smaller than *Stoat*. She was flying the Finnish flag, so her true nationality was not evident. Etienne had not noticed it, but *Jägure* had also returned to flying the Finnish flag, again somewhat disguising her Swedish adherence.

Colonel Borg gave an order in a loud voice. From the crew's response, Etienne knew that he must have ordered the ship cleared for action. Glancing at the opposing ship, it was evident to Etienne that her commander must have issued the same order.

Captain Borg gave another order, which was followed by the leading gun of *Jaguar*'s broadside firing a shot – presumably a ranging shot – at the other ship. A corresponding billow of smoke erupted from the other ship's side. Almost at once, there was a great crash near where Etienne was standing as the other ship's cannonball arrived, sending a vicious shower of slivers spreading far and wide. On the opposite ship, some damage had been done to the rigging so that one sail was flapping uncontrollably. Etienne could see sailors rushing to get the sail under control. At the same time, he could see that a new bundle of cloth was being hauled to the masthead. It broke open just as the Finnish flag started to be lowered. Rising in its place was the simple flag of the Russian Empire. Glancing aloft on *Jägure*, Etienne saw that Colonel Borg had ordered the equivalent change to fly the Swedish flag now.

Neither ship had fired under false colors, it could be argued, but it was also clear that each vessel had fired at an ally. At least, that was the interpretation that Colonel Borg could assume since the Russian ship immediately broke off the possible engagement by spinning into the wind, based on a helm order that was then accompanied by commands to come about*. At least, that was the interpretation that Etienne gave to what he could observe on the Russian ship.

Colonel Borg also gathered the same information. His string of orders had *Jägure* spin away from the encounter, and her oars pulled her in the opposite direction to the one that the Russian ship was taking. That the colonel was not happy was indicated by the outburst he made. Though Etienne could not understand a word, it was evident that Colonel Borg was swearing to high heaven about the turn of events. After a few minutes, he calmed down.

"Excuse me for my outburst, Commander Macreau," the Colonel said to Etienne. "I am afraid that I may have started a diplomatic incident that could lead to war. We must get back to our base as soon as possible, and you should take *Stoat* to meet with *Glaucus* without delay so you don't get embroiled in this mess."

Jägure continued to pull towards the opposite side of the waterway and her base. When the wind rose, she sailed, and when, towards nightfall, it dropped off, she resumed rowing. Dawn was breaking as she came in sight of the base. A young ensign came rushing along the quay and jumped aboard *Jägure* as soon as it was feasible. He had a message for Colonel Borg, who immediately transferred it to Etienne. The message contained a letter for Etienne from Giles. With a nod of permission or encouragement from the colonel, he opened the letter.

The message contained straightforward information. Giles had received his orders from the Admiralty. He was to proceed to St. Petersburg as quickly as possible. He wanted *Stoat* to join him at Karlskrona without returning to Stockholm. Etienne showed the letter to Colonel Borg.

"We'd better get you on your way without delay, Captain Macreau," declared the chief of the Galley Fleet. It has been a delight to have you with us."

"The pleasure has been all mine, Colonel," Etienne replied. "I have learned a great deal on my short visit to your fleet, material I could not have learned otherwise. Thank you very much. But as you see, I agree that I must get away as soon as there is a wind to allow *Stoat* to move."

"Oh, we can do better than that. I am sure. We towed you here from Stockholm, and we will tow you south among the islands until you find wind. Don't protest. It is the best way to have you obey your orders and for us to cement our friendship. I'll just give the orders to have the towing boats manned and ready. You go and tell your subordinates to prepare for the tow. Then I think you will have to return, and we can have a proper breakfast to bid you farewell."

Etienne did as Colonel Borg suggested. The breakfast included the many friends he had made on *Jägure* and featured a variety of the Swedish dishes that Etienne, to his surprise, continued to find excellent. The Swedes certainly did not cook in the French fashion, but Etienne almost felt that their cooking was just as good. The meal was washed down with beer, which he had learned already was excellent. Then, unfortunately, some farewell toasts needed to be drunk. The toasts were made in the abominable brainwine, and Etienne had had to respond in kind, draining a matching glass of the liquor every time. When this ceremony ended, and final farewells had been spoken, Etienne found that he was not quite able to walk a straight line as he made his way to *Stoat,* which was, luckily, moored immediately ahead of *Jägure*.

Etienne's only regret about his need to leave precipitously was that he would have no chance to see Miss Harvey, which he had hoped would be possible before leaving the Stockholm area. This hope was now out of the question. However, he could write to her about his thoughts and actions, and maybe she would reply. He had never been much of a correspondent. However, he remembered that Lady Dipton had confided in him that Giles had won her heart as much by his letters sent from his ship when she was simple Miss Moorhouse as any other way, and Giles's only title at the time was "Sir," which he had earned by means of which she then knew nothing. After all, Etienne was now a commander and had the right to call himself a "Count," even though his title was a French one. He knew how to write, so there was no reason for him not to write letters to Miss Harvey. If Etienne was careful not to indicate that he was contemplating marriage, he could keep his options open. After all, he looked forward to seeing St Petersburg. Stockholm and Sweden had proved to be much more interesting than he had expected. Maybe St. Petersburg would be even better. It was, after all, a much more important and exotic capital and one that he had never visited. Broadening his horizons before committing himself to one woman made a lot of sense!

Chapter XIX

Daphne and Catherine returned to London after only two weeks at Dipton. During that period, Catherine's pregnancy became ever more evident. They had held lengthy discussions about where Catherine would live after her baby was born, and she was ready to live on her own with her child. Hillcrest Grange was clearly out of the question. Not only did Catherine not want to live there, but the lease was in the name of her husband, so there was no immediate way to block him from entering the house. Dipton Hall's nursery would be full up when Daphne's baby arrived. While that could be accommodated in various ways, there was another reason not to have Catherine remain at Daphne's residence. Lady Clara, Giles's mother and Catherine's step-grandmother did not like Catherine, and the feeling was mutual. They would prefer to live under different roofs. Catherine would most like to live in London, where she could best develop her hopes of being a successful artist and where there were far more people with similar interests to hers than anywhere else in the country. The solution to their problem of what would be best for Catherine was to buy a house in London in which she would live but which would be owned by Giles. Captain Bolton could not visit his wife there legally, and a burly footman or butler would guarantee that he could not harass her at home.

The next issue was where the house should be in London. Catherine felt that there were very few artists in Mayfair, the area Daphne had favored as being close to Camshire House. Catherine's favorite place to start looking was Bloomsbury, where some of the artistic friends she had already made in London lived and had their studios.

Having decided on a course of action, Daphne saw no point in delaying the implementation of their plan. They left on the following Monday for their return journey to London. The first thing Daphne did on her first morning in Camshire House was to visit Mr. Snodgras's chambers in Chancery Lane. She could, of course, have summoned him to come to Camshire House, but it was more convenient to go to his chambers, where he kept the records of everything he undertook on Giles's behalf.

Mr. Snodgrass was already at work, and Daphne was ushered into his room without delay.

"What can I do for you today, Lady Dipton," the agent asked after the usual pleasantries had been exchanged.

"My niece by marriage, Mrs. Bolton, is with child. She will have the delivery at Dipton, but then she wants a townhouse in town where she can explore a career in painting."

"With Captain Bolton, my lady."

"Definitely not. That marriage has not been a success."

"I am sorry to hear it. You do realize that Captain Bolton has the right to live with his wife if she owns or rents a house, for legally, it is his."

"Does he? Even if she is staying as a guest in someone else's house? A relative who could probably ruin his naval career?"

"Ah, yes. I see what you are planning. In that case, Captain Bolton's rights over her would be greatly curtailed."

"Mr. Snodgras," Daphne asked, "Do you know of any suitable row houses that are available? We believe that Bloomsbury is the place to start looking. "

"Not really. I don't usually keep track of real estate in the city. I do have a colleague who specializes in it. He charges a fee only if a successful transaction happens, and then it is paid by the seller."

"Ask him to come to Camshire House tomorrow at nine, prepared to show us houses. I think it is better to consider ones that are for sale rather than for lease, at least to begin with. We want to make sure that Catherine's name appears on nothing to do with her house and that she has to deal only with us concerning any problems with it."

"I'll have to think about it some more, but that seems to be the best way that you can guarantee that Captain Bolton can't interfere with his estranged wife."

On her way back to Camshire House from the Lawyer's office, Daphne realized that she had never seen Bloomsbury in the daylight and wasn't even sure if she had ever been there for a ball or lecture. Indeed, she was not really sure exactly where it was. It might be a good idea if she did some exploring with Catherine that afternoon before the agent came to show them available properties.

Catherine was delighted with Daphne's suggestion that they go exploring in the carriage. Some tea and jam tarts rapidly filled any pangs of hunger they might be experiencing. There was, however, one problem. Daphne and Giles had yet to hire a coachman for their London home. They had been relying on their coachmen from Dipton and Giles's knowledge of Westminster to take them to the right place when a carriage was needed. Luckily, it turned out that one of the footmen that they had recently hired had parents living on the other side of Bloomsbury, and he was quite familiar with the area. Off they set, with

Daphne and Catherine inside the carriage and the footman on the bench with the coachmen. However, they had not gone far before Daphne realized that this was a stupid way to ride when they intended to see what various neighborhoods looked like.

Daphne stopped the carriage, and she and Catherine took places on the driver's bench while the footman was relegated to his proper place, standing on the step at the back of the carriage. Now, the ladies could see comfortably, and since it was a lovely clear summer day, they could enjoy their exploration far more than if they were confined to the dark interior of their vehicle. They headed north out of Camshire Square and soon reached Oxford Street, where they turned right. They proceeded through St. Giles to Bloomsbury. Now Catherine said that she would like to start at Bloomsbury Square and work outwards, going in expanding circles as they explored the neighborhood. The streets were lined with row houses, well kept up, any one of which would be suitable as her home and also near her friend Helen's address.

"These houses all look eminently worthwhile for our purpose from the outside," commented Daphne. As far as housing goes, they are at least as good as anything in Mayfair. Do you want to explore other areas, or do these houses suit you if some of them are available?"

"Any of these places would suit me," Catherine replied enthusiastically. "I would like one where the attic can be turned into a studio with skylights to illuminate it. I can't tell from the street how many have such a feature, if any. Do you suppose it could be added if a house only had a standard sort of attic?"

"Well," said Daphne, "tomorrow, we can find out what is available and what alterations are possible for any that attract you. Now, I don't think either of us has been to the British Museum, which, I believe, is near here.

"Do you know where it is?" she called back to the footman on the step.

"Yes, my lady," came the answer. His instructions to the coachman were clear. In minutes, the carriage drew up in front of the imposing building.

There was a large number of people at the entrance to the museum, some coming, some going, and some just enjoying the summer day while talking with friends. All turned to stare at the carriage, whose importance was indicated by the crest on the door. Even more interesting were the two very well-dressed ladies who were sitting with the driver on the bench. When the footman on the step jumped off as soon as the vehicle stopped and went not to open the carriage door but instead to help the two ladies alight from the bench, a murmur arose as everyone commented on the unusual sight of the ladies sitting on the bench while leaving the inside of the carriage vacant. Some of the watchers recognized Daphne from caricatures that had appeared in newspapers and periodicals that kept the curious informed of the doings of members of fashionable society. A few others could read the coat of arms and realized it fit the description of the one recently awarded to the Marquess of Dipton. One of the women must be the celebrated Lady Daphne Giles, Marchioness of Dipton. How like her to sit where the view was best rather than inside as the usual decorum dictated.

Some of the spectators cheered, and the lady in question responded by waving gayly at the crowd while companion seemed to shrink from the attention. Lady Dipton took the other lady's hand, tucked it under her arm, and set off for the museum entrance, followed by a third woman dressed as a lady's maid.

Daphne was astounded by what she found inside the museum. She had no idea that so many fascinating things existed all under one roof. Catherine was equally thrilled, but poor Betsey had to trail along behind the other two, utterly uninterested in the old, often damaged objects on display. When they were finally urged politely to leave so that the museum officials could close the building, their carriage was still waiting at the curb. Apparently, no one had dared to tell the Marchioness's driver to move on.

The following morning, the estate agent, a Mr. Innis, arrived promptly at nine o'clock. Daphne wasted no time, "Mr. Innis, we have narrowed down the area of our initial search to Bloomsbury. A row house. What do you have?"

"I have several fine properties of that sort with quite reasonable rents, my lady," replied Mr. Innis. "For some of the houses, I am the owner's representative, and for others, I can show the property, but you would have to deal with someone else, the landlord or his agent if you are interested.

"Good, Mr. Innis," replied Daphne. "However, we want fee-simple, not rental. It is for my niece, and we don't want any complications that landlords can make in adjusting the inside of the dwelling to suit her needs.

"I see. This preference is very unusual for row housing, my lady. Most of the vacancies are rentals, and when houses come up as fee-simple, it is usually one landlord who wants to sell the place to someone who intends to be the landlord with the existing tenants. Let me see what I have that would fit your desires."

Mr. Innis took out a notebook and flipped its many pages, searching for some particular types of entries. After several moments, he looked up. "I only have one such property available in Bloomsbury, my lady. Unfortunately, it is a rather wretched one."

"Why is that?"

"The previous tenant stopped paying the rent for the house and pretty well trashed the inside of the place. He was using it as some sort of an opium den, unknown to the landlord, and in the process badly scarred the walls and floors. The owner isn't prepared to undertake the repairs needed, figuring that he could never turn a profit on the place after paying to restore it to a proper state, for the rent he could charge would not be enough to want to continue with the nuisance of dealing with possibly difficult tenants which might be the only ones he could attract. So far, no one whom he would accept has been prepared to pay his price for a house that has a poor reputation.

Well, I know a builder who can probably set the house in order before my niece needs it. Let's have a look at the place. Richards, tell the coachman to bring the carriage to the front door.

They all piled into the carriage, with Betsey having to share the bench with the coachman. Before long, they turned into a street that Catherine recognized as being only one street away from the one on which her friend Helen lived. Halfway up the block, the carriage pulled up in front of a house. Daphne was the first one out of the carriage, and she noticed that the lace curtains on several houses twitched as curious neighbors tried to hide their interest. Perhaps it had not been such a good idea to drive up in the carriage with her coat of arms on it, but it couldn't be helped now. It was not unknown, after all, for some aristocrats to be landlords in London.

The house in question revealed a lack of maintenance in the form of peeling paint on the woodwork and ironwork and the need for tuck-pointing in the brickwork. Inside, the lack of proper upkeep was again evident, but there was no smell of rot or vermin. Daphne had told Catherine not to make any comments in the presence of the property agent, and they proceeded to examine the house from top to bottom. They even went into the garden at the back and examined the privy and the mews, which had room for a carriage and several horses with living quarters above.

When they had completed their inspection, Daphne suggested that Mr. Innis step outside while she conferred with Catherine and Mr. Snodgravel.

"What do you think of the place, Catherine?" asked Daphne.

"It's in terrible condition, of course, but I think the layout is perfect. But isn't it a bit large for just me?"

"Well, it won't be just you, of course. You will have your child, and that involves a nanny and a nursery maid to look after the child. And you will need a butler and a footman and a housekeeper and a cook and so on. They will certainly fill up the rooms on the third floor. And with your bedroom and the nursery, the second floor will be well used. Public or day rooms on the first floor and the kitchen in the basement should pretty well fill the place. Admittedly, you could do almost as well in a twenty-four-foot house as in this thirty-footer, but one of those is not available in Bloomsbury right now. We could, of course, see what is available in other parts of town, but I would guess that we won't find one that is as good at the price that we can likely get this one for. The question really is, do you like it?

"Yes, it would be perfect, especially if you can put a north-facing skylight in the fourth-floor ceiling."

"I'm sure that we can do that. Mr. Snodgravel, what do you think?"

"If you can get the property at a reasonable price, I think it would be a sound investment, even if you did not need a place for Mrs. Bolton. Given the state of the place, I would suggest that a fair price to start with would be £900. I did some investigation about row houses for sale in London, and there are not many unleased, freehold ones. Their sellers are asking much more, partly because they are undoubtedly in better condition."

"I agree. Get Mr. Innis back here, please."

The estate agent waited for Daphne to open the conversation. He was authorized to make an initial offer or counter-off of 1,300 guineas and to settle for £1,100. He expected some general small talk before anything serious was discussed. He had no intention of letting the prospective client have any idea of what he was authorized to accept.

"Mr. Innis, this property is in even worse condition than I expected," Daphne began. "It's going to require a lot of work! And, of course, in such a major task, one often finds flaws that have not been evident until work begins. The generally poor conditions in which this house has been kept make that danger especially likely here. Things like mold, dry rot, and so on are costly to fix once they have taken hold. If it were up to me, considering the place as an investment, I would just walk away, but Mrs. Bolton does see some possibilities and likes the location. What is your principal asking?"

"Thirteen hundred guineas, my lady"

"Out of the question! I am prepared to offer £700."

"That is ridiculously low," stated Mr. Innis. "I am authorized to make a counteroffer of twelve hundred guineas, but no less."

"If you are not authorized to accept my very reasonable offer on the spot, Mr. Innis, I would understand if you need to consult your principal. My offer remains open until ten o'clock tomorrow morning. Bring your agreement to Camshire House by then. If I don't hear from you by that time, I shall have to move on to other properties. Thank you for showing us this house."

Daphne led the way to the carriage. When they were all seated, Mr. Innis said, "My lady, I think that was a very low counteroffer you made."

"Do you? Well, the figure that he stated is undoubtedly not what his seller would accept, and it was far too high. I had to go quite low to shift him into a much more reasonable area.

"Catherine, you can profitably begin to plan any changes you want and how you would use the space," Daphne continued. "With luck, we can get the builders started very soon. They are almost finished with our new club." The following morning, Mr. Innis came to Camshire House at nine-thirty. Mr. Snodgravel had come earlier and was drinking coffee in the morning room and discussing other business with Daphne while they waited. Catherine joined them when she heard the knock on the front door.

After Mr. Innis and Catherine had been supplied with coffee and the footman had left the room, Daphne wasted no time in asking, "What is your counteroffer, Mr. Innis?"

"My principal was very reluctant to lower his price, my lady. He believes that your offer is quite divorced from market realities."

"Very well. I am not prepared to haggle. If the man you represent is not willing to come down a great deal, I will just have to look elsewhere. Do you have any suitable houses elsewhere in town, by any chance?" Daphne asked.

"Won't you at least listen to his offer?"

"Only if it is much closer to mine. Otherwise, we are wasting our time."

"Very well. I am authorized to offer 850 guineas."

"Too much! To avoid the effort of looking elsewhere, I will come up to £725."

"800 guineas"

"£750."

"750 guineas."

"Done. Mr. Snodgravel, please arrange a down payment of 75 guineas with the balance when the transfer of title is made. I trust that you and Mr. Innis can arrange for the title to be transferred quickly. Make sure to get the keys to the property and have several copies made.

"Come Catherine. We'll leave the men to deal with all the legal matters required to transfer the property to Giles's name. Mr. Snodgravel, please ask Mr. XXX, the builder, to come to this house at 2:30 tomorrow afternoon.

"Was that really your highest price, Daphne?" Catherine asked.

"No. If the seller had held firm, I would have come up very close to what he was asking. You will want to start on how you want the house to be as soon as possible. That way, we will have a better idea of what we want from the builder tomorrow."

Chapter XX

Glaucus and *Stoat* had a slow, uneventful trip from Sweden to the Gulf of Finland. Finally, they saw the frigate that guarded the entrance to the Neva River and the water access to St. Petersburg. As expected, they were instructed by the frigate stationed to guard the access to the capital to report to the great naval base of Kronstadt, where they were directed to anchor and wait for instructions. Word was sent upriver immediately to inform the Tsar's palace that their guest had arrived.

Giles received an invitation to see the friend he had made during his previous visit to Russia, Admiral Stroganoff. They had no problem picking up the same rapport that they had enjoyed. The admiral suggested that Giles join him for a private dinner so that they could catch up on each other's doings and discuss the military situation without worrying about unfriendly ears, which might well want to spread unfavorable rumors or gossip about the admiral.

The admiral has not been happy about his treatment during the period since he had last seen Giles. The Russian Baltic Fleet had seen very little action. He had hoped to be transferred to the Black Sea Fleet, but that had not happened. Admiral Stroganoff had also been disappointed that his fleet had been given no significant role in the campaign that led to the battle of Friedland and the humbling of Tsar Alexander in the Treaty of Tilset. He thought that his ships could have aided the Russian army significantly in that campaign and possibly turned the tide against Napoleon. Giles did not know what to say in reply other than to agree with his friend that his treatment by the Tsar and its odious consequences were appalling.

Admiral Stroganoff realized that Giles could not raise a criticism of Russia's naval strategy at a ceremony that affirmed the friendship that still existed between the two countries despite Russia having to join a system that would exclude trade with Britain. Before Giles returned to *Glaucus*, the admiral assured his guest that he would understand if Giles did not raise the recent lack of meaningful use of the Baltic Fleet with the Tsar. Giles, for his part, assured his friend that he sympathized with his plight but would avoid angering the Tsar by questioning his naval policies. Since, based on experience, it would be many days before Giles was allowed to proceed to St Petersburg, he assured the admiral that he looked forward to many more talks in the days ahead.

Admiral Stroganoff had remembered Giles's limited appreciation of vodka and had substituted a bottle of fine French cognac to be drunk following their dinner. Giles, luckily, had been sitting near a potted plant that adorned the admiral's quarters. He just hoped that sharing his brandy with the house plant when his host wasn't looking would not lead to the mysterious death of the plant. Giving the plant some of his hard liquor would certainly help with his head when he woke up the next morning.

Tsar Alexander must have been eager to get on with the ceremony of awarding Giles the Cross of St. Nicholas. After spending only one night in Kronstadt, *Glaucus* and *Stoat* were told to proceed upriver to the Tsar's summer palace of Peterhof. Not having to wait a long period to be invited upriver or to go by rowboat rather than by ship was very welcome to Giles. Getting underway in *Glaucus* was especially pleasant since he did not have to endure a headache while giving the orders to get his frigate moving upriver.

The two British ships were allowed to moor in front of the palace, which sat at the top of a steep bluff overlooking the river. A stream ran down from the front of the palace in a series of ponds with fountains, waterfalls, and cascades lined with statues of classical figures. The palace itself was huge.

Admiral Stroganoff had come with Giles on the trip upriver and accompanied him on the long walk to the palace, commenting on the features of the great complex that had been built by Tsar Peter the Great. On reaching the palace, Admiral Stroganoff teamed up with a man whose clothes suggested that he was a significant aristocrat assigned to leading guests into the imperial presence.

The noble functionary led the two sailors to the second floor by a magnificent staircase and showed them into a very large room. An elaborately decorated, oversized chair, sitting on a dais, proclaimed it to be the throne room. However, the Tsar was not sitting on the chair. He was standing chatting with some other people when their guide announced the arrival of the British sailors. The Tsar looked up and, with a smile on his face, beckoned Giles to join him.

Giles knew the protocol. He bowed deeply to the Tsar but did not kiss his hand or shake it.

"Good to see you again, my lord, the Marquess of Dipton." The Tsar opened the conversation in perfect English with just a hint of a foreign accent. "I am afraid that circumstances prevented me from bidding you a proper farewell on your previous visit to our country, but I am delighted to see you again."

The two men chatted together for a while. Then the Tsar politely excused himself, saying, "I am sure you can appreciate that, with all the problems that come from our general losing that battle at Friedland, I am still trying to lessen the impact of the treaties I had to sign at Tilset at the insistence of that upstart Napoleon. In fact, even awarding you with the Cross of St. Nicolas may violate that treaty, but I am sure that I can get away with it. So this afternoon, we shall get together in the Chapel of St. Nicolas here to award you the Cross. It's a very solemn occasion, with lots of priests and a magnificent choir, all men with deep voices. You'll enjoy it, I'm sure. After the ceremony, we will have a state dinner to commemorate the occasion.

"Now, I have to confer with all my advisors on what to do next since it does not seem that all the prayers of our priests are going to make Napoleon disappear. Prince Obolensky will be happy to show you around the grounds and offer some refreshments while you wait for the ceremony to begin. The palace grounds were laid out by my ancestor, Peter the Great, and feature many fountains."

The prince, who turned out to be the man who had first brought them into the throne room, guided them outside, stopping on the way at a room that conveniently offered refreshments for those who were thirsty. Prince Obolensky and Admiral Stroganov picked up glasses of what looked like water, but Giles suspected from the way the prince eagerly took the glass that, in fact, it was vodka. Giles accepted a glass of red wine.

The grounds of the palace were extensive, with many shaded walks among trees, bushes, flower beds, and many spectacular fountains. Giles was delighted. He did not notice when his two companions hung back for a moment. The next thing he knew, a fountain started up right beside him and seemed to be directed right at him. Sputtering, Giles leaped aside, but he was already soaked.

He was not amused by the laughter from the other two men.

"We should have warned you, Tsar Peter the Great liked practical jokes, and there are several fountains that are triggered by people walking where they are aimed," said

Prince Obolensky. "With experience, we know where they are, but anyone coming here for the first time is likely to get soaked several times."

The boisterous amusement was cut short when one of the laughers, it wasn't clear which one, forgot to be careful and triggered another vigorous spraying of water. Giles's two companions were now as wet as he was.

"We had all better go to somewhere sunny to try to dry off before the ceremony," Prince Obolensky suggested. They made their way back to the main entrance and went down to the dock. There, they turned around and made their way back up to the palace. By the time they arrived, they were only slightly damp. There was no time to do anything about that condition. They were expected in the throne room. At least they were no longer dripping water from their soaking.

The ceremony, Giles learned later, was very much abbreviated from what usually occurred when the Cross of St. Nicholas was awarded. The award was traditionally given during a lengthy church service that would serve, in this case, two purposes. It would celebrate Giles's sportsmanship in going to the rescue of some Russian ships in distress at the cost of forfeiting a winning position in a race that would demonstrate the superiority of the Royal Navy. More importantly, the real reason the Cross had been awarded was to demonstrate the strength of the alliance between Great Britain and Russia. Now, the second reason, if mentioned, threatened the agreement that Tsar Alexander had been forced to sign after the disastrous battle of Friedland. The award might puzzle the French, but it was unlikely to cause another rupture between France and Russia if it only seemed to be a rather strange celebration of sportsmanship of little importance in the broader world of warfare.

The ceremony was still impressive despite being greatly abbreviated. A clergyman in full regalia, who Giles learned later was the Patriarch of St. Petersburg, chanted a long, incomprehensible set of words, followed by some singing by a magnificent bass choir. Tsar Alexander then draped an elaborately bejeweled cross on a matching ribbon over Giles's head to rest on Giles's still-damp coat. He then gave a brief speech in English that notably did not contain any hint that Giles's country was allied with Alexander's.

After the ceremony, the Tsar said a few words to Giles and then disappeared, claiming that pressing matters having to do with the Treaty of Tilset required his attention. The British Ambassador, Lord Malthamton, took charge of Giles and explained that many British residents of St. Petersburg had been invited to a special reception to be held in another room of the palace to welcome Giles and Captain Macreau to Russia. It was a very restrained gathering. The merchants were very concerned with what the new relationship between the Tsar and Napoleon would mean for them. Giles was unable to reassure them since he knew less than they did about what had been happening while he had been making his way to St. Petersburg. He was pretty sure, however, that trade with Britain, which was the main reason most of them were in Russia, would likely be drastically curtailed. After a while, Admiral Stroganoff took command of Giles and Etienne, indicating that it was time they went to a state dinner arranged for Giles to reconnect with all the naval friends he had made on his previous visit to Russia. Etienne and the lieutenants from both ships of the Royal Navy had also been invited.

It was a rather glum dinner with the Russian captains. Giles had no major skirmishes to recount since all the fighting and maneuvering to deal with his Scottish adventure could not be mentioned. The Russians equally had nothing to reveal since they had had no role in the disastrous campaign against Napoleon, which had led to the present tricky diplomatic situation arising from Giles's being in St. Petersburg. This mournful state of affairs did not prevent toast after toast from being offered to better days ahead.

Giles woke with another pounding headache the following morning. Couldn't these Eastern Europeans celebrate or commiserate without endless toasts in their fiery alcohol, which, in his view, had no redeeming virtues? He was inclined to roll over and go back to sleep, but then he realized that someone was trying to wake him. He opened one eye, which, even to him, felt bloodshot, to see Mr. Lester standing over him. His first lieutenant looked to be in no better condition than Giles.

"Captain," Mr. Lester said crisply, in a way that worsened Giles's headache, "Admiral Stroganoff is here with an urgent message. You must get up and meet him."

Giles realized that the situation must be dire for his usually deferential lieutenant officer to give him what amounted to an order. "Right. Stall him while I get dressed. I'll be on deck as soon as I can."

Giles's servant had already laid out his everyday uniform. Giles struggled into it as quickly as he could. There was no time to shave, but he could brush his hair. Should he have a shot of brandy to dull his headache? Probably not: it just might make a bad situation worse.

Giles arrived on the quarter deck to find Admiral Stroganoff chatting amiably with Mr. Lester. The admiral looked clear-eyed and happy. How did these Russians do it? He must have drunk as much as Giles last night.

"Ah, Captain Giles. Rough night, isn't that what you say? Sorry to wake you, but my message is urgent.

Perhaps we should retire to your cabin while I relay my news."

Once settled in Giles's cabin, the admiral got straight to business: "Overnight, we received an urgent message from the west. It announces that your navy has attacked Copenhagen. The Tsar believes that this is the last straw. Russia must declare war on Great Britain and join Napoleon's coalition against your country. In principle, he should seize your ship, and it took quite a bit of effort on the part of his advisors to persuade him not to do so. It would be ridiculous, most of us felt, to give you the Cross of St Nicholas and then seize your ship and arrest you as an enemy officer. We persuaded him to wait for a while to arrest you, but we could only get him to wait until nightfall. If you are not west of Kronstadt by then, *Glaucus* will be seized, and you and your officers will be arrested and thrown into prison. I am sorry about this, but there is nothing I can do to make the situation better. Luckily, the wind is from the east, so you should be able to get past Kronstadt with time to spare.

"I appreciate your warning me, Admiral Smirnoff. We'll be away in plenty of time. I will also warn the merchant ships flying the Union Jack that they must leave immediately."

"Quite right, Captain Giles. Once you have given your orders, we should have a final toast to our being allies again soon, even though this is not the usual hour for such toasts," replied Admiral Smirnoff.

'Maybe,' thought Giles, 'the Russian ability to absorb large quantities of alcohol without consequence was more a matter of appearances than of reality. The suggested drink was a classic medicine for hangovers.'

Admiral Stroganoff took three large glasses of Giles's best brandy before taking leave of his good friend.

Giles had succeeded in surreptitiously diluting his glasses with water, so he suffered no repercussions from his early return to the bottle. Possibly, he felt better for the indulgence.

Giles turned to the immediate necessity of getting underway as quickly as possible after seeing the Admiral off *Glaucus*. Much to his surprise, none of his crew members had overstayed their shore leave. He sent the jolly boat to St. Petersburg to warn all the merchant ships to leave as soon as possible, even if they had not yet loaded all their cargo. They would rendezvous east of Kronstadt to sail in convoy with *Glaucus* and *Stoat*.

Within half an hour of Admiral Smirnoff's going ashore, Giles ordered boats into the water to tow *Glaucus* away from the quay and turn her to head downriver. Luckily, the wind was from the southeast, so that she could sail downriver. If it had been from the west, the crew would have had to row hard to tow her to safety beyond the Russian naval base.

As they passed Kronstadt, Giles sent Mr. Lester in the jolly boat to warn any British ships moored there to sail immediately. He then had *Glaucus* and *Stoat* heave-to in order to wait for escaping merchant ships to catch up with them, both those from St. Petersburg and the ones presently in Kronstadt. Giles doubted that any warships of the Russian navy would come after them. Still, he would not be surprised if messengers might have galloped downriver to warn privateers, who had probably been acting as pirates in the eastern parts of the Baltic Sea, that a host of prizes would soon be leaving the Niva River. At the end of the afternoon watch, Giles ordered the convoy to get underway, and they headed west.

It was a slow business as the little flotilla sailed away from the eastern end of the Baltic Sea to where they would turn north to head for the exit. The wind soon turned west when there was any wind at all, and their progress against it was slow. This late in the season, there was effectively no current to bear them westward, and they had much too far to go to contemplate towing the ships using their boats.

The days were getting noticeably shorter. Giles was in a quandary as they neared Denmark. He did not want to remain in the Baltic until the autumn storms might overwhelm some of his merchant ships, but he had no idea what the situation in Copenhagen was. Fishermen and other ships he stopped to get information told varying stories. All agreed that the British had attacked Copenhagen, not only by sea but also by land across the Island of Zealand as well. After that, the present situation was hazy. Giles would just have to proceed with his little group of two warships and thirteen merchant ships with no actual knowledge of what he would find when he reached Copenhagen. It might be in English hands, or it might now be held by Danes who would be furious about the unprovoked attack on themselves. Giles would just have to make the best of the uncertain situation.

Giles reckoned that he had three things he might do. First, he could wait until he had better information. Unfortunately, that option was accompanied by difficulties. Some of the merchant ships were running short of supplies because of the haste in which they had had to leave Russia and because of the slow progress they had made getting from St. Petersburg. Furthermore, the British might still be in Copenhagen, but they might well leave while he waited for news. Secondly, he could try to take his flotilla through the Great Belt. That route to get to the North Sea was longer and trickier, and it seemed to Giles that the Danes might have reacted to the British action at Copenhagen by moving artillery to prevent any passage through the Great

Belt. Finally, the British might still have a presence in Copenhagen, or the Danes had not recovered enough to prevent Giles's convoy from passing in the night close to the Swedish side of the Sound. If either were the present case, their escape from the Baltic was likely not to be obstructed. If he waited, the British might leave, and the Danes would start to improve the defense of their city.

The convoy headed towards Copenhagen. Giles timed his entry into the Sound so that his ships would pass Copenhagen early in the morning. All seemed quiet along the city's waterfront. As they approached, Giles could see several Union Jacks declaring that the city was still in British hands. As *Glaucus* came closer to the town, a boat pulled out from the line of battle ship at the main entrance to the harbor, which was flying an admiral's flag.

The boat carried the admiral's flag lieutenant, whose instructions were to find out what a pair of British warships and a convoy of merchant vessels were doing coming down the Sound from the south. The flag lieutenant informed Giles that the Danish fleet had been destroyed or taken captive and sailed away to England. The remaining British force was engaged in clearing up a final few details before returning their capital to the Danes and returning to England.

No one had warned the forces invading Denmark that *Glaucus* and *Stoat* were in the Baltic Sea on a mission to Russia. If Giles's ships hadn't been thrown out of Russia so suddenly, they would have found an outraged nation of Danes blocking their departure from the Baltic. Clearly, the British Government of the day didn't give a fig for the fate of the two British ships and their crews who would be stranded in the Baltic by their initiating war with Denmark.

Chapter XXI

The problem of what to do about Catherine's imminent giving-birth had been satisfactorily settled. Now, Daphne had nothing pressing to do until her own time to deliver a baby arrived. Or so she thought. However, when she had been home for less than two weeks, a letter arrived from Mr. Snodgravel, marked 'URGENT.' It was just as well that that announcement was on the message since otherwise, she would have left it on the pile of things to be done when she had more energy. This pregnancy was taking more from her than the previous ones.

. Mr. Snodgravel had written that three gentlemen's clubs had filed a complaint about the new club, objecting to the proposed club allowing women members and also for its providing overnight lodging for such members if required. The three clubs were Bunter's, which seemed to be the ringleader, Struddle's, and Brown's. Daphne was glad to see that the Club Giles belonged to was not among the complainers.

Mr. Snodgravel went on to state that there would be a meeting of the complainers and the Chief Magistrate of Westminster to hear the complaint and any objections to not letting the proposed undertaking go ahead. The hearing would be held two weeks from the date of the 'urgent' message. Mr. Snodgravel would, of course, attend that meeting, but he would appreciate having Daphne's reactions to the points that might be raised.

Daphne did not feel particularly strongly about the principle of having a club accepting women members. She thought it was a good idea if enough women were interested. Still, she was more interested in having a club for men with more serious interests than horse racing and gambling, which seemed to dominate the existing gentlemen's clubs. Surprisingly, Giles seemed to be more passionate about the provision for ladies' membership. But now that the principle of a club admitting women had been raised, she was not going to allow some prejudiced group of men to stand in her way. They had laid down the gauntlet: she was going to pick it up!

Daphne was not going to leave Mr. Snodgravel to defend the proposed club all by himself. She wouldn't even wait for the hearing date to go to London. She wanted to see what material she could gather, with or without Mr. Snodgravel's help, that would destroy the clubs' attack on Giles' and her idea. Instead, she returned to London on the day following the receipt of the ' urgent' letter.

The first thing Daphne did after her first night in Camshire House was to visit Mr. Snodgravel's chambers in Chancery Lane. She could, of course, have summoned him to come to Camshire House, but it was more convenient to go to his chambers, where he kept the records of everything he undertook on Giles's behalf.

Daphne arrived at Mr. Snodgravel's offices as early as she could while still being sure that Mr. Snodgravel would already be at work. She was ushered into his room without delay.

"What is all this nonsense about our new club?" she demanded even before she sat down. "We haven't even named it or finished its bylaws, let alone recruited many members."

"The gentlemen's clubs seem to be very threatened by your having a club where women can be members and wives of members, as well as members, can use the facilities and even stay overnight when they want to," the solicitor replied, though he must have remembered that this was what he had already written to Daphne. "It's mainly because they fear that their more hen-pecked members whose wives may insist that their husbands get memberships in the new club and drop their present clubs. Other members probably just see it as a threat to their way of life. That, at least, is what I gathered from talking to the Chief Magistrate. He has had the issue dropped in his lap by the municipal authorities, who received the original complaint.

"That sounds like a pretty thin case to me. By many accounts, the gentlemen's clubs are nothing but gambling dens. They are hardly bastions of morality."

"You are quite right, of course. But the clubs are places where their wives can't bother the gentlemen or cause a scene about how much money they are losing gambling. Though there are many bawdy houses in Westminster, no one with influence complains about them. That's what this group claims about the club you are planning: that it is a thinly disguised house of ill repute."

"I see. And that's the only complaint that can shut down a club."

"Yes. It is the only prohibited activity that would cause the forced closure of a club. That's how Giles got Green's Club closed, wasn't it?"

"No. In that case, that use of the facilities helped to break the lease so that Giles was able to terminate the club in those premises. However, if that is the law, the claim could be hard to fight, even though it is nonsense. I'll have to gather some dirt about these gentlemen's clubs that are harassing us. No, Mr. Snodgrass, it's better that I do it rather than you," Daphne added. "My sources are probably more informed about the underbelly of the ton than yours. Now, there is another matter that I would like to consult you on. Do you know Mrs. Marsdon's current address?"

"Yes, I do. Here it is. Let me write it down for you. May I ask why you want to see such an immoral woman, my lady?"

"Mrs. Marsden is my best source of well-informed gossip about the doings of the ton and their clubs and what really goes on behind their closed doors."

"Now, I will truly look forward to our meeting with the Chief Magistrate and the officers of the complaining clubs. Good luck with dealing with that bawd! She probably is the person who has the most compelling information against the clubs that made the complaint."

Daphne took a sedan chair, with another one for Betsy. to the address that Mr. Snodgravel had given her. It was a well-kept-up row house in St. James, which had been altered to include the houses on each side of it. Mrs. Marsten's business had been expanding since Daphne's first run-in with her. Without hesitation, Daphne strode up to the front door and knocked. When she gave her card to the butler, she was shown immediately into a richly furnished sitting room where Mrs. Marsten was having a cup of hot chocolate. Another was provided for Daphne, and after a very short general chat, they got down to the reason for Daphne's visit.

"You have heard about the new club that Giles and I are sponsoring," Daphne began.

"Of course. I also heard that some other clubs are trying to prevent it from opening. Claiming with blatant hypocrisy that you will be a threat to public morals."

"Yes. So, I was wondering if you knew any material that I could use as a counterattack."

Mrs. Marsden broke into laughter. "Defeat them at their own game? I like it! I do make a lot of money from the gentlemen's clubs, but I would make even more if they had to stop some of their more immoral practices and their members spend the money in my establishment. Just let me think a moment."

Mrs. Marsden turned out to have a wealth of knowledge about the shadier doings that went on in the most respectable gentlemen's clubs. Daphne was amazed; she had no idea about the seamy underbelly of the clubs. Mrs. Marsten's information would be highly embarrassing to the clubs if it became generally known among members of the ton. She also had ideas on how Daphne could make accusations of their moral turpitude stand up if they were contested. She promised to see if any of her women had other information that indicated that the gentlemen's clubs were not pillars of sexual morality.

Daphne, with some trepidation, asked whether the club where Giles was a member was equally immoral.

"No," Mrs. Marsden replied. "They wisely don't want any other members to be aware of what they do when they seek our sex away from home. That's not to say that I don't make a pretty penny from some of them, just that the club is not involved in that aspect of their lives."

When Daphne left on foot, with Betsey once more trailing behind her, she was confident that she had plenty of material to induce the clubs to withdraw their complaints. Now, she could turn her attention to other matters.

Several days later, Daphne's butler came to her work rook to tell her that a bulky letter had been received from Mrs. Marsden. It must include information relevant to her quashing the attempt to prevent the new club from opening. She forgot all about the financial statements she had been studying while she found out what the whoremonger had sent her.

The package confirmed some of the information that she had obtained when she visited Mrs. Marsden. The bawd had also learned of some easily provable cases where the clubs' moral stances were shown to be hypocritical. Indeed, the clubs were already doing what they accused Daphne's proposed club of wanting to do.

Daphne was well pleased. The meeting with the representatives of the gentlemen's clubs should put an end to any attempts to have the new club proscribed by the borough of Westminster. If all this information became public knowledge, it might take more than the grand stature of many of their members to save the clubs from having to close. Daphne was now looking forward to the meeting with the clubs' representatives.

Mr. Downing, the Chief Magistrate of Westminster, was the first to arrive for the hearing. He was closely followed by Mr. Snodgravel. The meeting would be held in the breakfast room since it had a convenient table for them to gather around. Daphne had coffee served while waiting for the other men to arrive. They discussed the wonders of the British Museum since both men turned out to be regular visitors to the collection.

The men representing the clubs arrived fifteen minutes late. Mr. Downing did not say anything about their tardiness, but he was clearly annoyed. One point for her side even before they started, Daphne thought. The oldest of the three representatives took the lead by introducing themselves: "Mr. Downing, it is good to see you again. For the other people here, I am Lord Harvey from Bunter's Club. This is Mr. Straddler from the Irving Club, and Mr. Vickers is from Brown's."

"I see," Mr. Downing took control of the meeting. "This is Lady Daphne Giles, Marchioness of Dipton, and

Mr. Snodgravel, Lord Dipton's agent. Now, exactly what is your complaint?"

Lord Harvey from Bunter's Club replied to the question without consulting the other club representatives. "As you know, Lord Dipton is proposing to open a new club in the premises where Green's Club used to be. The call for expression of interest in the club states that membership will be open to women as well as men, including single women. This provision is against all the traditions of clubs in London. After all, we are all known colloquially as 'gentlemen's clubs.' Having women in the same club as men would be most immoral.

"To make it worse, they even intend to have rooms where women can stay overnight! Not just rooms where male members can spend the night if they are from out of town or don't want to go home. No, there will be rooms for women as well where they can spend the night unchaperoned, on their own! Can you imagine it, Chief Magistrate? It's bound to be an utterly immoral environment! It's against all tradition and propriety! This rogue undertaking would harm the reputations of our valued institutions. You cannot permit it!

"It is not unusual for some types of establishments to prohibit women," Lord Harvey continued with less passion. "For example, coffee houses ban women from being on their premises and won't serve one if she happens to enter by mistake. The same provision should apply to all clubs as well. This shocking proposed club cannot be permitted! It flies in the face of an honored tradition and the whole purpose of gentlemen's clubs! You must prohibit this so-called club from opening. It will be nothing less than a … than a … than a brothel!"

Lord Harvey had worked himself into such a state of self-righteous indignation that his prominent wattles waggled in time with his horrified words. Daphne had a hard time not bursting out laughing at the image of a distraught rooster that popped into her head.

"Do any of you other gentlemen wish to add to Lord Harvey's presentation?" Mr. Downing asked calmly. The other representatives shook their heads, and Mr. Straddler commented that Lord Downing had presented their case very well.

"Lady Dipton, would you like to reply now, or would you rather wait to hear what the others have to say?" Mr. Downing asked, giving no hint as to what he thought of Lord Harvey's speech.

"Let me answer while his points are clear in our minds, Mr. Downing," Daphne replied. "First, the coffee houses ban women from their premises by their own decision, not by any law that I know of. There are, of course, tea shops like Gunther's for women, but they have no objection to having men as customers.

"More serious is the moral argument, which, to be frank, I consider offensive. First, the women's rooms will all be in a separate wing of the building where men will not be allowed, and there will be accommodation for the ladies' maids. There will be no question that propriety is maintained at all times.

"What I am horrified by is the hypocrisy of your moral claims, Lord Harvey. The majordomo of your club is happy to arrange for your members to be visited in their private bedrooms by women supplied by select whore mongers. He arranges for the ladies of the night to come through your trade entrance. I know that he extracts a substantial fee for the service. I don't know if he shares it with you, Lord Harvey, but it is widely believed that he does by the ladies who visit your club. You do not allow women in your more public rooms so that your members' wives cannot observe the other forms of debauchery your members indulge in, even though someone losing their fortune at cards has immediate, painful consequences for their spouses.

"Mr. Downing, I am sorry to have to reveal an equivalent lack of maintenance of the moral standard that Mr. Straddler claims on behalf of The Irving Club. Ladies of the night call at regular intervals at the tradesman's entrance to that club to see if there is a request for their services. Mr. Straddler, I have it on good authority that your majordomo arranges for one of your footmen to convey surreptitiously any women who are requested to the appropriate rooms. As a representative of the club, I would expect you to know about this custom, especially as I have it on good authority that you avail yourself of the service from time to time.

"Even more shocking, Mr. Vickers, is the situation at your club. As with all the clubs, Brown's Club employs a number of chambermaids. Indeed, you employ double the number that is needed for the usual tasks of chambermaids. The regular ones do not have rooms provided on the premises, though that is a common feature of clubs employing female staff. Instead, they are accommodated elsewhere. The bedrooms that they would typically occupy are filled each night by the other chamber maids who are available, for a substantial fee, to members of the club who rent rooms for the night and desire the company of compliant women. These women, I have it on good authority, do not engage in any housekeeping duties.

"I put it to you, Mr. Downing, that the complaint made by these three clubs is without merit and is based more on the danger of losing some of their shady dealings than on any moral grounds. In our case, every propriety will be maintained, and the women's wing will not be filled with the whores who seem to decorate the private rooms of these three gentlemen's clubs. Don't pretend to be shocked at my language, Mr. Stadler. You are, I am sure, familiar both with the term and what it refers to."

"Gentlemen, what do you have to say in reply to Lady Dipton's remarks?" asked the Chief Magistrate. He seemed to be struggling to keep a straight and impartial face.

"Pack of lies! Pack of lies!" huffed Lord Harvey. "Nothing to it!"

The other two representatives of gentlemen's clubs made similar noises.

"I am insulted, Mr. Downing," said Daphne. "These gentlemen have just accused me of slander. If they don't retract their accusations and drop their objections to our club immediately, I will have no choice but to sue them personally. My reputation is at stake, and I can get witnesses to my statements who are willing to testify in open court about the veracity of what I have been saying. The court proceedings, I am sure, will be widely reported by the newspapers."

"That's outrageous," shouted Lord Harvey.

"Lady Dipton is quite right, my lord," said Mr. Downing, mildly. "That was slander. I suggest that you apologize immediately. The only defense for slander is that the claims she made are true. Are they?

"As you know, Lady Dipton is not hesitant about testifying in open court. I am sure the newspapers will have a field day with such a juicy case. I might add that her first point is compelling as well. Private clubs can do what they want about membership, and that includes having women participate as members. We can have an open hearing on the matter if you wish, but that will also attract the newspapers, or you can withdraw your complaint."

"I think that we three should discuss this in private," announced Lord Harvey.

"Please use the drawing room," Daphne stated, ringing the bell for Mr. Richards.

The butler showed the three men out of the breakfast room, leaving the door open. It soon became evident why he had done so since no sooner had they left the breakfast room than Mr. Vickers was heard by everyone still at the table say, "Why the hell, Harvey, did you call her a liar? I know that what she said is true; you know it's true; only some of your self-righteous members don't know it's true."

"What did you expect me to do? Ignore it? Now shut up. Servants have ears!"

After a moment, the door to the drawing room was heard to close.

"Do you belong to one of the gentlemen's clubs, Mr. Downing?" Daphne asked to open a conversation to fill the time until the men representing the clubs returned.

"No. My job keeps me too busy, and anyway, I don't want to appear to be special friends with anyone who has business with me. Is your husband a member of one of them?"

"Yes, he is. But Giles uses it for lunch with people he wants to see, usually about business connected with his duties in the House of Lords or some unofficial matters having to do with the Admiralty. He is not much of a gambler and says wagering is a large part of what goes on in the various clubs. Is his club as debauched as the ones we are dealing with today?"

"No. I don't think so. Not that many of its members don't frequent ladies of the night, but I am pretty sure that they keep such activities out of the club," Mr. Downing replied. "If you are worried, you could always ask Mrs. Marsden."

At that point, the three men representing the clubs returned. Lord Harvey was again the spokesman, "Lady Dipton, I must apologize for the implication of the word I used that might be taken to be aimed at you. I should not have said what I did. I hope you will accept my apology."

"That depends on what else you have to say to us," Daphne replied tartly.

"Well, on the matter of this meeting," Lord Harvey continued, "we have discussed your points and find that we no longer have any objection to the proposed club. Indeed, we wish you and Lord Dipton every success in your venture. Mr. Downing, we have agreed to withdraw our objection to the proposed club."

"In that case, I shall ignore your insult, Lord Harvey," announced Daphne, "provided that I do not hear that you have been slandering me to anybody else in the future."

Mr. Downing rapped his knuckles on the table. "I think, Lady Dipton and gentlemen, that that concludes our business today. I shall mark your complaint as canceled at the complainer's wishes. I would advise you, Lord Harvey, not to bring such frivolous cases to me in the future."

The men turned and left the room, guided to the front door by Richards.

"Thank you, Lady Dipton," said Mr. Downing. "I have seldom enjoyed a hearing so much."

Mr. Snodgravel also took his leave. "It is always a pleasure to see you at work, my lady. Don't forget that the builder is coming this afternoon. I had a couple of keys cut for you for the house in Bloomsbury. Here they are."

Daphne was left to have a light luncheon with Catherine before her niece got involved again with the house in Bloomsbury and plans to remodel it. Now, Daphne was free to return to Dipton Hall. The trip to London had accomplished everything she wanted it to, but that wasn't what she really desired. She wanted Giles home, and she was worried about him. She had had no news of him for a long time, and the papers had been full of stories about a battle somewhere in Eastern Europe where Napoleon had beaten the Tsar of Russia, and there were concerns about how punishing the peace treaty would be. In addition, the papers were boasting that Britain had attacked Copenhagen and taken their fleet. Giles was in the middle of that part of the world where the fighting had occurred, she knew, because his voyage was to take him to St. Petersburg. She couldn't help worrying about him, even though she always told him that she didn't. Her anxiety had become exceptionally high since there had been no letter from him or other news about him in ages.

Chapter XXII

Giles decided not to waste time in Copenhagen. He wanted to get home as quickly as possible. The flag lieutenant who had met him as he passed the Danish capital had assured him that no Danish warship could intercept his little flotilla since they had all been taken away by the English or destroyed. The wind was from the west. If it continued, he could use just one long reach to bring *Glaucus* and *Stoat* to the point where he would have to turn west to navigate the Kattegat, which was the exit into the North Sea. It was also advantageous for the merchant ships accompanying *Glaucus*, which now were at risk from Danish as well as Dutch privateers and pirates. They would not have to beat slowly into a foul wind to get away from hostile waters.

Everything went smoothly as they sailed up the straight to leave Danish waters. The wind held from the west until they had got far enough north to clear the Skaw, the spit of land at the north end of the Jutland Peninsula. The wind then backed into the south enough that they could turn west with some hope of clearing the southwest corner of Norway on one long larboard tack.

It was a lovely clear night, with an almost full moon. Even sailing the course dictated by the ship in the group of merchantmen that could point lowest, they would clear the end of Norway on this tack without difficulty.

Dawn was just breaking when *Glaucus* was approaching the last Norwegian headland with *Stoat* close behind her. The convoy was sailing a bit to windward of the naval vessels. Giles had feared that, close to the Norwegian coast, a privateer might pop out of a little bay to quickly capture one of the merchant ships and successfully carry her to their home port if the naval vessels were to the south of the convoy. A cry came from the *Glaucus*'s masthead to say that a sail was emerging off the starboard bow above where the final Norwegian headland sloped into the sea. The sail was headed on a south-by-east course that would soon intercept *Glaucus*'s. The sail did not look like a merchant ship; it was more like a frigate's fore topsail, though it appeared to be larger than most of the foresails on frigates, including *Glaucus*'s.

Mr. Lester had the watch. As always, *Glaucus* had cleared for action before dawn. When no enemy could be spotted as it became light, the crew started to reverse the level of preparedness for combat, and Giles had gone below. Now, Mr. Lester ordered that the crew undo their recent work so that the frigate was again ready for battle and sent a messenger to tell Giles of the development.

Arriving on deck, Giles instructed the signal midshipman to inform *Stoat* that an enemy ship had been sighted. Then he stepped to the mainmast ratlines and climbed aloft. Reaching the top of the mast, he found that the lookout's call had been accurate. More and more of the other ship's sails were coming into sight as she moved south along the far side of the headland. Giles could see from the activity in her rigging that she was preparing for action, and he could see that an officer had joined the other ship's lookout and was staring at Giles through a telescope. Her masthead flag indicated that the unknown ship was Danish. So much for the claim made at Copenhagen that the British expedition had captured or destroyed all the ships of the Danish Navy.

The Danish ship looked quite a bit larger than Glaucus, not enough to be considered a ship of the line but possibly a small fourth rate, a forty-two of forty-four or some such rating. It was a size that had gone out of fashion with most navies, but Giles was pretty sure that was what he was looking at. As he was about to return to the deck, the lookout said, "Sir, there is another sail coming into sight."

Giles scanned the area to the north of the Danish ship that he had already seen. Sure enough, the foremast topsail of some other vessel was emerging from behind the steep slope that hid the rest of this new ship. But it wasn't the usual type of topsail like the first ship had been displaying. Instead, it was a jib-headed topsail, the sail between the gaff and the mast on a fore-and-aft rigged vessel. The new vessel was undoubtedly smaller than the first one, even smaller than *Glaucus*, and more like a brig, though a larger one than *Stoat*.

Giles returned to the deck and ordered the midshipman of the watch to signal *Stoat*. "Two enemy ships approaching from behind the headland. Clear for action. Close up to us." Then, Mr. Evans, signal to the convoy: "Disperse."

The minutes seemed to crawl by after the ship was cleared for action, and the sails reduced in anticipation of close-range action. The masthead reported that the vessels on the other side of the headland had not changed their course. The smaller one was catching up to the larger ship just as *Stoat* was closing on *Glaucus*. Mr. Brooks had been making calculations based on the speed at which *Glaucus* was moving and what he thought the larger Danish ship was achieving.

"Captain Giles," the master announced, "if she holds her course and with her reduced canvas, I calculate that the Dane will pass two cables ahead of us. Our course will take us too close to the shore for her to veer to some down our starboard side, but she can engage us to larboard. Of course, she can instead tack and wait for us to come up with her or just sail away."

"Is she faster than us, do you think, Mr. Brooks?" Giles asked.

"Maybe a little, but she is making more leeway than us. So we should be on more of a reach if we were to be on the same course."

"Well, we will just have to hold our course to see what she does. The Dane will likely pass ahead of us.

"Mr. Lester," Giles ordered. "Go to the bow and make sure that Mr. Dunsmuir is informed about what to expect. Help him to make the calculations so that the bow chasers are most effective."

A tense ten minutes followed that order. Everything was as ready as it could be when very little was known about the adversary that was about to emerge to starboard of *Glaucus*'s bow. Of the people on deck, only Giles had seen the enemy. The rest were left to speculate on what would soon be revealed and worry about the Danish ship, which, Giles had said, was likely to be more powerful than *Glaucus*. The tension was shown as men nervously redid tasks that had already been done perfectly and cracked and laughed at jokes that were not really funny.

Then, the bow of the Danish ship came into view. Surprisingly, the tension on *Glaucus* seemed to ease, even though, just from seeing her bowsprit, they could tell she was indeed significantly larger than *Glaucus*. Now they knew that only with superior seamanship and luck would they come out of the following short period safe to continue their journey.

The Danish ship continued to emerge from behind the headland. She was more like an oversized frigate than a ship of the line. A single line of gunports indicated her primary weapons.

"Mr. Lester," Giles roared, "Prepare to fire when you bear. Mr. Brooks, luff off until our bow chasers can hit her."

Glaucus turned slightly to starboard. The bow chasers roared, first the starboard one and moments later the larboard cannon. The shots must have been high, for there was no spray of splinters where the missiles landed. Some stays that were holding up the foremast had been severed. Giles could see Danish seamen racing to start repairing or replacing the cut lines, but so far, they did not seem to have hindered his opponent's sailing abilities.

Glaucus returned to her course before they could establish what damage the heavy-duty bow chasers had done. The crew of the bow chasers started reloading without waiting to see what effect their first shots might have had. They were almost ready to fire again when their opponents fired their broadside. The bow chasers roared out just after the Danish broadside struck home. Surprisingly, most of the Danish broadside missed, the cannonballs zipping down the two sides of *Glaucus* without doing any damage. However, two Danish shots did find their targets. One hit larboard gunwale* near the bow, sending a shower of deadly splinters across *Glaucus*'s foredeck. The second one clipped the starboard shrouds of the foremast. Since that was the leeward side of the ship, this damage had little effect on *Glaucus*'s immediate ability to keep fighting. Still, it did seriously limit her capability to maneuver since it would not be safe to come-about* until the damage was repaired.

Glaucus's bow chasers' two shots must have arrived just after her rival's balls had struck home. One of the balls missed completely, but the other one did real damage. It chewed a large bite out of the mizzen mast, spraying deadly splinters all over the quarterdeck. Mr.

Brooks speculated bloodthirstily that they must have wounded several Danish officers.

The immediate effect of the lucky bow-chaser shot was that the Danish ship had to furl her driver and mizzen topsail before she could maneuver safely to continue the battle. Her crew went urgently to work to work on the affected sails. In the meantime, the ship was being pushed around to point more downwind, and she was becoming the target for *Glaucus*'s broadside. Her only chance to destroy this British ship, or even to avoid her own defeat, was to turn more downwind so that her rival would have to tack to come after her. That is precisely what the Danes did. As she turned to larboard, their ship became into the arc of Glaucus's broadside. The target was not as close as Giles would have liked, but most of the guns were loaded and aimed at the Danish vessel.

"Larboard guns," bellowed Giles, "fire as you bear."

The guns exploded, not as evenly as Giles would have liked, but all aimed in the right direction, though not necessarily with the proper elevation. Some of the balls plowed harmlessly into the water between the two antagonists. Others hit the water but ricocheted off and hit the hull of the Danish ship, in one case hitting the edge of a gunport. Another one hit the rail and sent a cloud of deadly splinters skimming along the Danish ship's deck. Finally, some cannonballs went high through the other ship's rigging. Holes appeared in some of the sails, and, more importantly, it was clear that some lines had been severed. *Glaucus*'s opponent had been injured but was not seriously crippled.

Men rushed to the various lines controlling the sails on both vessels. Giles had to choose among several alternatives to his next move, and he had little time to deliberate. He could continue on his present course and likely get clean away from his more powerful opponent. He could go to the aid of *Stoat,* which was engaged with the large Danish brig. Finally, he could just sail away. Unfortunately, he had to remember the slow merchant ships from St. Petersburg that had accompanied him. The Danish ship would be delighted to round them up as prizes, so the last possibility was not open to him.

"Prepare to veer," Giles roared. *Glaucus* turned to larboard. Giles's decision-making had been swift enough that, as his ship turned downwind, her broadside again had a target: the stern of her rival. The ships were now somewhat farther apart, and the target was narrower than on the previous firing. Nevertheless, the broadside did some visible damage. The most spectacular was that the stern windows of the Danish captain's cabin disappeared. Everyone on board *Glaucus* could imagine the destruction wrought as the cannon balls blasted down the crowded gun deck. No one on *Glaucus* could see the further damage the cannonballs had done, but they all understood how catastrophic it must have been.

"Mr. Brooks," Giles addressed the master, "course to bring us alongside her."

The master's response came immediately in the action he took: Mr. Brooks must have anticipated what Giles would do next. The master gave helm and sail-handling orders that had *Glaucus* pointing slightly ahead of their opponent. As they closed with the other ship, she could be hit again by *Glaucus*'s unusually powerful bow chasers.

"Steer so that the bow chasers bear on her stern. Bow chasers, fire when you bear," Giles roared. The cannon both fired. Instantaneously, more damage appeared in the stern of the Danish ship, and no sign of her stern windows remained. *Glaucus* resumed her course. The aftermost Danish gun fired. The ball must have been aimed low because it passed just under the end of *Glaucus*'s bowsprit without doing any damage.

"Larboard guns, fire as you bear," Giles ordered. The foremost cannon of his ship's broadside struck just below the rival quarterdeck and produced a new, ragged hole just behind the gun that had fired uselessly to begin the next stage of the encounter. The Danish ship also began to fire as the British frigate moved up beside her. With the muzzle of the enemy cannon only yards away from its target this time, the ball hit *Glaucus*'s bowsprit squarely and wrenched it from its moorings. The lines holding the foremast were loosened, and the whole foremast threatened to go by the board.

"Starboard your helm. Lash the ships together," Giles ordered. "Mr. Macauley, get your marines out of the foremast fighting top."

"Mr. Lester," he shouted to the first lieutenant on the forecastle, where he had been directing the bow chasers. "Board her! Over the bow as soon as we touch."

The first lieutenant responded eagerly, leading the attack from *Glaucus*'s foredeck to the Danish quarterdeck, wildly swinging his sword as soon as he found his footing on the rival deck. Unfortunately, he had little experience in hand-to-hand fighting in close quarters. Mr. Lester's immediate opponent countered his initial lunge with his sword, and that left *Glaucus*'s first lieutenant open to a lunge by another Dane, which produced a fatal wound.

Picking up his cutlass as he went, Giles raced from the quarter deck to the main deck and then forward, with everyone following him. Up the steps to the fo'c'sle, he charged and then followed the boarders already fighting on the Danish ship's quarterdeck. The marines in the fighting tops on each side were shooting into the melees, adding to the carnage produced by the cutlasses that the crews on both sides had snatched up to fight their enemies. The greater experience and more intense training of the British sailors started to pay off for Giles's attackers. They overwhelmed the defenders on the quarter deck. Then, they let the marines clear the way with their rifles and bayonets to descend to the main deck.

The marines in the *Glaucus*'s foremast fighting top had delayed their departure from their now precarious post long enough to take aim and fire at the officers on the Danish ship's quarter deck. Their fire killed one lieutenant and hit the Danish captain in the shoulder. Then, the marines made their way down to the deck on ratlines that had gone somewhat slack. Nevertheless, they carried their rifles and ammunition boxes with them. The minute they reached the deck, they reloaded and fixed bayonets, preparing to cross onto the Danish quarterdeck. Ahead of them, a major part of *Glaucus's* crew, led by Giles, arrived on the foredeck. They were joined almost immediately by the marines from the other fighting tops. Without pausing, they all stormed across to their rival's quarterdeck. Surprisingly, many of the Danish sailors were still on the main deck, and Giles found he had a superior force on the quarter deck. In no time, his force got the better of their rivals.

The Danish captain shouted that he surrendered. Giles was bellowing to cease fighting since the Danes had given up when his right leg was knocked from under him. He collapsed on the deck. His right leg, just above the ankle, hurt incredibly, and Giles found that when he tried to rise, the leg refused to accept any weight. As he collapsed back onto the deck, he heard Mr. Macauley bellow, "The captain is down! Jenkins, Macdonald, and Butcher take him to the orlop at once."

Giles passed out from the pain as the marines lifted him. He regained consciousness just as the loblolly boys were lifting him onto the table where Mr. Maclean was waiting to treat him.

"Captain Giles," the surgeon greeted him. "A musket ball has hit you, probably shot from the fighting tops just after the surrender. It has shattered the bones. There is too much of a mess for me to try to set it, so I am going to have to amputate your foot and ankle. It is going to hurt abominably, but the alternative is that the wound becomes infected and will kill you. Even if that doesn't happen, your leg will be useless, and you will be in constant pain from it.

"I'll give you some laudanum, which will help the pain a bit. Here it is. It's very bitter, but it should do a great deal to reduce the agony of the procedure and reduce the shock to your system."

Giles drank the very bitter concoction that the surgeon gave him and lay back. The last thing he remembered hearing was the surgeon telling his assistants, two of the most muscular men on board, "Hold the patient down."

Giles slipped into a dreamlike state where he was vaguely aware of the pain in his right leg but thought it was funny. Somehow, he was still aware that he had been engaged in a savage fight before being injured, but it did not seem to matter anymore. There was, however, still a great deal of pain in his leg. Before the surgeon had finished, Giles lost consciousness.

Giles did not wake up until well into the morning of the next day. His leg hurt terribly, and he had a very annoying itch in his right heel. Mr. Rich, his most junior midshipman, was keeping watch at his bedside.

"Captain Giles," the youth exclaimed. "You are awake! How Do you feel?"

"Rotten. Did we win the battle with the Danish ship?"

"Yes, sir."

"And what happened to *Stoat*?"

"She was sunk, sir, but Commander Macreau captured the Danish ship he was attacking, so if he can keep that ship from sinking, he will have gained a valuable prize."

"Good! Ask Mr. Lester to visit me."

"I am afraid that Mr. Lester died in boarding the Danish ship, sir."

"Ah, yes, now I remember. And Mr. Stewart?"

"He was uninjured, sir, though he was at the forefront of the fighting. He accepted the Danish surrender and the officers' paroles. He is now on the Danish ship, trying to finish patching her up and redoing the rigging. She was almost sinking, and it was touch and go before it was clear that she could be saved. The Danish pumps and some of ours were just keeping ahead of the water pouring into her. He stopped that by fothering the worst of the holes in the hull, and the pumps have gained a lot on the water in her. *Glaucus* is not leaking, though the Danes did a lot of damage to our bow. I heard Mr. Stewart tell Mr. Brooks that we are almost ready to proceed, though we will need a dockyard to finish the repairs."

"All right, Mr. Rich. Is the master on *Glaucus*?"

"Yes, sir."

"Then, ask him to visit me when he has a chance."

"Aye, aye, sir." Mr. Rich seemed to be delighted to get away from Giles's cross-examination since he would know few of the answers if Giles wanted to probe more deeply.

Before Mr. Brooks could come to the captain's cabin, *Glaucus*'s surgeon, Mr. Maclean, could be heard announcing himself to the marine at Giles's door.

"I see you are awake," the surgeon remarked to Giles. "I had to take your leg off a bit above the ankle. A bullet, a musket ball, hit you, wrecking your ankle and shattering the end of your leg bones. I got to the wound quickly, and the loblolly boys had cleaned the area as well as they could. The bullet hole was also far enough down that I had enough good flesh to make an excellent pad. If we can keep gangrene out, we should have you up and active before too long. So far, the discharge from the tubes looks good, and you only have a very slight fever. It's early days yet, but I hope that you will be stamping around the deck very soon. How are you feeling?"

"Rotten! In a lot of pain, almost unendurable, in my leg, and a terrible itch in my right heel, which you say isn't there anymore."

"It isn't. That reaction to losing part of a limb is not uncommon. Somehow, something gets scrambled after an amputation, and one still feels things in the part that isn't there anymore."

"Can you give me some more of the laudanum that you gave me for the surgery?"

"I could. But I don't want to do so if you can stand the pain a little longer. There are some decisions you will have to make, and that drug does distort one's selections. After the decisions are all straightened away, I can give you some more, but that will be it. I am afraid that medicine is highly addictive. Once you become bound to laudanum, it is very challenging to get away from it, and the victim is only a shadow of himself. Laudanum is an extraction of opium, but far worse, and you will become a lotus eater if you take it too often."

"I didn't realize. I will try to endure the pain, especially as I know from others who have lost a limb that the pain will go away eventually.

"Now, what have been the casualties?"

"We had seventy-four serious casualties, sir," the surgeon replied. "Twenty-three dead so far, including Mr. Lester. Several others may not recover. I am afraid that your coxswain was among them."

"I'm sorry to hear that. He was a good man, and I was getting used to him and got on well with him. That total for casualties is a lot. Good men all! I know you will do your best to heal as many as you can. Any idea about how many the Danes lost?"

"No, sir. I also don't know how many casualties *Stoat* has suffered," the surgeon continued. "That must have been a very bloody fight too."

"More credit to Etienne for winning it. Especially when his own ship was sinking, or so Dr. Maclean told me. "What about the prisoners?"

"I don't know yet how many were injured so badly that we had to keep them aboard the two vessels. On Mr. Macreau's orders, all those who were uninjured or whose injuries were not serious were put in the Danish ships' boats. We kept the officers, of course, all of whom have given their paroles. Now, try to sleep. Everything is in good hands. After all, you trained us all to be able to carry on without you."

No sooner had Dr. Maclean departed than Mr. Brooks entered the cabin.

"Good to see you awake, Captain," the master greeted Giles. "The surgeon tells me that your prospects for recovery are excellent. Of course, you will not have your right foot anymore, but just look how far Captain Bush had got with only one leg."

"What is the situation on the capture?"

"She is a fine ship, sir. Quite a bit stronger than us, in fact. She received much of our last shots below the waterline, and while the mizzen did not go by the board immediately, it is taking a lot of work to stabilize it. It is a big feather in your cap to have taken her."

"What about the ship that Etienne captured?"

"Another powerful ship. It's certainly stronger than *Stoat*. A great addition to our navy, I am sure. Etienne fought her tooth and nail and then succeeded in boarding her even though *Stoat* was sinking. She will undoubtedly count towards getting Etienne posted captain soon."

"Glad to hear it. He has shown real ability commanding that brig."

"Speak of the devil, sir," responded the master. "Commander Macreau is here now."

"Captain Giles, sir," Etienne declared. "I am sorry that you have been wounded but glad that Mr. Maclean says you are likely to recover."

"Thank you, Etienne. I am told you have won quite a battle. Congratulations."

"Thank you, sir. *Haevner* is the name of the ship, I believe, though I have no idea how to pronounce it in Danish. She is a strange ship, best described as an overgrown schooner or maybe a small fore-and-aft rigged frigate. My only hope was to get alongside her and hope to take her by boarding. It worked when she tried to turn downwind to capture us. She misjudged a bit, and we were able to grapple. I gathered all our people on deck and luffed up to come alongside her. We fired no shot, so everyone was ready to board. The minute we were alongside her, we stormed onto her. Her crew was still primarily engaged in firing on *Stoat*, and they didn't abandon it soon enough. We got more than a foothold on her and were able to overcome the crew piecemeal by concentrating our attack one gun at a time. Anyway, we overcame them without very much loss of life to ourselves. They lost far more men than we did, so many that they surrendered pretty quickly. We only lost three men killed and another nine seriously injured. We tried to save *Stoat*, but we couldn't plug the holes quickly enough.

"We are now ready to sail," Etienne continued. "It took us some time to repair the rigging and some of the spars that were wrecked in our original attack. I consulted with Mr. Brooks as to what to do with the prisoners, for we had captured most of the enemy crew, more men than we had ourselves. We used *Haevner*'s boats to take all the Danish seamen away. It will be some time before they can get to shore and even more time before they can get to any major settlement to tell their tale. We should be long gone before there is any response from the Norwegians or the Danes."

"Mr Brooks, are we ready to get underway?"

"Yes, sir. Both us and the captured vessel. I believe that it must be a fourth-rate based on the definitions put out by the Admiralty. I would recommend that Mr. Stewart be given command of the prize with Mr. Rich as second lieutenant and Midshipman Rich as the third officer. I can stand watch for you until you become mobile again, and we can carry you on deck as required.

"Then, Mr. Brooks, set a course for England. I would prefer to go to Portsmouth if we can because of the superiority of the boatyards there and the hope that we may get Mr. Stewart's father to repair *Glaucus*. It is also much nearer Dipton, and Portsmouth is the base with which most of our crew are familiar, and I believe that includes your crew as well, Mr. Macreau."

"Yes, sir, it does."

"Then, I suggest we get underway as soon as possible."

Giles had been hanging on, ignoring his painful right leg as long as he could. As the door closed behind Mr. Brooks and Commander Macreau, he sank back into his bed of pain. He had to fight a desire to have the sentry recall Dr. Maclean to get another dose of the magic medicine. Luckily, before his will weakened, he passed out, not waking until the following morning when the pain was already less, and his prime want was water and some food despite the fact that his leg still hurt a great deal and his missing foot begged to be scratched.

Chapter XXIII

Daphne was struggling to keep up with the management of her husband's and uncle's affairs. It wasn't just that her swollen belly was placing her farther from the edge of the table where she worked on the accounts because she seemed to be much larger this time than in previous pregnancies. The real problem was that she couldn't concentrate, and she had difficulty paying full attention to any particular task for any length of time. Partly, but only partly, this was because she was being distracted by the unborn baby's kicking. This baby was much more active than her previous ones. At least, the birth was now due fairly soon, according to Mr. Jackson, who was her physician and would be acting as her male midwife. He had been puzzled, but not alarmed, at how large she had grown. He even thought that she might have twins. He had muttered that he might have heard two heartbeats when he pushed his ear against her womb the last time he had examined her.

It was a relief that Catherine had had her child after a fairly short labor and was already pretty well recovered from the ordeal of childbirth. Indeed, Catherine was chattering about how soon she would move to London. Just as well, Daphne thought to herself; she really wasn't interested in endlessly discussing how wonderful her niece's daughter was.

Partly, Daphne admitted to herself, her difficulty concentrating arose from her worry about Giles. She hadn't heard from him in ages, and the papers kept having pieces about the war going on in the part of the world where his voyage was taking him. She was concerned about him much more than on previous occasions when she had not heard from him for long periods. Maybe that was to be accounted for by the baby, too.

She had just resolved to force herself to get down to the accounts when she heard some sounds from the servants that suggested that Dipton Hall was about to receive visitors. She looked out the window of her workroom and saw that a traveling coach was coming up the drive. Could it be Giles at long last? She mustn't get her hopes up! She had been fooled before, so she couldn't wait to hear who was coming to Dipton Hall.

Daphne pushed herself up from her chair and waddled towards the front door. When she arrived, the coach had just come to a stop, and a footman was letting down the steps. First out was a youth who looked vaguely familiar to Daphne. Yes, she thought, he must be one of Giles's midshipmen. He turned around, and someone inside passed him a crutch that he handed to the footman. By this time, Daphne would usually have been dashing down the steps to greet her husband, but there could be no dashing in her present condition. She was even hesitant to go down the stairs without help. There was more movement in the coach, and a left foot appeared and found the step. Then, the owner of the foot appeared, and all was explained. It was Giles, but a Giles whose right leg ended in a bandaged stump. Daphne quite forgot about her fragile state as she tried to rush down the stairs to her husband. Luckily, Steves had his eye on her and, abandoning his usual staid mannerisms, acted immediately to steady her before she could trip.

Giles also reacted automatically. He jumped forward without thinking as he saw Daphne stumble. Prompt reaction by Midshipman Jenks saved his captain from crashing to the ground. The midshipman and the footman then helped Giles up to the top of the steps to meet Daphne where they embraced awkwardly.

"What happened to your leg?" Daphne asked at the same time that Giles asked, "When is the baby due?"

They laughed.

"You first," commanded Daphne.

"I took a bullet in a fight leaving Denmark, and Mr. Maclean had to amputate my foot and ankle. He says it has healed nicely, but it is still somewhat tender," Giles replied.

"I hope you are not downplaying how serious it is. You must see Mr. Jackson at once. Remember how much help he was with Captain Bush lost his leg."

"I will, but mine is not as serious as Bush's was. Right now, it has stopped hurting almost completely. Much more annoying is the desire to scratch the part that isn't there, but Bush had that, too, and it disappeared soon. Of course, he claimed that it was because you were teaching him how to dance. But that's enough about me. Now tell me about yourself."

"The baby's due any day now," stated Daphne. "Oh, Giles, I am so glad that you got home in time for the delivery! I have been so afraid for you!

"Oh, drat!" she exclaimed. "The baby wants to come now! My water has broken!"

Organized chaos broke out on Dipton Hall's portico. Giles took over: "Betsey," he ordered, "escort Lady Giles to our bedroom. Mr. Steeves, send someone to ask Mr. Jackson at once. Mrs. Wilson, make sure that everything is ready for the delivery."

"Giles, wait," Daphne interrupted. "The birth isn't that imminent. Steves, send someone to inform Mr. Jackson, but the messenger should also tell him that Captain Giles has had a leg amputation that I would like him to look at. But let's not alarm the children about what is happening.

" Look, Giles, Nanny has brought the children. This baby can wait a bit while you say hello to them."

Giles willingly took up her suggestion. Daphne was right. There was nothing that had to be done about her giving birth immediately. He had resolved never to be like his father, who always ignored Giles and his brother. Doing so did make the scene seem more normal and maybe prevented the children from worrying about Daphne's giving birth.

Giles first shook Hugh's hand formally and then picked him up, kissed him on the cheek, and spun him around until he shrieked with laughter, quite forgetting that this was not the way a young gentleman was supposed to act. Mary's hand was the next to get his attention, treating her very formally despite her giggles and then picking her up for a spin. He then picked up each of the younger children, but much more sedately since he wasn't sure how fragile they might be. Even so, he bounced them up and down a bit. While they had started out being very shy to him, before long, each one started laughing and shouting. Daphne watched this display with a happy grin. Any worry that the loss of his foot would cripple Giles seriously disappeared as she saw how easily he could play vigorously with the children.

It was over an hour before Mr. Jackson arrived. Most of that time was spent probing how Giles had been injured and how severe the handicap would be. Giles kept trying to change the subject to the arrangements made for Catherine, during which Daphne revealed how she had got the best of the gentlemen's clubs.

When Mr. Jackson arrived, the first thing he did was to take her pulse and feel her stomach.

"Everything is proceeding normally, Daphne," he declared, "but it is time for you to go upstairs to get ready for the main event. You've done this often enough to know what is in store. There is nothing to worry about."

Mr. Jackson rang the bell to summon Betsey to help Daphne go upstairs and then turned to Giles.

"No, no, Giles. There is no need for you upstairs yet. I want to examine that stump to make sure all is well. I know your Mr. Maclean is a very expert surgeon, especially for that sort of injury, but it never hurts to be careful. If anything is going wrong, I need to know about it as soon as possible."

Mr Jackson carefully unwrapped the dressings around Giles's stump and felt all over the puckers from the wounds. He pressed on several points with his finger while looking at Giles to see what reaction there might be. Giles wondered what was going on: Mr. Jackson's probings were not particularly painful, though the skin over the scars was still tender.

"I see that you are curious about what I am doing, Giles," Mr. Jackson said. "As wounds heal, the patient's reaction to pressure around them can tell me a lot about how well the recovery is going. In your case, it seems to be going exceptionally well. Of course, I know *Glaucus*'s surgeon's work, so I am not surprised.

"What we need to do now is get you better padding for the stump that makes it easier to rub salve into it and a better peg leg and way to hold it securely and comfortably. Your navy carpenters and leather workers are not as good as people who have been making horse harnesses all their lives. We are lucky to have an exceptionally able one here in Dipton. He made the leg that Captain Bush uses. I'll get him here in the next couple of days. There is no reason that you can't pretty well return to all your former activities except that you won't be able to run very well. No more cricket on the village green! But you can ride to hounds as recklessly as ever. Dancing the waltz might be more of a problem, but Captain Bush managed it, so you can, too.

"Now, we had better get upstairs to see how things are going. I presume that you want to be in the delivery room again?"

"Of course, as long as Daphne wants me there. I know it is unusual, but I think it helps Daphne, and it is far better for me than sitting down here getting drunk while listening to the shrieks coming down the stairs and fearing the worst."

The two men went up to the room off Daphne's bedroom, which served as the birthing room. Mr. Jackson's birthing cot* had already been set up, and Daphne had changed into the special clothes she would wear during the delivery.

"All ready, I see, Daphne," said Mr. Jackson. "You are getting to be an old hand at this. Have the contractions started yet?"

"No," Daphne replied and then winced with pain. "There was the first."

"Let's get a pattern started, and then I can time them," said Mr. Jackson. "It helps me to know how the labor is progressing."

Daphne felt another contraction five minutes or so later. It wasn't severe, not nearly as painful as she knew from past labors that the spasms would get, but it was further confirmation that the baby had determined that it was time to be born. That's how Daphne thought of the situation, though she knew that the baby couldn't decide anything yet. She felt it helped to bridge the huge gap between having a kicking lump in her stomach and having a newborn infant, already with distinctive features and its own voice, and in need of immediate attention from those designated to care for it.

"Giles, tell me how you got injured," Daphne asked, though she had already heard the story. "Indeed, tell me everything about your trip. I want to hear you tell it again, and it will keep me distracted from the more painful aspects of giving birth."

Giles complied. He started retelling the tale from the point at which he had left the Nore after the disastrous commencement of the voyage when he had to rescue a ship from the Godwin sands. He didn't know how many of his letters from the early part of the expedition had gotten through, but he knew from past occasions when he recounted his adventures on coming home that Daphne did not mind hearing him retell things she had already read about or that she had already heard told before.

The contractions were steadily getting more frequent as Giles droned on about his voyage, and Daphne started to moan louder as each one struck. She couldn't concentrate any longer on Giles's tale, and he started instead squeezing her hand and murmuring encouragement.

Mr. Jackson also told Daphne to concentrate on what was happening. "That's it, Daphne. Give a push when the contraction comes … now! …now! … alright, pause till the next one hits … good, almost there … now! Push hard! Keep pushing! … Good! Your child's head is appearing … now, another push! Big one! Again! There we go! … Daphne, congratulations! You have a boy, a perfectly formed baby boy!"

While Mr. Jackson busied himself with the immediate tasks required when a baby arrives in the world, Giles squeezed Daphne's hand. "Well done, darling! Well done! We are so lucky! You have been so brave! Now you can rest."

"Hold on, Giles," Mr. Jackson looked up from his task. "We are only half done."

"What do you mean?"

"Daphne is about to present you with twins. Sorry about that, Daphne, but you have another baby on the way. I suspected you might have twins, and you do. It will be arriving any minute now. Drink some water and try to relax until the contractions start again."

Daphne was lying back on the special birthing cot, exhausted. Could she take another birth, Giles wondered. He realized that she had no choice. The next baby had to be born, and that was all there was to it. It couldn't be put off until the next day or whenever it was convenient to welcome the additional baby into the world.

The wait for the next birth cycle to start was not long. Daphne's contractions began again, as did the moans and then the instructions to "push." The second birth did not take as long as the first one. Very soon, Mr. Jackson was poised to ease the second baby into the world. "Good news, Daphne!" he called. "This one is a girl, just as perfect as her brother."

"Can I see her?"

"Just let me cut the cord and clean her up. She is about the same size as her brother, and both are healthy and strong. Well-done!"

Giles leaned over and kissed Daphne. "I am so proud of you, darling," he said. "I am so happy that you waited until I was home to give birth."

"We'll let you rest now, Daphne, and get your strength back," Mr. Jackson declared. "The others can help you get to bed and look after everything. Come along, Giles. I think we have earned a good drink of your best Scotch whisky."

When the two men had settled in the drawing room with glasses of whiskey, Giles noticed for the first time that Mr. Jackson seemed to be exhausted. He had never thought of it, but the man who looked after all the medical needs of Dipton, for people of any status, and who also lent a hand when needed to deal with a sick or injured animal, was not young. After all, he had delivered Daphne.

"Long day, Mr. Jackson?" Giles asked. "You look exhausted."

"Yes. I was called out before dawn. It's a good tiredness, however. There is nothing happier in my line of work than successfully helping at a birth. You must also have been up very early to get here so soon."

"Yes, I was. I'll sleep well tonight."

"Will you be going back to sea soon? Or will your leg induce you to come ashore?"

"I don't know. My frigate, *Glaucus*, was severely damaged on my last voyage. They may have to get me another one. My leg won't stop me, of course. Many other officers have carried on after losing a limb: Lord Nelson, for one, and, of course, Captain Bush, for another. But I have very little confidence that my next assignment will be any better than my last one. I am furious with the government. There was no excuse for their going to war with Denmark just to steal their navy. All our trade with the Baltic is now in jeopardy, and with it, the navy supplies we get from that area. And all for what? The French haven't used their Brest Fleet yet, and the only admiral Napoleon had who was worth anything got stranded when no one came to his aid after he had escaped from Toulon*. Having the Danish fleet will not make much of a difference, certainly not enough to warrant stealing the fleet of a neutral country that was well-intentioned to us and was in a strategic position with respect to some of our most important trade.

"I think that I might be of more use trying to hold the government accountable in the House of Lords than serving doubtful purposes at sea, as was this last expedition. I have done my duty and more; now, I think I should have a chance to enjoy my family and estate. I appreciate that Daphne did not complain about my having to do my duty in the past, but I am sure that she would welcome my staying at home now. I should have plenty to do with our various endeavors in England to keep me busy."

Glossary

Amiens, Treaty of	Treaty between Britain and France ending the Napoleonic wars, signed in 1802.
Back a sail	Turning a sail so that the wind blows against the back side rather than the frontside so that the ship stops.
Birthing cot	many midwives took with them a framework or cot on which the mother could lie when giving birth. It was much firmer (and less lumpy) than the usual bed and easier to clean up after the birth had occurred
Belay (v.)	Tie down. Regularly used by mariners to also mean stop. Belaying pins were stout, removable rods that were often used as makeshift weapons.
Board(ing)(1)	Refers to attacking another ship by coming side to side so that men from one ship
	can attack the other one in an attempt to capture it.
	(2) in 'on board' it means present on a ship.
Boarding nets	Loose nets hung from the spars of a ship to prevent enemies from climbing aboard from boats.
Brig	A two-masted, square-rigged ship.

Carronade	A short gun, frequently mounted on a slider rather than a wheeled gun carriage, only used for close-in work. They were not usually counted in the number of guns by which a ship was rated.
Close (verb)	Closing with another ship (or fleet) was to sail towards it by the quickest path.
Close to the wind	A ship is sailing close to the wind when it is going upwind as much as it can without stalling. Slang meaning is that the action is almost illegal.
Cloth (drawn)	Refers to the stage of a meal when the final dish had been consumed, the tablecloth had been removed, and the men in attendance gathered together to imbibe liquor stronger than wine, usually accompanied by nuts and fruit. When ladies were present, they withdrew to the drawing room just before the cloth was drawn. It was often a time of more pointed conversation than occurred during the meal.
Come about	Turn into the wind and keep turning until the fore and aft rigged sails fill on the other tack.
Consol	A bond issued by the British Government with no stated redemption date, paying the holder a specified amount per annum. The term is short for Consolidated Fund.
Crosstrees	Two horizontal spars at the upper ends of a topmast to which are attached the shrouds of the topgallant mast

Cutting-out	Entering an enemy harbor in boats to capture a ship and sail her out to sea where t the warship would be waiting.
Dirk (midshipman's**)**	A short sword, part of a midshipman's uniform.
Entail	A provision that the inheritance of real property would go to specified members of a family (or another specified group) usually to the closest male relatives. An entail typically prevented the present owner from leaving the property to someone else, and it was usually put on a property to prevent the immediate heir from dissipating the inheritance but would pass it intact (more or less) to the next generation.
Exemptions	were Documents issued to merchant seamen and some others so that they would not be pressed into the navy. Even with them, seamen were often forcibly taken from merchant ships to serve in the navy.
Fighting both sides	occurs when a warship engages two (or more) enemies using the guns on both sides of the ship. Doing so requires a very large crew.
Fighting top	A Platform on the mast where the main mast met the top mast from which marines could fire their muskets on to the deck of an opposing ship.
Full and Bye	A sailing ship is sailing full and bye when it is as close to the wind as possible without the danger of the sails flapping with small changes to the wind. The same as 'close-hauled,' but the

	latter indicates adjusting the course for every small change in the wind.
Grapne	: A metal hook or set of hooks attached to a line that could be thrown and hooked onto the edge of another ship, a wall, or another object.
Gunroom	Place where the midshipmen berthed.
Helm alee	Turn a ship into the wind. (It sounds backwards, but originates from the time when ships had tillers which were pushed in the direction opposite to the desired turn.)
Holystone	On naval ships, the decks were scrubbed each morning using sandstone blocks. Since the crew had to perform the task on their knees, they were called holy stones and holystone became the verb to indicate the activity.
Jolly boat	A small lapstreake boat often suspended from the stern of a ship
Leeway	The sideways drift of a ship down wind of the desired course.
King's hard bargain	Refers to crew members who are ineffective or insubordinate.
Larboard	the left-hand side of the ship looking forward. Opposite of starboard. Now usually called "port."
Lead-line	A thin rope knotted at six-foot intervals with a piece of lead at the end. Used to measure the depth of water under a ship.
Line abreast	vessels sailing together in parallel.
Loblolly boys	Assistants to the surgeon
Lubber's hole	A hole in the top (q.v.) of a mast so that access can b e gained from below, either

	to get to the top of to be able to reach the next set of shrouds to clime farther up the masts. Experienced topmen avoided its use when climbing the mast, preferring to climb up the ropes on the outside of the top.
Luffing up	turning into the wind to stop a ship
Mews	Stables at the rear of mansions and row houses in te richer residential areas.
The Nore	Anchorage in the Thames estuary off the mouth of the Medway River. A major anchorage for the Royal Navy in the Age of Sail.
Oakum	Fibre, often hemp, soaked in tar, used for caulking ships' seams.
Pinnae	One of the types of boats carried by (or trailed behind) full-sized ships.
Quarterdeck	The highest deck of a war ship at the stern, province of the officers
Raft	Ships or boats are rafted together when they are tied side by side to each other.
Rake (a ship)	Fire a broadside into the bow or stern of an opponent who would not be able to return the fire.
Remove	Different dishes served at dinner. The more removes, the more elaborate and elegant the dinner was thought to be
Rout	A large, formal evening gathering. It had slightly risqué connotation.
Shrouds	A rope ladder formed by short lengths of rope tied tightly between the stays of a mast.

356

Sheet	A line controlling how much a sail is pulled in.
Skagerrak	East-wet passage from the North Sea Norway and Denmark
Stay(s)	(1) A line used to prevent a mast from falling over or being broken in the wind
	(2) Corsets
Steer by the course	Usually, sailing ships adjust the direction they are sailing according to the vagaries of the wind to avoid having to alter the set of all the sails frequently. "Steering by the course" indicates that the ship keeps heading in the same direction as indicated by the compass, and the sails have to be adjusted to suit that course as the wind varied.
Stern sheets	The after part of an open boat.
Step	Promotion from lieutenant to commander.
Spring (line)	A line attached to the anchor cable leading to the aft of the ship that can be used to turn it
Tack	(a) Change the direction in which a ship is sailing and the side of the ship from which the wind is blowing by turning towards the direction from which the wind is blowing.
	(b) (as in larboard of starboard tack) The side of the ship from which the wind is blowing when the ship is going to windward.
Taffrail	Railing at the stern of the quarter-deck.
Ton	That part of London society most in adhering to the latest fashions.

Tubs	Liquor was not usually smuggled in regular barrels but in smaller containers, made like a barrel, which could be carried by one man.
Tumblehome	The part of the hull of a ship that slopes inward toward the deck.
Turn of the glass	Time during the day on ships was measured via an hourglass – or rather a half-hour glass. It was counted from the start of each watch, and a bell was rung each time a half hour had passed when the glass had to be turned. The number indicated how many half-hours had passed since the start of the watch. Eight-bells was the signal that a watch had ended.
Wardroom	The area in a ship used by the commissioned officers of a ship when off-duty.
Watch	First watch: 8 p.m.- 12 midnight
	Middle watch: 12 midnight - 4 a.m.
	Morning watch 4 a.m. – 8 a.m.
	Forenoon watch: 8 a.m. – 12 noon
	Afternoon watch 12 noon – 4 p.m.
	First Dog watch 4 p.m. – 6 p.m.
	Second Dog watch 6 p.m. – 8 p.m.
	In each watch, time was marked off in half-hour segments so the one bell of the First watch would be 8:30 p.m., two bells would be 9:00 p.m., and so on.

	(2) Division of the crew. The crew was divided (usually) into two watches, the starboard watch and the larboard watch, which alternated when they worked (in normal circumstances) and when they were at leisure or asleep.
	3) the time when officers were on duty. Referred to as "being on watch" or "watch."
	(4) Police force on land.
Wear	The opposite of tack, where the maneuver of changing which side of a ship the wind is coming from is accomplished by turning away from the wind. instead of into it Sometimes spelled ware.
What Nelson said	"East of Gibraltar, all men are bachelors."
Yardarm	The end of a yard (the piece of wood to which the sail was attached on a square-rigged ship.) The yardarm was where a pully was fastened to allow a condemned person to be pulled up to kill him by strangulation. Naval hangings did not have a 'drop' to break the victim's neck.

Printed in Great Britain
by Amazon